REAGAN'S
WAR STORIES

REAGAN'S WAR STORIES

A Cold War Presidency

Benjamin Griffin

NAVAL INSTITUTE PRESS
ANNAPOLIS, MARYLAND

Naval Institute Press
291 Wood Road
Annapolis, MD 21402

Library of Congress Cataloging-in-Publication Data

Names: Griffin, Benjamin, 1984- author.
Title: Reagan's war stories : a Cold War presidency / Benjamin Griffin.
Other titles: Cold War presidency
Description: Annapolis, Maryland : Naval Institute Press, [2022] | Includes
    bibliographical references and index.
Identifiers: LCCN 2022010007 (print) | LCCN 2022010008 (ebook) | ISBN
    9781682477786 (hardcover) | ISBN 9781682477793 (ebook)
Subjects: LCSH: Reagan, Ronald--Books and reading. | Reagan,
    Ronald--Political and social views. | Politics and literature--United
    States--History--20th century. | Politics and culture--United
    States--History--20th century. | Rhetoric--Political aspects--United
    States--History--20th century. | National security--United
    States--Decision making--History--20th century. | United States--Foreign
    relations--1981-1989. | Cold War in popular culture--United States. |
    BISAC: HISTORY / United States / 20th Century | BIOGRAPHY &
    AUTOBIOGRAPHY / Political
Classification: LCC E877.2 .G75 2022 (print) | LCC E877.2 (ebook) | DDC
    973.927092 [B]--dc23/eng/20220518
LC record available at https://lccn.loc.gov/2022010007
LC ebook record available at https://lccn.loc.gov/2022010008

♾ Print editions meet the requirements of ANSI/NISO z39.48-1992 (Permanence of Paper).
Printed in the United States of America.

30 29 28 27 26 25 24 23 22   9 8 7 6 5 4 3 2 1

First printing

For Amibeth, Natalie, and Patrick.
Thank you for your love and patience.

CONTENTS

ACKNOWLEDGMENTS

I started research for this book in the summer of 1996. It began when my father handed a book-hungry twelve-year-old a hardback copy of *The Hunt for Red October*. I inhaled it and the rest of Clancy's books, introducing me to techno-thrillers and spy novels. While I certainly did not think about them in an academic way at the time, I am very glad to have lucked into a project that allowed me to categorize rereading them as "research."

While I was studying at the University of Texas, the faculty and my fellow students were incredible. Dr. Jeremi Suri, Dr. William Inboden, Dr. Mark Lawrence, Dr. H. W. Brands, and Dr. James Graham Wilson served as my dissertation committee and generously provided their expertise and guidance as the project grew from a vague idea about how fiction shapes thought to this book. Dr. Susan Colbourn, Dr. Carl Forsberg, Dr. James Martin, Dr. Simon Miles, and Dr. Emily Whalen all were excellent sounding boards and provided feedback and encouragement throughout. I am also very fortunate that I arrived in Austin in 2013, when the Clements Center for National Security opened on campus. It graciously funded research trips, helped arrange many of the interviews I conducted for the project, and have continued to support me long after I left the Forty Acres.

I taught in the History Department of the U.S. Academy from 2015 to 2018, and my superiors and colleagues there made this book immeasurably better. Brig. Gen. Ty Seidule, Col. Gail Yoshitani, and Col. Sean Sculley mentored me, making me become a better historian and officer. Dr. Stephanie Hinnezshitz twice ran "writing months" when I was stuck, kick-starting both the dissertation and book. Dr. Amanda Boczar helped me to frame my arguments better and tipped me off to a number of good sources and opportunities. Lt. Col. Rory McGovern, Maj. Greg Hope, Maj. Mike Kiser, and Maj. Dave Krueger are all excellent friends who listened to me talk endlessly about the project over drinks and games. Also, the Omar Bradley Foundation graciously provided a research grant. I am eagerly looking forward to returning to the department soon to work with such outstanding people again. Teaching some of America's finest young men and women is an absolute privilege, and I am grateful to have the opportunity to do so once more.

Glenn Griffith did an incredible job guiding me through the process of publishing this book. Ashley Baird, Pel Boyer, Robin Noonan, Jacqline Barnes, Jack Russell, Susan Corrado, and Adam Kane of the Naval Institute Press helped shape the book in innumerable ways. I am grateful for their time, expertise, and patience. I would also like to thank the peer reviewers, Dr. Stephen Randolph and one who remains anonymous, whose feedback on multiple drafts made this a much better book.

Most importantly, this book would not be possible without the support of my family. My wife, Amibeth Griffin, is an incredible woman and mother who not only showed remarkable patience with me as the project consumed nights and weekends, but also encouraged me throughout. Her love and support make me better. Our children, Natalie and Patrick, are joys, and I am proud of the people they are becoming. I am lucky to have all three in my life.

INTRODUCTION

STORYTELLER IN CHIEF

A confused, visibly aged President Reagan appears in an NBC interview from the Oval Office. Pressed about U.S. activities in Iran and Nicaragua and, what is worse, on his knowing or not knowing about them, he responds that his administration is "trying to find out what happened, because none of us know." Ending the interview, the seemingly senile president ushers the reporter from the office, expressing the hope that he had been informative, "given the very little that I know."[1] Momentarily alone, Reagan transforms. He straightens, and the mask of grandfatherly care vanishes, leaving a look of cold, menacing calculation.

Secretary of Defense Caspar Weinberger, Director of Central Intelligence William Casey, Chief of Staff Don Regan, and other principals and staffers then enter the office and sit as Reagan reveals a master plan to continue illegally supporting the Contras. The inept and confused advisors gradually fall asleep as the president speaks in fluent Arabic and German, calculates exchange rates instantly, and quotes Montesquieu on the danger of sharing knowledge. It is clear that Reagan not only knows what is going on but is the mastermind behind it.

The "interview" and "meeting" were not real but a *Saturday Night Live* skit that aired in December 1986. Like most good satire, the sketch highlighted an important reality: that it was unclear to many Americans who was in charge in the Reagan White House. Though personally popular, Reagan remained an enigma, both to the public and within his own administration. Throughout his two terms in office, bureaucratic chaos and personal rivalries persisted in the public eye. Tell-all books by disgruntled former officials painted the president as an intellectual lightweight who drew on his acting background to convey the ideas and words of shadowy figures who were the power behind the throne.

David Stockman's 1986 *The Triumph of Politics: Why the Reagan Revolution Failed* offers a good example. Stockman left Congress in 1981 to join the administration as the director of the Office of Management and Budget but resigned in 1985, frustrated at his declining influence and the country's continued deficit spending. His book made a case that those around Reagan "made him stumble into the wrong camp," that the president "had no business trying to make a revolution" and lacked the will to lead one.[2] The book debuted in the top spot on the *New York Times* nonfiction best-sellers' list, and Stockman played a prominent role in a media blitz promoting the book and decrying the failure of Reagan's leadership.[3]

In its review of the book, the *New York Times* agreed that Reagan was incapable of directing his administration and found Stockman's "Reagan stories . . . priceless."[4] The book portrayed Reagan sitting silently in meetings until he heard a magic word, like "welfare" or "Medicare." On cue, Reagan would launch into an anecdote "not applicable to his task of governance."[5] Stockman and the *New York Times* saw Reagan's use of stories and jokes as proof that he had "totally misunderstood the preceding conversation."[6] Reagan's preference for spinning yarns was therefore a sign of intellectual weakness and proof he was not the ideological or policy driver of the administration.

However, this charge, far from an accurate indictment of presidential incapacity, reflects a major misunderstanding of how Reagan thought and communicated. Reagan likely never saw the *SNL* sketch and would have been even less likely to enjoy its portrayal of him, but he did recognize the value of jokes to convey messages. Throughout his life, Reagan used narrative as a primary means of thinking about the world and communicating his vision. He believed that compelling stories could convey essential truths and messages and offered him a memorable way to explain his ideas. Reagan continually sought stories and jokes that could express his vision, keeping his favorites on index cards in a box in his desk for future reference.

George Shultz, who served as secretary of state from 1982 to 1989 and was one of Reagan's most trusted and important advisors, recognized the importance of stories to the president. He saw Reagan as recognizing that "stories create meaning" and believing that "facts are the unassembled parts" of a story waiting for a master to piece them into something greater. Shultz viewed Reagan's use of stories positively, as a way to impart a larger message—unconcerned that sometimes for Reagan the message was simply more important than the facts.[7]

Caspar Weinberger agreed. Serving as secretary of defense from 1981 to 1987, Weinberger was instrumental in implementing the administration's plan to reinvigorate America's military. He saw Reagan's stories and jokes as critical to the "high standing and popularity" the president enjoyed with the public and as facilitating policy making and international relations. His accessible and immersive communication style created "an atmosphere" that made stakes seem less and counterparts less distant, in a way that led to "vital agreements that neither logic, nor table pounding, nor cajoling could bring about."[8] Though unorthodox, Reagan's approach was essential to the success of the administration. To Weinberger and Shultz, Reagan was much closer to the SNL mastermind than the smiling figurehead of The Triumph of Politics.

Reagan's unusual approach contributed greatly, however, to ambiguity about his mental capacity and inspired a widespread belief that he was the "amiable dunce" that former secretary of defense Clark Clifford labeled him.[9] Even his official biographer, Edmund Morris, had a dim view of his subject's intellect. "How much does Dutch really know?" Morris asked, doubting that there would be anything of value to future historians in Reagan's diaries.[10] He went further in a 2011 op-ed that sought to dismantle the "sentimental colossus [Reagan's] acolytes are trying to erect," insisting that the Reagan he knew was a man "of no ego and little charisma."[11]

Recent scholarship provides a more nuanced view. It finds that contrary to Morris' fears, Reagan's writings offered deep insight into his thoughts and feelings while occupying the Oval Office. Historian John Patrick Diggins admits to a "belated respect" for Reagan's "boldness" and surprise to have found in him "an intelligent sensitive mind, with passionate convictions."[12] Similarly, though critical of Reagan overall, Rick Perlstein finds the president to be simultaneously a rescuer and a divider, a person whose ability to "reimagine the morass in front of him as a tableau of moral clarity" was unique among modern political figures.[13]

In his survey of the Cold War, John Lewis Gaddis argues that Reagan, Mikhail Gorbachev, and Pope John Paul II recognized the Cold War as theater and that "like all good actors, they brought the play at last to an end."[14] Gaddis speculates that it took "dramatizations" by all three men to "remove the mental blinders" of their constituencies.[15] While this characterization risks oversimplifying the motivations behind Reagan's "Peace through Strength," Pope John Paul II's World Youth Day, and Gorbachev's policy of perestroika, it accurately represents the importance of performance and stagecraft in politics and international relations. Reagan's background as an actor and storyteller undoubtedly played a critical role in how he achieved his largest policy objectives. His Hollywood past also provided critics an easy way to malign his intellect, agency, and capability.

With increasing frequency, scholars of the Reagan administration are highlighting the importance of the vision and imagination of Reagan himself. At his best, he combined keen insight and synthesized knowledge to create relatable and durable visions of the world and its future. Communicating his visions memorably and widely, he upended orthodox views and brought lasting change. Reagan did this most successfully on issues of American-Soviet relations, arms control, and sharing his vision of the potential of the United States. At other times, indifference, poor understanding, or lack of creativity led Reagan to abdicate responsibility or pursue poorly conceived and ultimately disastrous agendas. His administration's policy in Latin America, its handling of the AIDS crisis, and its ignorance of racial issues speak to Reagan's failures of imagination.

Reagan's ability to tell memorable stories had long been essential to his success. He began his career as a radio broadcaster before becoming a movie star and then a politician. Reagan's tales forged connections with his audiences, be they moviegoers, rival politicians, or world leaders; all were left identifying with the character he portrayed or understanding, if not always agreeing with, the message he sought to impart. He hoped his audiences would repeat the stories, and their messages, widely. Reagan saw himself as a fabulist and believed the right one would inevitably lead people to his way of thinking.

Reagan used fiction broadly, particularly highlighting stories that spoke to his life experiences or that he otherwise related to. These narratives largely ended happily for the protagonists; the good guys always won. The stories helped form his value system and his sense of how the broader world operated. Fiction reinforced Reagan's own experience and convinced him of the basic correctness of his views on subjects like freedom, religion, and the military. Stories also provided Reagan with a creative space in which to develop and test policy. They offered him a way to visualize information presented to him in more conventional formats. Fiction often served as framework with which to "wargame" ideas and think about policy in a concrete way. The ability to insert himself into a narrative humanized policy for Reagan and led him to seek more creative solutions. Through stories, Reagan gained the confidence in his policies necessary to challenge orthodox political views. Fictional accounts were essential to his presidential leadership. He used movies, novels, jokes, and other cultural vehicles to communicate ideas to his staff and build consensus among his closest advisors.

Finally, Reagan sought to use popular culture to mobilize broad support for his administration's objectives. He and others in his administration promoted narratives that portrayed their policy goals favorably and attacked elements of popular culture they deemed hostile. Reagan viewed such narratives as essential to restoring national will generally and, specifically, to sustaining his policies. He spoke frequently about the state of television and movies and consistently called on them to embrace his definitions of patriotism and liberty.

At first glance, the idea of a president making substantial use of fiction to develop and communicate policy is disconcerting. Using imagined worlds, often shaped to suit specific audiences, to influence the real one seems dangerous: attempting to cross the unbridgeable chasm between fact and fantasy could only result in a disastrous fall. Indeed, sometimes it did, as Reagan's use of fiction in Latin America and Africa demonstrate. However, popular fiction and culture draw greatly on the real world and can both distill complicated issues into simpler problems and reveal nuance that opens viable paths that conventional wisdom declared impossible.

This recognition was not unique to Reagan. Throughout the early Cold War, the United States leveraged fiction as a means to convey its worldview and attack the Soviet Union. The Central Intelligence Agency (CIA) financed the publication and distribution of works like George Orwell's *Animal Farm* and Boris Pasternak's *Doctor Zhivago*, recognizing these works as powerful and memorable critiques of the Soviet Union. Historian Duncan White notes in

Cold Warriors that "cultural policies on both sides of the Iron Curtain lent great power to literature."[16] Similarly, Christina Klein argues that books, plays, and movies of the period "presented the Cold War as something that ordinary Americans could take part in," inviting them to become invested in the conflict on a personal level.[17] Fiction translated abstract global power structures and distant events "into personal terms and [imbued] them with sentiment."[18] Reagan in the 1950s, as his anticommunist views hardened, was both a producer and consumer of the content highlighted by Klein and White. Fiction's role in shaping his view is then at least to some extent a sign of strategic policy that succeeded.

Particularly in a democratic society, it is difficult to wield power effectively without supporting popular-culture narratives. Edward Said views this fact as sinister in his *Culture and Imperialism*. He asserts that neither a novel nor the concept of imperialism could exist without the other, that they draw on the authority and power of society to create in each other both legibility and legitimacy.[19] Melani McAlister's survey of American cultural portrayals of the Middle East agrees. She finds that "popular culture actively assists the construction of narratives that help policy make sense in a given moment" and, further, that pop culture is constantly interacting with and responding to "other fields in the larger social system."[20] In the view of both scholars, the link between popular culture and policy is almost entirely negative—understandably, given the heavy emphasis on the Middle East in their work. The failures of the Reagan administration in Lebanon and Iran and its often-racist portrayal of Middle Eastern peoples and nations in the 1980s strongly support their argument.

However, there are positives to the symbiosis of policy and culture. Charles Hill, a senior advisor to Reagan and Shultz and who was heavily involved in policy on Russia, argues that the relationship between literature and statecraft is reciprocal.[21] He recognizes that literature informed the actions of leaders, actions that in turn influenced future writing. Though Hill does lament the state of popular culture in general, feeling it has evicted literature "from its place in the pantheon of arts," he acknowledges that works with mass appeal accelerate the process and can create more responsive policy.[22] Popular culture can also model the realistic outcomes and perhaps feasibility of policies in an accessible and visible manner. This is particularly useful in defense planning, for which narratives can offer de facto "wargames" that allow strategists to visualize concepts without actual warfare or large-scale exercises. Positive cultural portrayals reinforce leaders' confidence in each initiative, while the opposite can urge the need for a new course.

Political scientists Paul Musgrave and J. Furman Daniel argue that popular culture can provide its audience "synthetic experiences," which are "impression, ideas, and pseudo-recollections about the world derived from exposure to narrative texts."[23] The new experience of the audience can "reinforce, induce, and even replace identities and beliefs" related to how individuals interpret and act in the "real world."[24] In this sense, popular culture does for policy makers what wargames do for military planners—offering a broadly representative, but immersive, environment in which to work through problems.

A strong narrative builds empathy. It can expose consumers to aspects of culture and societies with which they are unfamiliar and bring fresh perspective on conflict. Close identification with characters in stories can translate into real-world understanding of and curiosity about different peoples and societies. Effective and well-constructed narratives can counter the dehumanizing effect of prolonged conflict. Policy stemming from this nuanced and complex view is likely to be all the more imaginative and successful for having done so.

Empathy and experience gleaned from stories are not, however, determinative of future action. They are among the many inputs, ideas, and skills on which an individual can draw. Their influence depends on openness to new ideas and experiences, an often impossibly high hurdle. It is also possible that fiction could have a detrimental effect. Stereotypical depictions, one-dimensional portrayals, or works actively seeking to elicit a hostile response create darker possibilities for fiction's employment in policy. Less malicious but still damaging is the way in which unrealistic or inaccurate narratives can create unwarranted confidence. Finally, interpretation of fiction is uniquely personal; there is a risk of misinterpretation when leaders assert it as a common language with advisors. Used incorrectly in policy making, narratives can exacerbate tensions and destroy well-intentioned initiatives.

Reagan and his administration are a showcase for both the good and ill that comes of consciously incorporating fiction into policy making. During his time in office, Reagan paid close attention to the portrayal in popular culture of both his policies and the United States. He and his advisors actively worked to shape these depictions into favorable ones. The administration elevated works that played up the party line and ferociously attacked negative representations.

This pattern began from the moment of Reagan's election and continued throughout his two terms in office.

Surveying the landscape of popular culture following his decisive victory over the incumbent Jimmy Carter, Reagan saw in film, television, and novels narratives with open hostility to his ideas. He felt revulsion for recent movies about the Vietnam War. Films like *Apocalypse Now* and *The Deer Hunter* were clear examples of the "reprehensible pandering" of Hollywood to "anti-militarism and anti-Americanism."[25] The themes in both movies of moral equivalency and the impotence of American power directly undercut the narrative of rebirth Reagan sought to advance. If the messages Americans took from their entertainment did not change drastically, Reagan would find it difficult to achieve his policy goals.

Fortunately for Reagan, most members of the American public were ready for a new narrative. The 1970s had left them battered and drained. Military embarrassments in Vietnam, Cambodia, and Iran raised difficult questions about the capacity of the United States to exert its will even on minor powers, let alone the Soviet Union. Communism seemed on the march. New communist states were emerging in Southeast Asia, and military insurgencies were advancing in Angola, Afghanistan, and Nicaragua. Americans doubted their ability to win the Cold War. The fallout of the oil embargo by the Organization of Petroleum Exporting Countries too showed that American economic might was not unchallengeable. Small states now had the power to affect drastically the lives of everyday Americans and inflict lasting harm on the U.S. economy. These military and economic insults to American prestige and power in the 1970s created an enthusiastic audience for Reagan's message of optimism and rebirth.

Hollywood recognized this enthusiasm. Throughout Reagan's time in office a large segment of popular culture reflected the resurgent American nationalism his administration encouraged. Movies like *Rocky IV*, *Rambo: First Blood Part II*, and *Top Gun* encouraged those who desired to move beyond the self-questioning of the previous decade toward an embrace of exceptionalism. Even the toy industry took up Reagan's optimistic language about American power. Hasbro rebooted the "G.I. Joe" action figure in 1983, having suspended the line because of the unpopularity of the military during Vietnam.

Novelist Tom Clancy may be the best representation of this trend. During the Reagan administration, this obscure insurance agent became one of the best-selling and best-known authors on the planet. A 1985 public endorsement from Reagan for Clancy's *The Hunt for Red October* helped catapult the book atop best-seller lists. Clancy was to follow up that success by releasing a new book every year through the end of the decade. His books certainly support the idea that pop culture helps make policy comprehensible to the public. Despite frequent criticism for their paragraphs of technobabble, Clancy's novels enthusiastically and consciously embraced Reagan's policy goals and presented them in entertaining and resonant ways. They found a readership not just within the public but also in the halls of the Pentagon, CIA Headquarters in Langley, Virginia, and Congress; they were also favorites of the president. Jack Ryan's adventures became evidence to Reagan that his policies were not only popular but were also working as intended and could achieve their goal of winning the Cold War.

□ ▦ ■

Reagan's War Stories argues that the complex relationship between culture and policy remains underexamined, to the detriment of historical inquiry. Closer examination can help answer questions about how policy originates and is sustained. The study also argues that fiction is a potentially valuable and constructive tool for developing effective, nuanced approaches to complex problems. Narratives provide creative space in which to explore unconventional and imaginative solutions. The use of imagination and creativity in policy development encourages consideration of a broader range of options and evaluation of unexpected contingencies. However, heavy reliance on fictional narratives in strategic policy making also creates risks. Unrealistic or simplistic narratives yield options that are similarly narrow and ineffective. Narrow reading can also limit the empathy of a leader toward a given audience, which, if it leads to the use of stereotypes, can have disastrous results.

Reagan's presidency shows the best and worst of using narrative to drive and communicate policy. His consumption of stories relating to the Soviet Union, the United States and its military, and technology paired well with the information he received in briefings and from his close advisors. As a result, Reagan saw opportunities and took political risks that helped end the Cold War in an American victory. In contrast, Reagan's reading of westerns, Rudyard Kipling, and adventure stories painted an oversimplified picture of the developing world. His focus on cowboy stories as a model for Latin America drove policies that were both illegal and responsible for significant hardship, even death, for the people of the region.

As a whole, this book is primarily concerned with how Reagan used and reacted to middlebrow books; it argues that his reading played a significant role in both the development of his worldview and his leadership in office. More specifically, it seeks to illuminate why narrative helped Reagan in Europe but led to disaster in the global South. To these ends, a first group of chapters examines the period from his adolescence through the 1950s, tracing the evolution of Reagan's views on religion, technology, freedom, communism, and military service.

The first chapter, "Raised on Mars," looks at Reagan from his early boyhood through the end of World War II. In these years the future president demonstrated a predilection for stories that cast him as heroic and destined for greatness. He established a lifelong pattern of seeking out comforting stories that ended happily and reaffirmed his self-worth and worldview. The chapter then examines Reagan's relationship with the works of Harold Bell Wright and Edgar Rice Burroughs, each of whom helped an adolescent Reagan identify the sort of man he wanted to be. Wright's stories about the nature of Christianity gave Reagan a religious framework that he was to follow all his life. Burroughs' Mars novels kindled a lifelong love of science fiction and a fascination with technology. The hero in most of them, John Carter, became the archetype of Reagan's ideal protagonist.

Chapter 2, "Friendly Witness," explores the development of Reagan's anticommunism. Following the war, Reagan viewed communism and the Soviet Union as an existential threat to individual liberty. Reagan's increased political activism between 1945 and 1953 brought personal and starkly negative encounters with communists. His reading of *Witness*, a work of nonfiction by Whittaker Chambers, and the fictional *Darkness at Noon*, by Arthur Koestler, assured Reagan that his personal experiences were not aberrations but rather indicative of how communists operated throughout the globe.

Chapter 3, "Cowboy Values," looks at how westerns and similar genres offered Reagan a model by which to counter communism. His reading of Louis L'Amour's westerns and of James Michener's accounts of the Korean War, as well as his reflections on works of Rudyard Kipling, read in childhood, taught him to see resisting communism as a moral imperative and to define the Cold

War as a simple struggle between "white hats" and "black hats." He wanted the United States to do the morally right thing, without regard to reward or long-term influence. The chapter also explores the negative consequences of the narrowness of Reagan's reading. His efforts to apply the morality of westerns and his single-minded focus on the Soviet Union would lead to policy in Africa and Latin America that ranged from tone-deaf to disastrous.

The remaining chapters address the Reagan administration in detail, using the works of Tom Clancy as the key to how Reagan and his advisors developed their initiatives and built support for them. It also explores how the complicated relationship between leaders, authors, and the public played out. Each influences the others, making it difficult either to determine the origins of ideas or assign responsibility for their success or failure. Clancy's open embrace of Reagan's ideology, Reagan's public declarations of support for Clancy's work, and the significant popularity of that work make Clancy a particularly useful analytical tool for tracing how fiction both influences and is influenced by the broader geopolitical environment.

Chapter 4, "Up from the Depths," uses Clancy's first novel, *The Hunt for Red October*, to show how Reagan both inspired and used fiction. Clancy, as he wrote the book, consciously adopted themes of Reagan's first term. The work reinforces Reagan's first-term efforts to shift the American public's perception of their military and to draw attention to the importance of technology in a potential Cold War conflict. Reagan saw in the book's success validation of the success of his own first term and a sign that the will of Americans to fight the Cold War had returned.

Clancy influenced Reagan even more directly with his second book, *Red Storm Rising*. This book's chapter 5, "Techno-Thriller Rising," shows how Reagan used the novel to think about a potential conventional (i.e., without nuclear weapons) war between the North Atlantic Treaty Organization (NATO) and the Warsaw Pact. Clancy's portrayal of the U.S. Army's emerging doctrine of "AirLand Battle" and of the dominance of the United States in technology convinced Reagan of the ability of NATO to defeat the Soviet Union and its allies conventionally. The realization spurred his efforts to seek the abolition of nuclear weapons, a lifetime ambition. *Red Storm Rising* was for Reagan critical creative space in which he could reach conclusions about U.S. power that were wildly different from, and more optimistic than, "received opinion." Reagan's conclusions in turn spurred diplomacy and directly contributed to the fact that the Cold War ended without, as had long been feared, the outbreak of war.

Chapter 6, "Pebbles from Space," explores how popular culture shaped the debate over Reagan's Strategic Defense Initiative (SDI). This missile-defense proposal produced a public split and vocal argument in the science-fiction community. Politicians and journalists sought out the opinion of writers in the genre, treating Robert Heinlein, Arthur C. Clarke, and Isaac Asimov as credible and important voices in space policy. Defense hawks, for their part, seized on Clancy's fourth book, *The Cardinal of the Kremlin*, for its positive portrayal of SDI. Supporters in the military and government actively enhanced Clancy's credibility, in the belief that his mass-market appeal could build durable support not only for SDI but for persistent high levels of defense spending. Caspar Weinberger tried to emulate Clancy's success by writing a novel of his own, based on a collection of fictional vignettes that were thinly veiled policy proposals. The debate over SDI thus demonstrates the ability of policy makers to inspire works of popular culture and of those works to shift public opinion.

This book concludes with a brief examination of the legacy and consequences of Reagan's relationship with popular culture. It examines the evolving way in which Americans engage with their military and with the creeping militarization of U.S. foreign policy. The conclusion also argues that Reagan's use of fiction positively contributed to the peaceful end of the Cold War and helped restore Americans' belief in their nation's global mission. It also, however, created precedent for the oversimplification of policy discourse and led many to disengage from in-depth discussion of foreign intervention. Finally, the conclusion attempts to make a case for popular culture as a source of inspiration for policy. Employed deliberately and in conjunction with more conventional influences, it can challenge assumptions and increase understanding of potentially impacted groups. The result can be a nuanced and flexible strategy that employs a broad range of assets. Used correctly, fiction can help create policies that will ensure the good guys do indeed win.

1

RAISED ON MARS

Reagan and the Power of Narrative

S hortly after the new year began in 1989, Reagan addressed the nation from the Oval Office for the thirty-fourth and final time. He was ending his time in office, having recovered popularity lost amid the Iran-Contra scandal by means of a remarkable foreign policy, and saw his vice president elected to replace him. Few presidents manage to depart the White House on such a high note. Reagan's farewell address was valedictory, and for the last time he sought to impart his vision to the American public. Predictably, he chose to open with a story that embodied everything he believed about the United States.

Reagan told of a floundering boat overloaded with refugees from Vietnam. The "leaky little boat," tossed about by "choppy seas," seems doomed and its passengers imminently bound for a watery grave rather than the freedom they seek. Fortunately, a "young, smart, fiercely observant" sailor on board the aircraft carrier USS *Midway* spots the vessel, and the U.S. Navy swoops in to save the refugees. Safe on board, a refugee sees the sailor and enthusiastically greets him: "Hello, American Sailor. Hello freedom man"—for Reagan, a "small moment, with a big meaning."[1]

The likely apocryphal story was rich in symbolism, and in this short anecdote Reagan conveyed what he viewed as the core message and accomplishment of his administration. Here is American military on display—the story improbably features an aircraft carrier, an instantly recognizable symbol of American power, performing the rescue. But the use of the *Midway* in particular recalls World War II and America's role in saving the world from fascism and remaking the global order. Reagan's emphasis on the sailor's intelligence, youth, and ability represented the vast improvement in the morale and readiness of the U.S. military during the 1980s.

The refugee's origin in Vietnam is crucial to the story. It reflects Reagan's optimism that after massive increases in defense spending and success in Grenada, the United States had vanquished Vietnam Syndrome. The story also shows Reagan's belief that the sense of moral equivalence between the United States and communist states prevalent in the 1970s was now banished. No one would brave the open sea in a "leaky little boat" without the firm belief that a better life awaited. Reagan intended the story to convey that the world, and more importantly Americans themselves, had "rediscovered" the United States stood again for freedom.[2] The story occupied just eight lines in Reagan's speech but carried immense weight. It set the tone for the remainder of the address and memorably portrayed how Reagan saw the nation: a parable in a paragraph.

Elsewhere in his farewell Reagan reminded his audience that "life has a way of reminding you of big things through small incidents." He followed with an anecdote from his trip to Moscow, where people had recognized Nancy and himself and greeted them in a way that left them both "just about swept away by the warmth" before KGB (Committee of State Security) personnel intervened and dispersed the crowd.[3] Reagan took the idea from this brief interaction that the average Russian wanted peace but that the Soviet government remained communist and a threat. Throughout his life, he had found ideas of geopolitical importance in his day-to-day activities. The ability to relate the commonplace to complicated concepts and beliefs had played a key role in building Reagan's reputation as the "Great Communicator."

He searched for stories that embodied his belief in small moments with big meanings. Once Reagan found such a story, he would capture it on an index card and keep it in small boxes in his office with other quotes and jokes he had trapped.[4] Then he would free it during a speech or a meeting, hoping others would see the same meaning in the moment. Stories like that of the sailor and the refugee were important to Reagan. He used them not just to communicate his ideas with the American people but also to see how well his policies were working and to imagine how his actions or those of his administration would work in the near future. Factualness was not the most important aspect of a good Reagan story, and he would often change details of his stories to increase their impact.

This loose relationship with facts provided ample fodder for criticism of the president. Some also took it as evidence of a tendentious and unintelligent mind. David Stockman's tell-all about his time as Office of Management and Budget director argues that Reagan "had no business trying to make a revolution," as he could be easily made to "stumble into the wrong camp."[5] Advisors could "take skillful advantage of the president's capacity for befuddlement" to advance their own, often expensive, policy preferences. In one instance that Stockman describes, Weinberger used cartoons to represent a fiscal proposal from Office of Budget and Management as "a four-eyed wimp, who looked like Woody Allen, carrying a tiny rifle." The secretary of defense's own proposed budget "was G.I. Joe himself," carrying an M-60 machine gun. Stockman felt the "intellectually reprehensible" and "demeaning" display was responsible for his inability to get Reagan to seek a smaller budget for the Pentagon.[6]

Foreign leaders and dignitaries too recognized Reagan's preference for simple stories. Anatoly Dobrynin, longtime Soviet ambassador to the United States, disliked the president's "habit of borrowing dubious quotations" to illustrate points.[7] British officials who encountered it even sought to conceal Reagan's use of fiction, fearing it would embarrass the president if word leaked. They categorized as "particularly sensitive" a portion of Prime Minister Margaret Thatcher's post-Reykjavík call to Reagan in which the president had recommended the prime minister read *Red Storm Rising* by Tom Clancy to understand his viewpoint.[8] Thatcher herself and her private secretary, Charles Powell, agreed that others would take Reagan's resorting to a novel to understand the world as evidence that his "grasp of strategy must be pretty limited."[9]

Reagan disregarded such criticism, and his most senior advisors agreed with his choice to emphasize narrative and fiction. Both Shultz and Weinberger recognized that Reagan's stories effectively conveyed his larger messages and created better environments for negotiation and discussion of policy. In their own memoirs, both praised Reagan as an effective storyteller and argued that his delivering messages in this way was essential to his "high standing and deserved popularity" with the public.[10] Reagan's stories created "meaning" and helped "impart a larger message."[11] To Shultz and Weinberger, Reagan's story-telling made him a modern-day Aesop, teaching through fables rich in meaning to the American and global publics.

Near the end of his farewell address, Reagan returned to the importance of narrative. He feared that for many "younger parents . . . an unambivalent appreciation of America" was no longer something to teach their children. Similarly, he worried that "for those who create the popular culture, well-grounded patriotism [was] no longer the style."[12] These fears stemmed from Reagan's feelings rather than firm evidence. It would be difficult to characterize films and TV from the 1980s as anti-American; in fact, both frequently told stories of capable, virtuous American military might abroad and wholesome life in suburbia at home. Reagan's fears more likely stemmed from the shift in storytelling about the United States in the 1960s and 1970s and his belief that change, for good or ill, takes only one generation.

In his speech he admitted as much, stating that America's "spirit was back" but not yet "re-institutionalized." Enshrining his version of "well-grounded patriotism" would require filmmakers to return to a time when "movies celebrated democratic values and implicitly reinforced the idea that America was special." He longed for the simple narratives of his youth, the ones in which he saw himself, that had shaped his values. Reagan did not recognize that the easy identities he found in those books were not universal, that the stories he championed took no account of the nation's diversity and did not capture why other nations might view America differently. He firmly, and wrongly, believed that all Americans would react to such stories in the same way he had himself as a young man, when he had found religion in the works of Harold Bell Wright and love of technology and belief in freedom in those of Edgar Rice Burroughs. Reagan believed in the power of the right story.

A HOME BETWEEN THE COVERS

It seems odd at first glance to describe as an avid reader a politician known for his work in Hollywood and love of the screen, a man regarded by critics as an intellectual lightweight at best and, at worst, an amiable dunce. Reagan is partially to blame for this, as he disliked talking about books in public or being seen to read. Lou Cannon, a reporter who covered Reagan in both Sacramento and Washington, DC, and later wrote two biographies of him, believes this reluctance came in part from a "reader's conceit that books were secret personal treasure."[13] Nancy Reagan encouraged it, fearing that being seen as a bookworm would harm Reagan's appeal. Nevertheless, Reagan was a lifelong lover of books and rarely without one to read.

Reading was an essential part of his childhood and something that gave him great joy. Throughout his life, he fondly recalled "one evening when all the funny black marks on the paper clicked into place." His mother, Nelle, "was proud enough to canvass the neighbors and get them to come over" and see her son's new talent. While an article about the 1916 Preparedness Day Bombing in San Francisco would have been grim fare for a five-year-old to read publicly, Reagan's joy in his mother's pride that day remained evident every time he told the story.[14]

Reagan idolized his mother throughout his life, and she was a stabilizing influence on his early years. His father, Jack, found little success as a traveling salesman, moving his family throughout the Midwest in search of a stable job. Jack's alcoholism created problems for the family, and he was an often-absent figure in Reagan's childhood. Although his father was "the best raconteur [Reagan] ever heard" and had a "wry mordant humor," Reagan took his love of stories from his mother.[15] She was "the dean of dramatic recitals for the county" and saw the performances and reading as her "sole relaxation from her family and charitable duties."[16] Her reassurance to her son as they moved from town to town was that "he would never be lonely . . . if [he] enjoyed reading."[17]

This was particularly useful advice for a young boy who was frequently a newcomer and outsider and in any case tended toward introversion. Reagan took it to heart, devouring books from the local library. He would share Nelle's words of wisdom to others throughout his long time in the public eye. While governor of California he told Nancy Reynolds, his assistant for electronic media and a confidante of Nancy Reagan, that "if you have a book around you never lack for friends."[18] A 1971 letter to the children of Troy, Michigan, emphasized this idea of friendship. In it Reagan told the children that "books are often our best friends" and that a world without them would be one "without light."[19] He longed for these friends in the Oval Office as well. A letter early in his presidency declared that he "could think of no greater torture than being isolated" in a room "without something to read."[20]

Reagan was very particular about the types of books that could be his "friends." A novel needed to meet two main criteria: it had to have a protagonist in whom Reagan could see himself, and the good guys had to win. After all, as a young boy he had seen books as an escape from an alcoholic father, poverty, and his own shyness and loneliness. Reagan latched on to stories that featured men he wanted to be. His protagonists were archetypically male, strong, intelligent, and morally upright. They were not tragic; indeed, their virtues guaranteed success. Writing to the director of the Mobile, Alabama, public library in 1977, Reagan admitted he was still a "sucker for hero worship." He was conscious of the fact his early reading had given him "an abiding belief in the triumph of good over evil" and a certainty that heroes found success by living to high "standards of morality and fair play."[21]

Such "hero worship" provided a young Reagan with an alternate model of masculinity to that of his father. He generally spoke well of his father in later years, but more from Reagan's aversion to negativity than true affection. A formative moment for Reagan was finding Jack drunk, "dead to the world," lying in snow "flat on his back on the front porch" of their family home in Dixon, Illinois. Dragging his father to a warm bed, Reagan later recalled, he realized what his father's absences and "loud voices in the night meant."[22] The incident is a leading one in Reagan's first autobiography, *Where's the Rest of Me?*, and it marks the moment he rejected his father as a potential role model. Tom Reed, a longtime advisor, believes that the incident and having been the child of an alcoholic father contributed to Reagan's difficulty in making deep, lasting friendships. The unwillingness to open himself to people meant that Reagan's paperback friends took on greater importance.

As he looked for valid role models, Reagan settled into a relatively narrow type of book. He inhaled pulp adventure and science fiction and read religious ones given to him by his mother. The protagonists of the novels were uniformly White and male, and plots tended to feature themes of the "White Man's Burden." Given the state of publishing when Reagan was growing up in the 1910s and 1920s, this was perhaps preordained, but in later years Reagan never broadened his reading to incorporate more diverse protagonists, themes, and backgrounds. Their absence contributed greatly to his tone deafness on issues of race, sexuality, and class during his presidency. Additionally, his desire for unnuanced morality plays provided him a framework inadequate to the complexity of the world.

Reagan found his friends in the "house of magic," the Dixon public library.[23] In 1977 Reagan gave a telling and self-aware response to Dallas Baillio, the director of the Mobile public library. Baillio had asked a hundred prominent Americans to name the books that influenced them growing up. Reagan confessed to Baillio that his first thought had been to list classic literature he read and enjoyed but that "none were forthcoming."[24] Instead, he came clean about his reading habits, highlighting his love for King Arthur stories, Sherlock Holmes, and Mark Twain. Of all the books he read as a young man, however, he held one series in highest regard: Edgar Rice Burroughs' sagas of John Carter of Mars.

BOYHOOD ON BARSOOM

In November 1985 it was finally time for Reagan to meet with a general secretary of the Communist Party of the Soviet Union. Over the previous four years, the combination of a geriatric Soviet leadership class and a strategic environment viewed as less than ideal by the White House prevented Reagan from sitting down with his Soviet counterpart. The ascent of the reformist Mikhail Gorbachev and a sense in the Reagan administration that in its first term it had closed several strategic gaps set the stage for a high-stakes summit in Geneva.

After a day of tense discussions, the delegations attended a dinner hosted by the Gorbachevs. Conversation generally centered on lighter fare and polite comments about how each side was glad to be in Geneva speaking with the other. In this relaxed setting Reagan mused with Gorbachev and Soviet foreign minister Eduard Shevardnadze about what would happen if aliens used the February 1986 return of Halley's Comet to attack earth. He felt certain such a threat could not help but "unite all the peoples of the world."[25] The Soviet leader pledged that in such a situation the Union of Soviet Socialist Republics (USSR) would help defend the earth. Reagan responded that the United States would do the same.

Reagan's scenario seemed better suited to a science-fiction novel than a dinner at a bilateral summit. However, it fits in the context of his subsequent comments, in which he mentioned the seventeenth chapter of the biblical Book of Acts, which describes all the peoples of earth as being made of one blood, and quoted Theodore Roosevelt to the effect that the true goal of nations is peace with self-respect. Finally, he noted that the day was the forty-third anniversary of the beginning of the Soviet counterattack at Stalingrad, evoking a time when the Americans and Soviets allied against a common threat and the

USSR had "turned the war around." He expressed hope that this summit could mark "another turning point for all mankind."[26]

The "alien" anecdote was, then, an attempt to build rapport and show that agreement was possible in the face of dire emergency, not a senile flight of fancy. It is likely that Reagan considered that the aliens had already arrived, in the form of nuclear weapons: he had often tried to include references to "little green men" in draft speeches in the context of arms control.[27] Reagan's frequent connection of alien invasion with policy speaks to his lifelong love of the science-fiction genre. He was particularly taken with its seemingly miraculous uses of technology.

In his letter to the director of the Mobile public library, Reagan went out of his way to express his love for "science fiction, 'John Carter Warlord of Mars' and all the other John Carter books."[28] He similarly fondly recalled "frequent trips to the strange kingdoms" of Mars in a letter to a resident of his old hometown, Dixon.[29] In it he expressed surprise that John Carter stories had fallen out of vogue. Reagan recognized Burroughs' important role in the popularity of science fiction generally and felt that the author's portrayal of the Red Planet and its marvelous technologies still held real value seventy years later.

Legendary science-fiction writer Ray Bradbury agreed with Reagan's view. Speaking in 2010, he called Burroughs "the most influential writer in the entire history of the world." He thought so because ten-year-olds "fell in love with John Carter and Tarzan and decided to be something romantic." Burroughs had inspired not only Bradbury and others writing in the genre but also legions of scientists, astronauts, and, as Reagan exemplifies, politicians. In Bradbury's estimation, John Carter "put us on the moon." Bradbury was being intentionally hyperbolic, knowing that ranking pulp stories above Shakespeare or Tolstoy "upsets everyone terribly." However, he had a point: if books like *Princess of Mars* were not high literary achievements, they did leave a mark on the world. They "gave romance and adventure to a whole generation of boys," inspiring them to "become special."[30] This was certainly true in Reagan's case, and it is no accident that he would be drawn more to John Carter than to Tarzan. It would be hard for a boy to travel much farther from a troubled home than to the red soil of Mars.

Burroughs himself had come to writing relatively late in life, not publishing his first story until he was thirty-five. His first passion was the military, where he hoped to make a career. He earned an appointment to the U.S. Military Academy but failed the entrance exams, dashing his hopes of becoming an officer. Instead, he enlisted in the Seventh Cavalry, serving in Arizona. Service in the Southwest did not agree with him, and Burroughs left the Army in 1897.[31] News that Theodore Roosevelt was raising a regiment for the Spanish-American War spurred Burroughs to seek a return to the military, but the Rough Rider declined his request to join, wary of overrecruiting the regiment.[32]

Over the next fifteen years Burroughs struggled to find a career path, working at various times with his father's battery company and as a prospector, railroad policeman, and salesman. Facing financial ruin, he turned to writing and in 1911 sold "A Princess of Mars" to The All-Story magazine for four hundred dollars for serial publication. Publishers rejected it in book form; one of them, Houghton Mifflin, found it "not at all probable" that it could "make use of the story of a Virginia soldier of fortune miraculously transported to Mars." Its editors believed the concept too fantastical, that audiences would reject such a silly premise. The publishers misjudged the audience. Burroughs' John Carter stories caused sales of The All-Story magazine to spike to new highs. The first book editions of John Carter's adventures on Mars would appear in 1917.

"A Princess of Mars" tells the story of John Carter, a former Confederate cavalryman transported to the Red Planet. Burroughs (as the novel's speaker) presents Carter as his uncle and claims to have received the manuscript from him with strict instructions not to print it until twenty-one years after Carter's "death." The writings reveal that Carter had found a magical way to travel to Mars and once there had discovered that in the planet's lesser gravity he had superior strength and speed. His impressive physical feats strike awe into the first Martians he encounters, who eventually make him a chief. Carter then rescues and woos Dejah Thoris, the eponymous princess, and becomes a leader of one of the planet's technologically advanced city-states. The book ends in a cliffhanger, with Carter racing to restore the dying planet's massive oxygen generator, blacking out, and awakening back on earth unsure if he had saved Dejah Thoris, their child, and the Red Planet (which its inhabitants know as Barsoom).[33]

Fortunately for devoted readers, Burroughs received another manuscript from his "uncle." Carter tells Burroughs to use his discretion in publishing them, because many "Earth men have not yet progressed to a point where they can comprehend" Carter's adventures and that he was "not to feel aggrieved if they laugh at you"—a dig at the publishers who previously rejected Burroughs' sub-missions.[34] The new book, *The Gods of Mars*, and its sequel, *Warlord of Mars*, see Carter dismantle the existing power structures on Mars and debunk the planet's religion. By the end of the initial trilogy, Carter is widely beloved on the planet and acclaimed as the "Warlord of Barsoom." The *Warlord of Mars* ends with Carter standing above his rapturous people kissing his queen, Dejah Thoris, "a world's most beautiful woman."[35]

Burroughs drew many elements from his own life in creating the John Carter of his stories. Both are cavalrymen, though Burroughs opted to make John Carter an ex-Confederate, perhaps to capitalize on the contemporary resurgence of Lost Cause mythology. The description of the Arizona setting of the opening episode bears strong evidence of Burrough's service there. Carter's dire financial straits at the start of *"A Princess of Mars"*—he is in Arizona pros-pecting for gold—matches Burroughs' post-Army life as well. The books blend science fiction with western tropes prominent in popular literature at the time. Most of Carter's path matches that of a "white hat" in a cowboy story, the gun-man coming into town to save it.

Burroughs also employed the damaging racial tropes common to pulp stories. The Apaches who set upon Carter in the first pages are portrayed as superstitious and backward but also fierce fighters and remorseless killers. His escape leads to his discovery of both a rich vein of gold and, inadvertently, instantaneous conveyance to Barsoom. There Carter falls in with a local tribe, the Tharks, clearly intended to stand in for Native Americans. Its chieftain, Tars Tarkas, plays the role of the "noble savage" who teaches Carter how to survive and whom in return Carter elevates, with his green race, into civilization—specifically, that of Dejah Thoris' red race, whose cities he soon encounters. Throughout the series race is a major theme; Burroughs introduces different Martian societies whose global roles are defined by color. Carter's actions in raising the stations of the green Martians and destroying the false beliefs of nearly the entire planet supported contemporary ideas about the "White Man's Burden," as held up by Rudyard Kipling. Throughout the John Carter books, stand-ins for Native Americans, African Americans, and peoples throughout the then-colonized world are "civilized" through the moral fortitude of a White Southerner. Burroughs pairs with Kipling as unapologetic cheerleaders for imperialism. Ronald Reagan's reading of Burroughs, as well as of Kipling, in these contexts was to create a damaging legacy, by which he would seek to apply the simplistic view of non-White peoples needing rescue to policy making for the entire global South.

Carter himself may be the archetype of the hero Reagan would admit to worshipping. This cavalryman is "a splendid specimen of manhood," whose steel-gray eyes reflect a combination of "strong and loyal character" with "fire and initiative."[36] Throughout his adventures Carter throws himself into danger to save his friends and allies. His loyalty extends to his Martian hound (equivalent), which he saves from certain death by fighting a giant, six-limbed white ape. Mars' most dangerous predators are no deterrent to a man protecting his dog. Carter also upholds early-twentieth-century notions of feminine honor. He protects Dejah Thoris from assault when she is held prisoner by the Tharks, even at risk to his personal position with the tribe. He spurns advances from other women and dislikes sexual forwardness. John Carter follows a simple moral code and uses it to transform the focus of society from violence and strength to honor and justice. For Reagan, these novels provided the sort of easy narrative that formed his "abiding belief in the triumph of good over evil."[37]

Reagan and many other children of his generation saw the man they wanted to be in Carter and imagined themselves in his sandals. The way Burroughs presented ideas of parental love in his narratives also likely increased their appeal to Reagan. Thark society is initially communal, with no affection between parents and their young. Martians of all races are oviparous; after they hatch, young Tharks are claimed at random and have no idea who their parents are. Only Sola, a Thark female who becomes a close confidante of Carter, shows "characteristics of sympathy, kindliness, and affection."[38] This is because she, unique to her people, had known her actual mother's love. Unfortunately, her mother had been found raising her and executed, but still refused to reveal where she had hidden Sola or the identity of her partner. In Burroughs' personal world, maternal love is defined by sacrifice and is responsible for instilling basic virtue.

Fathers are absent or at least distant figures on Barsoom. Sola's father is in fact Tars Tarkas, who is absent from her life not by intention but because he does not know she is still alive. Sola, who knows her parentage, watches him and sees that "his great love is as strong in his breast" for his lost family even after much time passes and takes pride in his efforts to change Thark society. Still, for much of the first book he remains an untouchable figure. Carter is himself a distant father to the son conceived late in the novel with Dejah Thoris. Transported unwillingly back to earth, he is unable to return for ten years. He first meets his son, Carthoris, when he is already a young man. Carthoris' only knowledge of Carter is what Dejah Thoris had "described to [him] a thousand times"—his stature, manner, and fighting prowess. Even after fighting alongside his father, however, Carthoris confesses that Carter's ability is not what most impresses him, rather that Carter's first words to him were of Dejah Thoris. Carthoris valued this fidelity to his mother over anything Carter could provide him directly.

Reagan likely strongly identified with Burrough's implicit message that mothers instill virtue in their children. Carthoris and Sola become heroes thanks to lessons from their mothers and idealized images of their absent, untouchable fathers. Jack Reagan had not been removed from his family in a literal sense, but his alcoholism created emotional absences keenly felt by a young Reagan. Nelle worked to keep an idealized version of Jack alive in his sons' eyes. She blamed the absences on "something that was beyond his control." The "bouts with the dark demon in the bottle" held him aloof from his family just as the void of space separated Carter from Carthoris. Nelle's stories, though, created hope for the permanent, triumphant return of the "bluff and hearty man [Reagan] knew and loved."[39]

Imaginative technology was part of the appeal of John Carter series to not only Reagan but a wide audience as well. Burroughs filled Mars with flying battleships, disintegration rays, and atmosphere factories. A secretive yellow race in arctic regions lives in cities with thick clear domes, shields to protect them from aerial threats and polar weather. The books offered readers a glimpse of things that could be, fueling their imagination. Importantly, though, in the series technology alone does not ensure success: it is Carter's intelligence and devotion to freedom that allow him to adapt to the new technologies and to create alliances. This combination of technology and an appealing vision of a free society fuel his rise among the Martians and the defeat of those who would oppress Martians and maintain the status quo. Reagan latched on to this pairing and made it central to how he talked about the future of the United States.

Speaking to the graduating class of U.S. Air Force Academy cadets in 1984, Reagan declared that "technology plus freedom equals opportunity and progress." Only the limits of their "own courage and imagination" could hold the new officers back, and Reagan believed that they, and American society, had ample reserves of both. He knew this to be true because, as he reminded the audience, in his lifetime he had witnessed aviation go from "open cockpits to lunar landings" and rocketry from the science fiction to space shuttles.[40] His childhood imaginings were now hard reality.

Imagination was critically important to Reagan's policy and a strong influence on it. Biographer Lou Cannon argues that Reagan resisted cuts to National Aeronautics and Space Administration "because spaceflight appealed to his own imagination."[41] A letter he wrote to a critic of NASA funding in the 1970s supports this sense. Reagan told the writer, "Man's great yearning to explore the great unknown should not be curbed because he can't tell in detail what he hopes to find."[42] The desire to explore the unknown and imagine its possibilities fit Reagan's version of American exceptionalism; he linked it to the foundational myth of pioneers and "rugged individualism" on the frontier.

Reagan drew on the linkage as he comforted the nation in the wake of the 1986 *Challenger* explosion. He told the grieving nation that "we've grown used to the wonders in this century" and that "it's hard to dazzle us," because of the great leaps technology had made in so short a period. NASA still had the power to dazzle, though, because its explorations had "only just begun." Its scientists and astronauts, and by proxy all Americans, were pioneers engaged in exploration and discovery. As he would in his farewell address, Reagan evoked the image of small wooden craft at sea: just as the Vietnamese refugees had been like the Pilgrims on *Mayflower*, so were the fallen astronauts like Sir Francis Drake, whose "great frontiers were the oceans."[43] What Reagan admired in the astronauts was the special spirit with which they paired imagination and technology in the service of their nation.

Reagan's ability to communicate this vision poignantly and relatably made the speech one of his most effective and memorable. In *The Impossible Presidency*, Jeremi Suri sees a great strength of Reagan in how he "married traditional values of self-sufficiency and individual freedom with modern technologies of science and war."[44] The speeches at the Air Force Academy and after the *Challenger* explosion show this well. In both, Reagan draws on American self-perceptions about the making of the nation, links them to freedom, and then promises that with technology a great future, as yet only imagined, was in reach. This way of approaching policy fixed Reagan's executive focus on vision and creativity rather than policy detail.

His reading of Burroughs is not solely responsible for this mindset, but the ex-Confederate warlord of Mars did exert significant influence on how Reagan thought about the world. It is perhaps unsurprising then that Edmund Morris chose in his unorthodox but official biography to introduce Reagan during one of his interviews with the president lost in a memory of being a lifeguard by a river, sitting under an old oak tree eating a hamburger and reading *A Princess of Mars*.[45] To Morris, that is where Reagan began. Morris then imagines leaving the interview to research the question of whether or not Burroughs' cities under protective domes influenced Reagan's thoughts on protection of the nation from nuclear attack.

RELIGIOUS FICTION

On March 30, 1981, Reagan ventured into politically hostile territory. He sought to convince members of the American Federation of Labor and Congress of Industrial Organizations (AFL-CIO) gathered in the Washington Hilton of the need for massive cuts to federal spending—cuts that would mean no money for large infrastructure programs and their union jobs. His own past as a union leader and supporter of organized labor did not avail him as he sought to explain his plan to navigate the ongoing economic crisis. In an unusually specific speech by his standards, Reagan painted a dire picture with references to statistics and Soviet defense spending. The speech fell flat. He convinced few, if any, in the room to support his budget.[46] The failure was unfortunate but not disastrous, and the speech would likely soon be forgotten. Then a would-be assassin struck.

As Reagan exited the Hilton, John Hinckley opened fire with a revolver. His first six shots missed their intended target but did hit a Secret Service agent, a District of Columbia police officer, and Press Secretary James Brady, who received a wound so severe that he would die of its effects thirty-three years later. One bullet struck the presidential limousine, but it splintered on the vehicle's protective armor, and a fragment hit Reagan, lodging in his lung. His security detail, quickly realizing that the situation was grave, drove him to the nearby George Washington University Hospital rather than the Walter Reed Army Medical Center (as then known), five miles away in city traffic. Reagan was rushed into surgery. A successful operation and, for the seventy-year-old president, a remarkably rapid recovery had him active again in time to address a joint session of Congress a month later on his economic plan. The bipartisan and nationwide outpouring of support for the wounded president led to the passage of his agenda. It is likely Hinckley's bullet fragment did far more than Reagan's Hilton speech could have to achieve that result.

A fantasy sparked by a fictional character inspired Hinckley to plan his attack. He fixated on Jodie Foster who, as a thirteen-year-old actress in the 1976 film *Taxi Driver*, played a sex-trafficked child. After stalking the actress when she attended Yale, Hinckley decided to emulate *Taxi Driver*'s antihero and carry out an assassination to gain her attention. Just as in the film former Marine Travis Bickle failed to kill Senator Palantine, Hinckley failed to kill Reagan, and his attempt rightly horrified Foster. The film itself was an example of the sort of 1970s pop culture that Reagan liked to rail at, believing that its embrace of antiheroes and negative depictions of (in this case former) military personnel was damaging and dangerous. In this extreme case, a violent and severely mentally ill man showed Reagan was right about the power of narratives. Certainly, most people would not and did not resort to violent action, but *Taxi Driver* did help define the national mood, both capturing how many Americans felt and expanding that feeling to others. Additionally, the mortal danger he experienced almost certainly increased Reagan's conviction that stories in popular culture mattered.

Even in the hospital Reagan communicated with jokes and stories. He told Nancy that he had forgotten to duck, and just before the operation expressed his hope to the surgical team that they were all Republicans.[47] Good humor and efforts at reassurance aside, the attempt on his life had the profound effect on Reagan that might be expected. On April 11, writing in his diary for the first time after the attack, Reagan credited God with saving his life and wrote, "whatever happens now I owe my life to God and will try to serve him in every way I can."[48] Reagan came to believe he survived the attempt because he had a special mission to perform as president. In his second autobiography, *An American Life*, he expressed his sense that perhaps he was meant to use the "years God [had] given [him] to reduce the threat of nuclear war."[49] Reagan believed he was on a mission from above and that the way to show his faith was with great acts.

This fit with how Reagan viewed religion broadly. He felt actions mattered more than church attendance or knowledge of Scripture. His beliefs originated in a book he read around the same time he first sought escape on John Carter's

Barsoom. Nelle Reagan gave him a copy of Harold Bell Wright's *That Printer of Udell's*, and in it Reagan found another hero worthy of worship, the protagonist, Dick Falkner. Reagan expressed to Wright's daughter-in-law in 1984, his admiration for the author's work and acknowledged "it [had] an impact he would always remember." Falkner was a "role model" who was to lead Reagan to embrace religion. *That Printer of Udell's* "played a definite part" in creating the Reagan who found a mission from God in 1981.[50]

Though largely forgotten now, Wright was one of the most popular writers of his day. Nelle and Ronald Reagan were far from the only people to read his books in the 1910s and find a deeper faith; Wright, pastor of a series of small churches, was the first American author to sell a million copies of a book. Wright came from a broken home, with an alcoholic father. His mother had died when he was eleven, after which he lived with relations and worked odd jobs. Frequently abused and angry at the exploitation he experienced, he finally found himself working in a printer's shop. There he also made a series of choices that eventually led him to the ministry.

He was "called to" a number of pulpits, but at length, in Pittsburg, Kansas, he came to recognize his sermons were not moving his flock. He sought a way to make his preaching more relevant, to apply Christian tenets and began using his own life story as the basis for fictional examples in his sermons. Eventually Wright collected them as a book—a thinly veiled autobiography—and sold it to the Book Supply Company of Chicago, which released it in 1903 as *That Printer of Udell's*.[51]

In it Dick Falkner serves as Wright's avatar. The book opens with the protagonist's mother dying of consumption in a small cabin. She dies in mid-prayer, beseeching, "God, take ker' o' Dick," who mourns briefly but then looks at his alcoholic father passed out drunk in the small cabin. Realizing that now his dad could not "hurt Maw anymore," the ten-year-old takes his dog and leaves.[52] The novel then advances sixteen years to reveal a Falkner who has become a bitter, violent young man. When a fellow transient insults his mother's memory Falkner threatens to kill him, and in the altercation that ensues Falkner learns that his father had died recently. Falkner then reflects on all the times when "inspired by his mother" he nearly broke free from evil only to be "dragged back by the training and memory of his father."[53] The news of his father's passing frees Falkner from this cycle, and he resolves to become a new man.

It is easy to see the appeal of this opening chapter to a young Reagan. As the novel opens, its hero is the same age as Reagan, who could see his own family in the saintly mother and drunken father of Dick Falkner. Of course, Nelle Reagan was still alive, though she had nearly died, as Reagan could vividly recall, during the Spanish Flu pandemic.[54] Wright's emphasis on values instilled by maternal love echoed Burroughs in the John Carter novels. Another thing that appealed to Reagan about Wright's novel: it was a novel of redemption and remaking for a boy from such a home. The preacher's story of Dick Falkner making himself into a worthy man helped Reagan imagine a path he too could follow.

The rest of Wright's narrative sees Falkner arrive in the town of Boyd, where churchgoers reject his requests for work, despite having just received a sermon on the need to help the poorest. The only person in town who offers anything other than bland platitudes is George Udell, who does not attend church. Udell gives Falkner work (in his print shop), food, and shelter and slowly teaches him to be a better man. Falkner becomes a youth leader in the church, and in time seeks to court Amy, the daughter of the town's wealthiest merchant. The father rejects their relationship, driving Amy to run away. Unable to fend for herself she winds up in a brothel. Falkner finds her and convinces her she can return, with the promise that though "we have each fallen" all can be "forgiven and accepted" if they choose virtuous action in the future.[55] Amy's father, though outwardly religious, is more concerned with his pride than "his daughter's salvation from sin" and still seeks to oppose her marriage to a man who "came to this town as a common tramp."[56] Dick eventually wins approval, and by the end of the novel the town has elected him to the U.S. House of Representatives. The novel closes with the married Dick and Amy pausing on their journey to Washington to visit the graves of Dick's parents and so complete his reconciliation.

That Printer of Udell's changed Reagan's life. His ability to find himself, and hope, in Wright's narrative made him a "practical Christian."[57] Shortly after reading it he chose to join his mother's denomination, the Disciples of Christ, the denomination in which Wright ministered.[58] The novel contributed to the young Reagan's "abiding belief in the triumph of good over evil" and showed him the path to that victory.[59] Victory, and faith, required action. The townspeople of Boyd failed to be good Christians because they went to church but did not act on their faith outside it. They were no better than the drunks, con men, and murderers Falkner encountered as a transient. The fallen Falkner and Amy redeemed themselves, and ultimately their town, through action backed by faith.

Reagan's speeches embraced this idea throughout his political career. His prospects skyrocketed with his 1964 televised campaign speech in support of the Republican nominee for president, Barry Goldwater. It was titled "A Time for Choosing," and in it he criticized "well-meaning politicians" who pursued a "policy of accommodation" that sought "peace at any price." In apocalyptic language, Reagan promised that such accommodation would only ensure the United States would fall into "a thousand years of darkness." Reagan asked his viewers at home if Moses should have asked the Israelites to endure a thousand more years of slavery or if Christ should have refused the cross. Reagan believed the answers were obvious, that action taken in the name of faith was greater than even the most beautiful and best-intentioned prayer. Only through action could Americans make their "rendezvous with destiny."[60]

The famous "Evil Empire" speech of 1983 to the National Association of Evangelicals cast the need for action, this time in the Cold War, in similar terms. Reagan drew on C. S. Lewis' "unforgettable" *Screwtape Letters* to remind his audience it is due not to "sordid dens of crime" that evil does not triumph but rather to the "quiet men in white collars" who speak in "soothing terms of brotherhood." Evangelicals needed to "beware the temptation of pride," the deadly sin that doomed the father of Wright's character Amy, as they "blithely declare [themselves] above it all." Only if they chose to "speak out against those who would place the United States in a position of military and moral inferiority" could the United States prevail in the Cold War. Victory required action.[61]

Religion drove Reagan's vision of the Cold War. Faith was important to him, but concrete activity in the name of that faith mattered more. This followed from the fact that Reagan did not find his faith in pews or the words of a preacher but in the printed words of a book. What he found in the pages of *That Printer of Udell's* helps explain why Reagan felt called to show his devotion in a hospital bed with a dangerous bullet wound. John Patrick Diggins finds Reagan's religious beliefs "baffling," seeming to "offer a Christianity without Christ and the crucifixion."[62] Diggins felt Reagan's religiosity was "without reference to sin, evil, suffering, or sacrifice."[63] Reagan's views and practice were indeed unconventional, but his speeches throughout his career make clear that sin and sacrifice were important parts of his faith. His optimism caused him not to dwell on them, however, notwithstanding his occasional apocalyptic language, but instead to focus on humanity toward others as a general good. This made anything threatening liberty a prime evil in the context of his faith (communism being the worst). His beliefs rested on the need to identify these evils and act against them. At its best, this impulse allowed Reagan to reestablish the moral high ground of the United States in the Cold War and so inspire oppressed peoples in Eastern Europe. At its worst, it led him to act instead of listening and understanding, leading his administration to support morally repugnant regimes and, at least tacitly, perpetrators of horrific evils.

LEARNING TO TELL THE STORY

It was April 1935, and Reagan was panicking. He was in the broadcast booth for WHO Radio Des Moines calling an early-season Cubs game.[64] They were facing their archrival St. Louis Cardinals, who had future Hall-of-Famer Dizzy Dean on the mound. The game was tied in the ninth with Auggie Galan striding to the plate. At this moment of high drama, WHO's telegraph feed cut out, leaving Reagan no way to know what was happening three hundred miles away in Chicago. Needing to fill the airtime to prevent his listening audience from finding the game on a different station, Reagan made up the action. For over six minutes Reagan conjured an epic battle between Dean and Galan, who kept fouling off the Cardinal ace's pitches to avoid striking out or hitting an easily fieldable ball. One nearly left the park for what would have been a home run had it only been in fair territory, and Reagan "described in detail the redheaded kid who had scrambled" for the souvenir.[65]

Finally, the telegraph feed returned, revealing that Galan had in fact flied out to the left fielder on the first pitch he saw. Reagan reported that as if it happened on the next pitch and resumed calling the game from the feed. A modern broadcaster would not be able to get away with such a thing, particularly so inflating Dean's pitch count. However, Reagan's act was not unusual for the time. Broadcast rights were not managed in the same way they are today, and numerous stations broadcast each game. Few of these play-by-play men ever called a game from the park where it was actually played, say, Wrigley Field. Instead, they created stories from information passed from the site in two- or three-letter codes by telegraph. Simply translating "SC1" into "Curve ball, strike one," would not make for compelling listening.[66] Instead, Reagan had to imagine the sights, sounds, and smells of the ballpark and create an immersive story for his listeners. A fan hearing "Dutch" Reagan over the radio could re-create correctly the box score of a game but would have a completely different understanding of how it had unfolded than that of a spectator. Most of Reagan's broadcasts contained only the smallest pieces of truth, but these pieces were the ones that mattered most.

The April 24, 1935, game stands out as Reagan's favorite memory from his days of calling baseball in Des Moines. He recounted the story often. It appears in his autobiography and in letters he wrote from the White House; he even told it to Harry Caray during a 1988 Cubs–Pirates game.[67] On the surface it is odd that this was the game he returned to. It was a relatively meaningless game in a year filled with dramatic Cubs moments. The team closed out September on a twenty-one-game winning streak that allowed them to run down the Cardinals in the standings and claim the National League pennant.[68] They would fall to the Detroit Tigers in six games at the World Series, but at least during his presidency Reagan could lay claim to being one of the few living broadcasters who had called a Cubs World Series game. The team reached the Series in 1938 and 1945, before making its fans wait seventy-one years to see them return.[69] Reagan had experienced something Cubs fans and Harry Caray yearned for, but, sitting next to the legendary broadcaster, he chose to tell the story of a lazy fly ball.

Galan's pop out was vivid to Reagan because that moment had affected him personally. The dead feed was the most pressure he ever felt calling a game. If he had been calling games from the press box at Wrigley instead of in Iowa, it would likely have been the tension and emotion in the park during the September run and World Series that left him with memories, but as it was, those were distant abstractions. Reagan learned best when he could put himself into a story. His broadcasting experience taught him the importance of creating compelling narratives to convey messages.

Reagan's understanding of blending message with narrative led to his hiring as a broadcaster. Shortly after graduating from Eureka College he auditioned with WOC Radio in Davenport, Iowa. Reagan exaggerated his college football prowess to the station manager, who, thinking Reagan had been a starter rather than a benchwarmer, invited him to audition for a football play-by-play position. With the instruction to "tell us about a game and make [us] see it," Reagan entered the booth. Having limited time to impress the manager, Reagan created "a dream game" with the "kind of climax" that would "permit a little excitement to creep in."[70] Drawing on a game from the previous season between Eureka College and Western State, he described a "chill wind" blowing through the stadium as the teams battled in a tight contest. Reagan set up his alma mater for a dramatic "college-try" finish as the clock expired. The play succeeds, thanks in part to Reagan's leveling a linebacker "with a block that could be felt in the press box"—and the good guys win.[71]

Duly impressed by Reagan's flair for the dramatic, the station manager assigned Reagan to call a University of Iowa game the next week. Reagan "played it straight" in the first quarter, but after trading off with another broadcaster for the second quarter he realized he needed to tell a better story. Reagan changed his approach in the third quarter, throwing himself into the broadcast and calling the game so compellingly the station manager telegraphed him to call the rest of it by himself. Afterward, Reagan was hired full-time with a pay raise.[72] The decision to change his broadcasting style midgame reflected Reagan's recognition of the importance of how a story is told. His job was to play in "the theater of the mind," and captivating his audience would require dramatic liberties.[73] His success in this role would lead to a job at WHO and the chance to speak to a larger audience. This in turn set him on the path to tell even grander stories on the silver screen.

After the 1935 season, WHO dispatched Reagan to the Cubs spring training in Catalina, California. He sent back letters to be read on the air detailing player life there. Learning about a "smart-bottomed young reporter" on the receiving end of a "one-punch fight" made fans feel more connected to the team, and the stories helped Reagan expand his audience.[74] His success on that trip led to another opportunity in 1936, and this time he leveraged connections to get an agent and a screen test with Warner Brothers. Thanks to creative embellishment of his acting background and his agent's willingness to tell "little white lies," Reagan received a contract paying him two hundred dollars per week.[75] The merging of reality and fiction in Reagan's time as a radio broadcaster had helped him achieve his life's ambition, reinforcing his belief that content mattered less than the message that conveyed it.

Working as an actor did little to dissuade Reagan from this belief. Though his star peaked with a supporting role in the 1942 Oscar-nominated *Kings Row*, on the way he had spent over two decades immersed in the creation and telling of stories. He saw firsthand how these narratives could influence the public. During World War II Reagan (an Army reservist exempted by poor vision from combat duty) served with the First Motion Picture Unit in Hollywood making training and propaganda films. He later expressed pride in how these films reduced the time it took to train new soldiers and pilots. The unit was also involved in editing war footage into newsreels. Reagan recognized that images of an aircraft on fire with "the pilot vainly trying to get out of the cockpit" could not see a wide release.[76] The unit needed to produce a clean and triumphant narrative of the war, one that avoided shocking the sensibilities of the American public.

Also, Reagan starred in *This Is the Army*, a sequel to Irving Berlin's musical from World War I, *Yip, Yip, Yaphank*. The movie, featuring Kate Smith's iconic performance of "God Bless America," was meant to raise funds for Army Emergency Relief and more broadly to build support for the war effort.[77] Reagan took immense pride in his unit's role and understandably believed its mission was an important one. However, he would come to regret his role in one aspect of his unit's success, a concerted effort to present the Soviet Union to an initially skeptical public as an acceptable ally and "friend."

In a 1944 radio broadcast, Reagan played a frontline infantryman. He encounters Secretary of the Treasury Henry Morgenthau (reading the part himself), who predicts that Germany and Japan will surrender unconditionally to end the war. When Reagan's character expresses doubt, Morgenthau promises him that he would find the "answer in Russia," where the Soviets represented the "final assurance of the future of free men." The broadcast was meant to reassure Americans that their Soviet allies were acting in the name of justice and freedom on the Eastern Front; Morgenthau credits them with "removing some of the worst stains from the face of the earth."[78] This rosy assessment glossed over the horrific conduct of the Red Army as it advanced toward Berlin. While the Soviets certainly did play a pivotal and likely decisive role in destroying the Nazi regime, they also left an appalling trail of murdered innocents and raped women. The Roosevelt administration, including Morgenthau, were aware of these atrocities but believed winning the war was more important than holding the Soviets accountable—which would have been arguably impossible at the time in any case.[79] As a result, the administration consciously pushed the false narrative of the Red Army as a righteous, moral force. Radio programs like Reagan's were a key elements of this effort; Morgenthau even wrote Reagan that their show had been the "most effective program of its kind since the beginning of the war."[80]

Hollywood during the war bolstered favorable perceptions not only of the Red Army but of the Soviet system. While Reagan was not directly involved in the latter, his studio and his boss, Warner Brothers and Jack Warner, respectively, were—providing Reagan with a glimpse of the process. The studio produced *Mission to Moscow* based on the memoir of Joseph Davies, a Franklin D. Roosevelt confidant, of his time as ambassador to the Soviet Union during the Great Terror.[81] The product portrayed the Soviet Union and Joseph Stalin so favorably that it earned the nickname "Submission to Moscow." Stalin certainly approved, and when Davies presented him with a copy of the film the dictator authorized its release throughout the Soviet Union.[82] A decade later, in a fear-tinged political environment, the film would be used against Hollywood by the House Un-American Activities Committee (HUAC) as proof that filmmakers were aggressively supporting communism in the United States. However, it was certainly the type of movie the government had wanted made at the time.

Reagan showed similar hypocrisy. While there is no indication that he had objected at the time to his role in building support for the Soviet Union, he became in the era of McCarthyism a vocal critic of that effort. He would argue that films like *Mission to Moscow* were "agitprop" ("agitation-propaganda" in the Russian portmanteau) and the result of what happened if someone "in the story department approved a script . . . without lookin' too closely at what was written between the lines."[83] He spent most of a 1985 session with Edmund Morris talking about the film. To Jack Matlock and other advisors Reagan argued that the film and other productions like it had created a deep reluctance on the part of political leaders to criticize the Soviets both during the war and immediately after. Politicians did not want to be out of step with the narrative Hollywood advanced.[84]

Reagan's first decade in Hollywood and service in World War II, then, reinforced his belief in the ability of fiction to spread important messages. In the next decade in the movie business he would undergo a political transformation, from New Deal Democrat to Goldwater Republican. He was to assert that the Democratic Party left him, but this was not the case. The move was another response to a combination of personal experience and compelling narrative.

His "hero worship" of sympathetic protagonists continued. An adult Reagan found new John Carters and Dick Falkners in the pages of Michener, Koestler, Chambers, and L'Amour. These authors would exert a profound influence on how the increasingly politically active Reagan thought about the world and the place of the United States in it.

2

FRIENDLY WITNESS

Politics, Belief, and Narrative

Reagan in December 1983 stood in front of a room full of heroes where he was to receive the Patriot Award. He was addressing the Medal of Honor Society, and the audience of around 650 included several recipients of their nation's highest military honor. The president used the occasion and audience to highlight the stark difference he saw between what American and Soviet societies valued.[1] Reagan believed that the contrast demonstrated the "great difference" between the Cold War rivals and showed the United States was "morally strong with a creed and vision" but the Soviet Union was not.[2] He told his audience two stories to illustrate the point.

He first told of a newspaper article in the 1960s that had left him confused. A Spaniard had recently been decorated as a Hero of the Soviet Union, the Soviet equivalent of the Medal of Honor. There was little in the man's biography to merit such a high accolade; he was working in Moscow as an interpreter following an eight-year period where he resided uneventfully in Cuba. It took another article to show Reagan the actions that earned the man his medal. The Spaniard in question was Ramon Mercader, the assassin in 1940 of the exiled Leon Trotsky, whom Stalin had considered a deadly enemy because of his competing interpretation of communist ideology. That the Soviets would grant "their highest honor to a political assassin" told Reagan that theirs was a morally insidious society.[3]

To contrast this, Reagan reflected on his own service and on a citation for the Medal of Honor he had carried with him ever since first reading it. A doomed B-17 four-engine bomber was limping over the English Channel, returning to its base in England after bombing targets in Germany. Knowing the plane would not make it back, the pilot ordered the crew to bail out. As he and the copilot stood at the open door to jump, they heard the belly gunner cry out. Too gravely wounded to be evacuated, the young airman was fated to die. The wounded man begged to not be left alone. The pilot, sensing his fear, turned from the door, sat next to him, and said, "Never mind, son, we'll ride it down together." Reagan paused briefly here, then added, "Congressional Medal of Honor, posthumously awarded." The president believed the granting by the United States of its highest honor to a "man who would sacrifice his life simply to bring comfort to a boy who had to die" spoke to the exceptional "moral and spiritual character" of the country. It showed a "bedrock of strength" that a nation that honored assassins could not match.[4]

Reagan's stories painted a dramatic and powerful contrast for his audience. They drove home his belief about the stark moral difference between the superpowers in a way that was recognizable and memorable. There is a problem with the story, though. Reagan's B-17 and its doomed boy and the heroic pilot never existed. No aviator was awarded a Medal of Honor in World War II for sacrificing himself to comfort a doomed crewmate.[5] The origin of Reagan's story is unclear; various accounts tie it to an issue of *Reader's Digest* or a movie Reagan worked on.[6] The president certainly did not read about it as part of his official duties, but wherever he came across it, he latched on to it, and he retold it frequently.

Choosing to tell a story about a fictional Medal of Honor recipient in a room full of people whose actual citations would serve just as well is odd. It is in keeping, though, with the way Reagan approached storytelling. Factual accuracy was unimportant to him if the story was memorable and had a message he liked. It also showed his preference for familiar narratives and clear heroes with whom he could identify. The B-17 struggling over the channel fit this perfectly and embodies the values Reagan wanted to highlight. The heroic pilot demonstrated a selflessness that spoke to Reagan's sense that individual freedom would produce bonds and communities that would transcend the fear and tyranny imposed by communism.

He first used the story in 1952 to the graduating class of William Woods College, an all-girls institution in Fulton, Missouri—the city where just six years earlier Winston Churchill had famously declared, "An Iron Curtain has descended across the continent" of Europe. Reagan discussed the Cold War in similarly stark terms. He used the story of the bomber to evoke the type of men the nation needed. Reagan exhorted the women in his audience to embrace a different sort of "momism" that would produce a generation of men willing to sacrifice themselves for their comrades. In doing so they would "strike a match" to "help push back the darkness." Drawing on his belief that women in general, and mothers in particular, instill values in men, he told the young women that their actions could help more people realize the United States represented "the last best hope of man on earth."[7]

The rhetoric and imagery of the speech strikingly resembles his 1964 televised address "A Time for Choosing," the speech that sparked Reagan's meteoric political ascent. In it he demanded action to maintain the United States as, again, "the last best hope of man on earth." Failure would ensure that the nation would instead take "the last step into a thousand years of darkness."[8] Reagan thought that Americans, like the women of William Woods, could strike a match and provide the light needed to keep hope and freedom alive. He consistently cast the Cold War in Manichaean terms, as a struggle of light against darkness. In doing so he was drawing on the rhetoric of his personal hero among the founding fathers: Thomas Paine.

Reagan's reading of Paine strongly influenced his ideas of freedom and liberty. Intellectual historian John Patrick Diggins notes that Reagan would often "quote Paine to prove that the government had become alienated from the people."[9] Paine was actually referring to a monarchy that ruled over colonies, not to a democracy, but Reagan saw similarities in both domestic politics and foreign relations. As his William Woods speech indicated, Reagan felt that the purest expression of freedom came at the individual and community level, which he thought communism suppressed. Sharing Paine's disregard for nuance and proclivity to action, Reagan consistently adopted a view of communism as monolithic and something to fight everywhere and at any cost.

He frequently described the United States as mankind's "last best hope." Variants appear in the William Woods commencement, "A Time for Choosing," the "Evil Empire" speech, and his second inaugural. The phrase draws on another of Reagan's political idols, Abraham Lincoln. In his Second Annual Address to Congress on December 1, 1862, the president called for a constitutional amendment to abolish slavery. He told the assembled members of Congress that "giving freedom to the slave" would "assure freedom to the free." The proposed amendment, then, represented a choice to "nobly save or meanly lose the last best hope of earth."[10] Lincoln and Reagan asked their respective audiences to make a conscious decision to preserve the United States as a symbol for others.

This framing built on Paine's call in *Common Sense* to "receive the fugitive and prepare in time an asylum for mankind."[11] The image of the newly united colonies as collectively an asylum resonated powerfully with Reagan. It conveyed a sense of destiny and held out an opportunity for greatness in a way that he embraced and employed in his own speeches. Reagan would frequently quote Paine's belief that Americans had the "power to begin the world again." He would add the idea came from "the dark days of the American Revolution, when it didn't seem possible that the nation would come into being."[12] He explicitly linked Valley Forge with the Cold War and the Americans of those "dark days" with those now "disturbed but not dismayed" at the direction of the country.[13]

Historian Steven Hayward thinks Reagan's love of Paine was evidence of his own "idiosyncratic and unorthodox" conservatism.[14] Diggins, similarly, holds that Reagan loved the "blasphemous rebel" because "Paine saw freedom as the birth of the new and the death of the old."[15] Paine's work, in their view, encouraged Reagan to believe in "hope, experiment, and freedom" rather than the "history, precedent, and order" of traditional conservatives.[16] This is largely accurate. Throughout his presidency Reagan expressed optimism in the boundless creativity of a free people to overcome any challenge. If unencumbered, he felt, the ingenuity and ideology of Americans would usher in a golden age. Only the Soviet Union and its totalitarian ideology threatened this prospect.

Reagan's embrace of the rhetoric and imagery of the Revolutionary and Civil Wars demonstrate the immense significance he attached to the Cold War. In his view, the conflict was an existential struggle whose outcome would determine not just the future of American ideology and freedom but also the fate of the world. He arrived at this conviction by way of a convergence of his personal postwar experiences and his reading. Throughout the late 1940s, Reagan encountered communists in Hollywood and in the pages of the books he read. He found in guilds and organizations in California echoes of the stories told by Whittaker Chambers and Arthur Koestler. These commonalities led him to conclude that "there could be no security anywhere in the free world" unless the United States was willing to refuse to deal with the "slave masters" in Moscow and resisted the temptations of appeasement and accommodation.[17]

SKIRMISHING ON THE PICKET LINE

Following the war Reagan settled back into his movie career, largely accepting he would not rise to what would now be called the A-list, but could enjoy a long, lucrative career telling stories. He also increasingly paid attention to behind-the-scenes labor relations and industry contracts. This interest led the Screen Actors Guild (SAG) to appoint him to a panel mediating a dispute between two industry unions over the right to erect sets for movies and television. In one report to the SAG board Reagan denounced the presence of communists in the Conference of Studio Unions (CSU), one of the parties involved in the dispute. His report and opposition drew attention inside that union and marked Reagan as an enemy.

Later that year Reagan was preparing to film *Night unto Night*, a romance that the *New York Times* would later review as "a somber hodge-podge, distinguished by some of the most blatant dialogue of the season."[18] On set, he received a phone call from an angry union worker. The caller threatened that if Reagan did not withdraw his report and his opposition to the CSU he would never work again. A shaken Reagan returned to the studio and after talks with the studio police began to carry a pistol, concerned that partisans in the CSU were planning to mar his face with acid.[19]

In 1985, Reagan explained to his counselor how this and other experiences during the strike "opened [his] eyes" to the true nature of communism.[20] He had a firsthand view of the strike and knew the parties involved well. Reagan's work as a mediator and growing involvement in SAG would soon take him to the presidency of the organization in 1947, a role he would hold for over ten years and six terms in office. In the postwar period Hollywood, like much of the nation, faced significant challenges with labor relations. Between 1945 and 1948 disputes between labor and management and intra-union competition led to frequent strikes that touched nearly every aspect of moviemaking.

The strike in which the dispute between the CSU and the International Alliance of Theatrical Stage Employees (IATSE) over who had the right to erect sets was one of the more intense. *Time* magazine, which referred to it as "like an old-fashioned serial," devoted considerable space to CSU leader Herb Sorrell, a former prizefighter who's "politics [were] of the far left" and was frequently accused of being a communist.[21] The next year a subcommittee of the House Committee on Education and Labor would call him to testify in response to such allegations, which Sorrell called "phony" lies intended to "tangle [him] up."[22]

However, during that testimony Sorrell did express admiration for union people who were openly communist and held to that politically risky position when challenged. In the charged environment of the hearing the union boss tried to walk a fine line, testifying on one hand that "he had no use for communism" but arguing, on the other, there was no utility in seeking to "eliminate the communist."[23] Sorrell risked being publicly "soft on communism" in part because of his personal views but also because the support of communists was important to his union's survival. He admitted there were in fact communists in the CSU and that they wielded an outsize influence. Sorrell praised how they "come out and whip the whole membership in line." Communists also helped "substantially with contributions."[24] Financing came, for example, from Vicente Lombardo Toledano, the leader of the Confederation of Mexican Workers, who had established ties to Soviet spy agencies.[25] The local chapter of the Communist Party in Los Angeles also supported Sorrell. Max Silver, its director, testified that the "Communist Party was very much interested in the success" of the CSU, hoping to make it "a nerve center" to allow "party policy and party people" to wield influence in Hollywood.[26]

Efforts to mediate between the CSU and the IATSE failed; the CSU refused to accept the ultimate determination, which was in favor of the IATSE. Its members turned to violence along the picket line; angry workers blocked studio gates, "scattered tacks in the path of movie star's automobiles," "threw coffee in faces of line-crossers," and "stoned the buses of rival AFL workers."[27] The scene in front of Warner Brothers Studio was particularly fraught; Reagan would recall strikers there employing "clubs, chains, bottles, bricks, and two-by-fours" to enforce the picket line.[28] CSU members also attacked IATSE members even far from the studio and vandalized their homes.

The strike exposed an ideological divide within SAG. As Reagan prepared an update for the guild's leadership, his friend Bill Holden (remembered as the actor William Holden, later very prominent) informed him of a planned meeting of guild members who were communists or "fellow travelers" (sympathizers but not party members, "intellectual communists"). The two decided to crash the meeting, held at the home of a mutual friend, Ida Lupino (an English actress, already famous). Lupino (who, Reagan asserted, was "not one of Them") greeted the two warmly, but Reagan and Holden were clearly not welcome to others in the room. Reagan attempted to "spike their guns with regard to brainwashing," by delivering to the group his draft report.[29] The presentation did not sway the audience.

While there was certainly a communist presence in SAG and other unions in postwar Hollywood, Reagan's personal encounters gave him a sense of threat out of proportion to the reality. It is unlikely that a guild significantly influenced by communist members would elect Reagan as its head. Reagan's own testimony (as a friendly witness, alongside other well-known Hollywood figures, such as Walt Disney) before the HUAC underlines this. While he was aware that the communist presence in SAG was confined to a "small clique," for him the threat was not in the numbers of activists but in their "more or less following the tactics that [Reagan associated] with the Communist Party."[30] He felt their efforts to intimidate citizens and subvert democratic norms threatened individual freedom. However, there is little on record to suggest that the threat posed by the exercise of communists of their political rights would ever achieve in Hollywood the scale of control and influence Reagan feared, and it certainly did not justify the decade of fear and suspicion both in the industry and the country.

Reagan's wariness of the "usual tactics" of communists—that is, trying to "run a majority of an organization with a well-organized minority"—came from his work with the American Veteran's Committee (AVC) and Hollywood Independent Citizens Committee of Arts, Sciences, and Professions (HICCASP). At a meeting of the AVC board, of which he was a member, Reagan spoke against communism and called on its members to do the same, on the spot. The response chilled him: a previously enthusiastic crowd went silent. Shortly after, he quarreled with the board over its decision to limit an upcoming strike meeting to "a small working majority" rather than the full membership. Reagan viewed this as "an old communist trick" of giving the illusion of majority support for a radical agenda.[31]

It was, however, his encounter with communists in HICCASP that had the more profound impact on Reagan. Initially honored to be accepted in a group with such an illustrious membership, he was shocked by stridently anti-American and pro-Soviet sentiments expressed during meetings. A musician offered to recite the constitution of the USSR to show it was more democratic than that of the United States. A screenwriter, likely Dalton Trumbo, went even further and declared he would volunteer to fight for Russia in the event of war between the USSR and United States. When Trumbo and another writer, John Howard Lawson, opposed an anticommunist resolution put by Reagan and Jimmy Roosevelt (a businessman and son of Franklin D. Roosevelt) and prevented the full membership from voting on it on the grounds it was not a "politically sophisticated enough [group] to make this decision," Reagan, Roosevelt, and Olivia de Haviland (one of the leading actresses of the day) resigned.[32]

Reagan's ill feelings toward Trumbo were mutual and lasted well beyond their times in HICCASP. In 1960 *Playboy* published an article by Trumbo decrying the studio blacklist of the late 1940s and 1950s against movie figures with allegedly "unpatriotic" view, comparing it to the witch trials of seventeenth-century Salem, Massachusetts. He believed Americans needed to hunt for witches, from "an instinct as deep as the sexual drive, almost as fun, and often safer"; the blacklist, he wrote, was "like a shroud" that the hypocritical Hollywood used to turn people who were actually its betters into "good and faithful servant[s]."[33] Reagan read the article and wrote Hugh Hefner, *Playboy's* publisher, to rebut. Disingenuously claiming there was no blacklist, he criticized Trumbo for seeking to employ "subversion and stealth" to impose rule "on an unwilling people." Reagan further alleged that Trumbo was a "traitor," that he "looked upon the death of American soldiers in Korea [i.e., in the 1950–53 Korean War] as a victory."[34]

These experiences with Trumbo, Sorrell, and others left Reagan convinced he knew how communists operated and that he could recognize the tactics they would employ to subvert democracy. He found further confirmation in the works of Arthur Koestler. Reagan met the author at a 1948 event hosted by the world-famous Henry Fonda, James Cagney, and Joan Fontaine.[35] The anticommunist message of Koestler matched his own beliefs, and his own observations matched the tactics of Soviet operatives as Koestler described them. *Darkness at Noon* and *The God That Failed* provided Reagan with realistic narratives that synched with his own beliefs and experiences. These stories helped expand his idea of the nature and scope of the threat posed by the Soviet Union.

Koestler, a Hungarian-born British citizen, had joined the Communist Party in Germany in disgust at the disintegration of the post–World War I Weimar Republic and the financial toll the hyperinflation of those years had taken on his family. He sought to sell the "World Revolution like vacuum cleaners."[36] His writing talent earned him a trip to the Soviet Union, where attempts were made to convince him the country was "an artist's paradise."[37] The rise of Hitler prevented Koestler from returning to Germany; instead he moved to France, where he got a job as a correspondent covering the Spanish Civil War. The Nationalist forces of Francisco Franco captured the writer, imprisoning him for four months. In jail he broke with communism: men, he realized, should not "be treated as units in operations of political arithmetic."[38] He became appalled at the way communism suppressed individual agency and demanded adherence to the party before all. After his release, Koestler returned to France, where he was promptly arrested for his prior communist activities. He spent several months in internment camps before British authorities secured his release. In the camps Koestler began work on *Darkness at Noon*, a novel that explored why he had left the party and leveled a damning accusation that communism destroyed the very people it purported to defend.

The book tells the story of the arrest, interrogation, and execution of a hero of the 1917 Bolshevik Revolution. Its doomed protagonist, Nicolas Rubashov, had become a high-ranking official in the Soviet Union during the Great Terror. The novel opens with Rubashov awakening from a dream of being imprisoned by three members of the Gestapo, only to realize he is in fact surrounded by three officers from the People's Commissariat of Internal Affairs, the NKVD. Both the dream Nazis and real Soviets are thugs, men for whom the "brutality was no longer put on but natural."[39] The book frequently equates the Nazi and Soviet regimes, and Koestler's experience with both lent the descriptions credibility.

Betrayal is a primary theme of the work, emerging from Koestler's own sense of how ideology and regimes had betrayed Andalusian peasants in the Spanish Civil War and his revulsion for the Moscow show trials between 1936 and 1938. In the book, the regime over time betrays Rubashov and his fellow heroes of the revolution, tracing the process by device of a repeatedly doctored photo from which the delegates to the first Communist Party congresses successively disappear as Stalin purges them. Each victim has disagreed with Stalin and by extension the party, an irredeemable fault having only one punishment. Rubashov is not in these terms innocent himself. Time in the KGB's prison forces him to contemplate his own long history of betrayals of young idealists, seasoned revolutionaries, union organizers, and lovers to their deaths. But he had done so in the name of the party, as part of an "inert and unerring" river flowing toward a goal, leaving "corpses of the drowned" in its wake.[40] After all, Rubashov recognizes, "the Party can never be mistaken," even now, when it accuses him of being a traitor.[41]

Rubashov accepts that "history treads into dust" those who resist its flow and accepts his part in it is now to die at the hands of a state he had helped create. His interrogator, Gletkin, offers the condemned man a piece of solace: "One day when it can do no more harm, the material of the secret archives will be published" and redeem Rubashov and his generation of revolutionaries.[42] The jailer's words were to prove prescient in real life, though not in the manner the character would expect. The collapse of the Soviet Union and resultant opening of its secret archives would show the remarkable accuracy of Koestler's account of a purged hero of the revolution turned potential rival to Stalin.

The show trials of 1936–38 of Soviet leaders like Nikolai Bukharin and Mikhail Tukhachevsky, depicted favorably in *Mission to Moscow*, would be revealed as artificial, staged to mask a power grab by Stalin and elevate a new generation of leadership loyal to him. Writing to Stalin his final letter, Bukharin praised the dictator, calling the purge "a great and bold idea."[43] Historians J. Arch Getty and Oleg Naumov note that the letter "explicitly recognized that the campaign against enemies was constructed and not reflective of political reality."[44] Knowing there were no serious internal threats to the USSR but that he was to die anyway, Bukharin still confessed. He told Stalin that he had "no intention of recanting anything" (he had opposed Stalin's program of agricultural collectivization) but was "innocent of the crimes [he had] admitted." Recanting "would be petty," given the "universal historical tasks" the party had before it.[45] Knowing as he did that millions of innocents faced false accusations, punishment, and death, Bukharin believed it was in the best interest of the party to slaughter its own.

The survival of the letter in archives until they were opened the 1990s allowed historians to understand the purges in a manner completely different from the official Soviet narrative. It explicitly confirmed previous arguments that the slaughter had been motivated not by fear of enemies but rather the consolidation of power. It is remarkable, considering Koestler did not have access to the archives, that his fictional interrogations bear so many similarities to Bukharin's experience. The author used his own experiences and understanding of the regime to craft a compelling and accurate narrative.

Darkness at Noon's focus on the duplicitous nature of communism appealed to Reagan. Koestler's portrayal of a party actively suppressing its membership, not in the name of revolution but to increase the power of its leading members, matched Reagan's experience in HICCASP and the AVC. Similarly, the frequent resort to violence also seemed to line up with what he saw during the CSU strike. Both *Darkness* and Koestler's autobiographical essay, *The God That Failed*, allowed Reagan to put himself into a larger narrative that meshed with his own present. He used these works as his own interactions with communists expanded to a global scope. They helped him conceptualize the goals and methods of the Soviet Union in a personal way that fixed that superpower in his mind as freedom's archenemy.

Koestler's works also laid the framework for a more nuanced view of the people who lived under Soviet rule. Throughout his life, Reagan made clear distinctions between the evils of the communist system, which was irredeemable, and those who fell under its sway, whom he felt could be saved. Authors like Koestler and George Orwell, who had also broken with the Soviet Union and communism because of the Spanish Civil War, stood as examples of how such people could find their way back to freedom. It was shortly after reading *Darkness* and meeting Koestler that Reagan would begin to work with the Motion Picture Industry Council (MPIC) to rehabilitate communists.[46] The most prominent beneficiary was Edward Dmytryk, one of Trumbo's associates and one of the blacklisted "Hollywood Ten" (who in 1947 had refused to answer questions from HUAC about their affiliations).

Dmytryk, a film director who had joined the party in 1944, believed himself to be one of 150 "intellectual communists" in Hollywood at that time. His desire to "make honest pictures about people" had led to several interactions with communist groups in the '30s and '40s, leading to his recruitment. Dmytryk spent little time in the party, which demanded changes he refused to make to a film he was working on. He also refused to testify before HUAC, which charged him with contempt of Congress. After a brief flight to England, he returned to serve a six-month sentence in 1950. While imprisoned with other members of the blacklist, he was shocked by their "conditioned thinking," their insistence that the newly begun Korean War was a result of aggression by United States–backed South Korea and not Soviet-supported North Korea.[47] With the Chinese entry into the war, Dmytryk completed both his break with the ideology and his prison sentence. He signed a full affidavit about his activity and returned to Hollywood, seeking to restart his career.

In a *Saturday Evening Post* confessional, Dmytryk envisioned an "Ex-Communists Anonymous," to help those trying to quit the bloc.[48] An MPIC committee started by Roy Brewer (a trade union leader) and Reagan sought to be exactly that. Reagan appreciated that the director was "heroic" for acknowledging that communism only used "humanitarian trappings" to mask an "ugly reality."[49] This made Dmytryk a perfect subject for the committee, but his cooperation with it led to significant backlash from communist groups. This response only deepened Reagan's enmity for communists, and through MPIC his committee released a letter that argued it took "courage and desire and time for an American to work free of the tentacles of the Communist Party." Reagan and his committee stood prepared to help and wanted those seeking an exit to know that "you too can be free men again."[50]

During this time, Reagan also became increasingly sympathetic to those who lived under communist regimes, believing there to be a gap between the system and its people. Koestler's work deepened this sense, using Rubashov's porter, Vassilii, as a stand-in for ordinary Soviets. Vassilii fondly recalls his service with the "little bearded Partisan commander" Rubashov once was and his fiery rhetoric on the battlefield. However, the porter could no longer find in him the inspirational leader amid the "long and difficult to understand" speeches of later years.[51] Vassilii's loyalty is to the man, not the system. Vassilii does remain, though, loyal to one system, his Orthodox faith. He intones silent and un-Marxist "amens" at the end of party speeches. At news of his master's death, the loyal servant mutters a silent prayer, refusing to condemn the man, whatever the will of the system. Reagan, who believed in demonstrating faith through action, took this to be a sign of active resistance to a godless regime and evidence that faith could help win the Cold War.

TESTIMONIALS OF FAITH

A pumpkin patch is a strange thing to start a political fight over and an even stranger thing to become a national landmark. Yet in 1988, as his time in office wound down, Reagan started a minor political kerfuffle over a patch of dirt in Maryland. The farm in question belonged to Whittaker Chambers, who had hidden there evidence of Alger Hiss' spying. The location was inaccessible to the public, and no marker or remnant of the pumpkin in which Chambers hid the evidence recalled the event. In any case, its role as a cache site to support testimony in Congress hardly seemed to merit inclusion on a Register of Historic Places that in Maryland alone included houses owned by Clara Barton and Edgar Allen Poe, the U.S. Naval Academy, and the home where a black indentured servant sewed the flag that inspired "The Star-Spangled Banner." The National Park Service advisory board unanimously rejected the inclusion of Chambers' Pipe Creek Farm on the list of landmarks.[52]

Reagan was undeterred. He insisted on recognition for the site and pressured his secretary of the interior, Donald Hodel, to arrange it. The secretary obliged, marking the first time in its history the Interior Department ignored a unanimous recommendation from the advisory board.[53] Critics immediately decried the action as both "an unprecedented politicization of the program" and an "unwise mix of history and ideology."[54] It yielded Reagan no tangible political gain and was, indeed, an unnecessary distraction. However, for the president it was important to honor the legacy of a man who had helped shape his own views on how the United States could win the Cold War.

Reagan believed that religious faith would provide the will for peoples across the world to unite against communism and persevere against the ideology's usual tactics of subversion and oppression. He took this idea directly from the work of Whittaker Chambers. In a 1981 address to the Conservative Political Action Conference (CPAC), he quoted the lapsed communist's assertion that the answer to the problem of communism was the West's "faith in God and the freedom He enjoins."[55] The quote was a favorite, presumably on an index card, and Reagan employed it frequently in his presidency. Most notably, it made a return appearance in his 1983 "Evil Empire" speech to the National Association of Evangelicals in Orlando.[56] Chambers' influence on Reagan went beyond catchphrases for speeches, though. The president would often quote verbatim to his staff from Chambers' memoir *Witness*. Those closest to Reagan recognized that he used them both to explain his enmity toward communism and to show how the United States could defeat the USSR in the Cold War.[57]

Chambers' political beliefs, like Reagan's, drew significantly on early reading. Victor Hugo's *Les Misérables* left a lasting impression on him as a young boy, as a "great act of human spirit" that would later in life provide the "forces that carried [him] into the Communist Party" and then offer the way out. It forced Chambers to deal with "two seemingly irreconcilable things—Christianity and revolution."[58] He opted for revolution first, joining the party at Columbia University and then in 1932 choosing to work for the Soviet General Staff's Main Intelligence Directorate, the GRU, as a spy "courier."

Working in Washington, DC, in the mid-1930s, Chambers built a network that included State Department employees Alger Hiss and Julian Wadleigh and economist Harry Dexter White. All provided Chambers with material bearing on U.S. policy; Hiss and White, who rose to prominent positions in the government, proved exceptionally valuable agents. Chambers, however, amid his great success in recruiting spies, began to doubt his cause. The Spanish Civil War and purges in the Soviet Union led him to fear the party and his own handler, Boris Bykov, who delighted in tormenting Chambers with ominous threats from Moscow. Finally, Bykov implied that Chambers' support for the recently executed Bukharin made him a party heretic; Chambers, fearing GRU agents would assassinate him, skipped his next meeting and fled with his family to Florida.[59]

Chambers eventually landed a job working with *Time* magazine but was still afraid of his former spymasters, especially after the likely assassination of his friend Walter Krivitsky. Seeking to live openly, Chambers attempted to arrange with American authorities a pardon in exchange for exposing the Soviet underground in the United States. These efforts yielded no fruit despite interviews with officials at the State Department and FBI. From his perch at *Time* Chambers attacked fellow travelers and the Stalin regime even during World War II, when Soviets and Americans fought together. He returned to government attention in 1947 when his replacement as a courier for the Soviets, Elizabeth Bentley, identified him as her predecessor. Ultimately, Chambers' appearance before HUAC revealed all he knew about the workings of Soviet intelligence and identified spies in his former network. He declared that both White and Hiss were seeking to wield "power and influence" in the U.S. government, the better to achieve the "paramount objectives" of the Communist Party.[60]

Over the decade since Chambers stopped working as a spy, Hiss and White had in fact risen to prominence. Hiss was a key adviser to Secretary of State Dean Acheson, and White was the lead American negotiator at the July 1944 Bretton Woods Conference, which established the framework of the postwar economic order. Chambers produced evidence of Hiss' activities by retrieving film with photos of copied State Department documents Hiss had passed to Chambers. The former spy had in mid-1948 hidden the film in a hollowed-out pumpkin on his farm and dramatically led HUAC investigators to it in 1948. Despite strident denials and support from the Washington establishment, Hiss was found guilty of perjury and served three years in a federal penitentiary. White died of a heart attack while traveling to testify before HUAC a second time. Soviet archives later revealed that both men had been valued agents and that Hiss, code-named "ALES," had even met with Soviet operatives while attending the 1945 Yalta Conference.[61]

Time fired Chambers after his testimony, and he began to write a memoir to replace his lost earnings. *Witness* told the story of his time as a communist and of why he left the party. The *Saturday Evening Post* quickly procured serialization rights for the astronomical sum of $75,000 and published the first chapter in an issue with, for the first time in its modern history, no illustration on the cover.[62] The book version rocketed up the *New York Times* best-sellers list and would be the ninth-best-selling book of 1952.[63] For Reagan, who read it shortly after publication, it cemented his conviction that the United States urgently needed to defeat the Soviet Union.

The memoir reads like a spy novel and so was an immersive narrative in which Reagan could picture himself. Ruthless, exploitive Soviet agents behaved like the communists Reagan had seen in Hollywood. Reagan also identified with Chambers' decision to arm himself and with Chambers' description of the paranoia he had felt, feelings that matched Reagan's own in the wake of the phone call to the set of *Night unto Night*. *Witness* described Boris Bykov as a controlling figure obsessed with settling accounts and exercising power; Reagan viewed Herb Sorrell in much the same way, as an obnoxious, rude man with "delusions of grandeur."[64] Both Sorrell and Bykov reveled in brutality and thought of subordinates like "ammunition—easily expendable."[65] These men deceived their followers, manipulating their loyalty and good faith to expend them as "cannon fodder in this war" of competing ideologies.[66]

Intellectual communists too looked the same in Chambers' tale as in Hollywood. Alger Hiss had lectured Chambers about loyalty to Bykov; the writer sensed that Hiss was incapable of criticizing the Soviet Union, because of the "transforming power of anything Russian" on intellectuals. For his part, Chambers gradually came to the realization that Hiss was one "who affected to act, think, and speak" for the "plain men and women of the nation."[67] He also perceived that Hiss' socioeconomic class enabled his spying. His peers "snapped their minds shut" to the possibility of his guilt, unable to believe someone with his skills and gifts could work for the Soviets. "The forces of enlightenment" dismissed the danger, "calling every allusion to it a witch hunt."[68]

Reagan recalled Dalton Trumbo and other communists in HICCASP in a similar light. HICCASP members indulged in a snobbery and elitism that Reagan saw as undemocratic and dangerous. Reagan had been appalled by Dmytryk's revelation that some of the Hollywood Ten cheered the sudden advances of the North Koreans, reveling in the deaths of American soldiers. He accordingly resented portrayals of his and others' efforts against communists as witch hunts. That Trumbo had written in *Playboy* that he was guiltless and being unfairly persecuted by people like Reagan infuriated the future president—one who disingenuously claimed there was no blacklist.[69] That willful lack of self-awareness is, in retrospect, very much to the point. If Trumbo was a communist and his opinions on the Korean War were distasteful, neither was illegal. The threat of communists in Hollywood certainly never in reality rose to the level of a national security threat, nor was it likely to have. The suppression of the Hollywood Ten, then, was an unconstitutional and dangerous act by Congress, and Reagan contributed to it. The lessons Reagan took from the experience would calcify and leave him, once in the White House, markedly inflexible in policy.

Moreover, Reagan's strong identification with the plight of Chambers went only so far. He viewed the writer as a "tragic and lonely" figure who believed he had abandoned, albeit in the name of what was right, what he had seen, and still saw, as "the winning side." Chambers' gloom on that point was something Reagan could not accept. The future president found himself "too optimistic to agree" that the United States would not prevail.[70] The good guys would win.

Reagan did, however, wholeheartedly agree with Chambers' belief that the fight would be difficult. He learned firsthand of the "fierce vindictiveness of [communism's] revolutionary temper" on a speaking tour for General Electric (GE).[71] Reagan experienced significant pushback to his inclusion of the Tennessee Valley Authority as an example of government waste; GE was threatened with the loss of millions in government contracts if it did not force him to drop the claim. Despite assurances from the chief executive officer of GE that the story could remain, Reagan chose to drop it—there were, after all, "a hundred examples of overgrown government"— but lamented how little time, the incident showed, remained to "save freedom."[72]

Organized labor too increasingly targeted the former SAG president. The AFL-CIO's committee on political education mentioned Reagan in a book purporting to "give the lowdown on Right-Wing extremist speakers." The committee urged affiliated unions "to head off and prevent the appearance" of Reagan at forums with their workers.[73] Given that much of Reagan's time was spent going to speak at unionized GE factories, this posed a potential threat to his work. Other unions took their cue from the AFL-CIO book as well. A teacher's union in St. Paul, Minnesota, passed a resolution demanding he not be allowed to speak, declaring him a "controversial personality" with nothing of value to offer a school assembly.[74] When the speech took place as planned, the union then demanded that the secretary of the American Communist Party receive an equal opportunity.

The AFL-CIO resistance to Reagan in Minnesota and its labeling him as an extremist was galling to Reagan in light of his history with the organization. In addition to having led a union that was on good terms with AFL-CIO, Reagan had supported its causes. In a 1948 broadcast for the AFL-affiliated International Ladies Garment Workers Union, Reagan had stumped for Hubert Humphrey, then running for the Senate. Reagan presented Humphrey as his "friend from Minneapolis" and a staunch opponent of the 1947 Taft-Hartley Act, which had restricted the activities of unions.[75] The strident opposition from a group with which Reagan had worked left him feeling betrayed. It also reinforced his belief that leftist groups did not support free speech but rather insisted on rigid adherence to a "party line," mirroring Chambers' and Koestler's views of the Communist Party.

Reagan saw the fight against communism as Chambers did. He shared the writer's sense that the present moment was a turning point that would determine "whether the whole world was to become free" or be "completely destroyed or completely changed."[76] It was in the year *Witness* appeared that Reagan spoke to the graduating class at William Woods, and his rhetoric there echoed the book's apocalyptic language ("the last best hope").[77] His 1982 speech to CPAC directly quoted the Chambers passage on the fate of the world.[78] Reagan used quotes from *Witness* to guide his staff in drafting National Security Decision Directive 32, which outline the administration's Cold War strategy, as a way of emphasizing that the country was at a pivotal moment in history.[79] The result was a document declaring the United States would take aggressive action "to contain and reverse" the Soviet Union and communism.[80]

However, to Reagan, *Witness* did even more than reveal communism as the "concentrated evil" of the time.[81] Moreover, and this would have surprised the pessimistic Chambers, Reagan saw in it the path to winning the Cold War. This path had to do with religion. In his book's introduction Chambers described communism as "man's second oldest faith," a tantalizing, though fraudulent, "vision of Man without God." This had been part of its allure to Chambers but also part of why he left the party; he came to believe "political freedom as the Western world has known it" derived from the Bible and that religion and freedom were indivisible.[82] This essentially Judeo-Christian view was certainly exclusionary, in that it implied that freedom to worship or not was in itself inimical to freedom, but it appealed strongly to Reagan, who saw his own faith in similar terms.

Like Reagan, Chambers had found his faith in fiction. His reading of *Les Misérables*, and its bishop who has converted his palace into a hospital, resonated with him and would do so even through his time in the Communist Party. The writer notes the character of the bishop was "invisibly present" with him as he left the party, it having been a religious revelation that drove it. One morning Chambers had realized the "immense design" of even his infant daughter's ear and felt as though "the finger of God was first laid upon [his] forehead."[83] That his handlers had wanted him and his wife to abort the child to avoid interference with party work revealed to Chambers a stark and irreconcilable difference between his revitalized faith and the communist ideology to which he had given his adult life.

This account became a favorite of Reagan's. How Chambers came to his faith paralleled how Reagan had discovered it in *That Printer of Udell's*; also, the path Chambers took from communism was one Reagan sought to inspire others to follow. It became a shorthand, in speeches and with his staff, for Reagan's emphasis on faith in the Cold War. When speechwriters included different passages of *Witness* in their drafts, Reagan would personally cross them out and insert his favorite, about Chambers seeing design in his infant daughter's ear.[84]

Reagan most prominently laid out his view of the Cold War as a religious conflict in his address to the National Association of Evangelicals in 1983. It was this speech that labeled the Soviet Union as an "evil empire," and it did so largely in religious terms. Its framing of the Cold War in such stark moral terms enraged Soviet leaders (though the Soviet ambassador to the United States, Anatoly Dobrynin, did allow that Reagan was simply "giving them a dose of their own medicine").[85] They perceived the speech as part of an "uncompromising new ideological offensive" and as indicative that Reagan was "deliberately and persistently" seeking "a break with the past."[86] In that, the Soviet leaders were correct: Reagan intended his words to challenge the sense of moral equivalency among Americans and return to the rhetoric of the 1950s, when American leaders had cast the conflict in terms of a faith-filled Western world against godless communism.

The "Evil Empire" speech was more than red meat for what would today be called "the base"; Reagan wanted to shake the whole of what he saw as a complacent evangelical population. In his view, too many accepted the existence of communism and, more dangerously, were willing both to accommodate and work with it. A reference to C. S. Lewis' *The Screwtape Letters* highlighted this perception. He accused listeners of "blithely declaring [themselves] above it all" and choosing simply to blame both sides. To Reagan, support for the ongoing nuclear-freeze movement and acceptance of détente in the 1970s were immoral and irreligious for churchgoers, as surrenders to "the temptation of pride."[87]

Reagan sought to convey to the evangelicals that in its true nature the Cold War was a spiritual conflict and that those who would place "the United States in a position of military and moral inferiority" to the Soviets were helping ensure the global demise of freedom. He drew on Chambers, to the effect that the only way to prevail was to ensure the Western world's "faith in God and the freedom He enjoins" were greater than "communism's faith in man." If the country was going to embrace Thomas Paine's conviction that it had the power to "begin the world over again," more of its citizens would need to embrace Chambers' belief that here was a battle between the world's two oldest faiths and that it was religion that held out the hope of freedom.[88]

In Koestler and Chambers, Reagan found imaginative experiences that built on his own recent experiences with communists in Hollywood. Also, Reagan encountered both writers' work at a time the U.S. government was actively casting the conflict in religious terms. The 1950s saw the adoption of "In God We Trust" as the national motto and the inclusion of ". . . under God" to the Pledge of Allegiance. Historian Will Inboden notes that many American policy makers and politicians of the period "believed their nation had a divine calling to oppose the Soviet Union and to reshape the world according to divine design."[89] This environment combined with his own experience and belief to make Reagan receptive to Koestler and Chambers.

The two authors had great respect for each other. Koestler believed if *Witness* had gone "unwritten [it] would leave a hole in the world," and Chambers saw in Koestler's *Darkness at Noon* a fellow writer trying to atone.[90] When Reagan gave Chambers a posthumous Presidential Medal of Freedom in 1984, he quoted Koestler's remarks on learning of his fellow writer's death that the "witness is gone but the testimony will stand."[91] Chambers, Reagan declared, had "changed the face and soul of the nation."[92]

The moral clarity Reagan found in Chambers and Koestler was, nevertheless, a double-edged sword. While it suggested clear rhetoric with which Reagan communicated his views and thereby did much to reframe the Cold War in the 1980s, it instilled in Reagan an unnuanced view of communism. The president never intellectually challenged the ideas that communism was monolithic or that anyone who opposed it was a potential partner for the United States. The Manichaean model would have fit well in the pages of pulp novels and westerns but was unsuited to the complexity of the actual world. Reagan's inflexibility here created in him a notion of the Americans as the wearing the white hats and any communist a black one and that the white hats needed to go to any length to win. This viewpoint would undermine U.S. objectives throughout the global South and create an environment in which malign actors were enabled to inflict great suffering.

COWBOY VALUES

Donning a Gray Hat

United Nations Resolution 2758 enraged Governor Reagan of California. The October 1971 vote elevated the communist People's Republic of China to membership in the United Nations (UN) and a seat on the Security Council, expelling Taiwan from the organization. Reagan, a longtime supporter of the Republic of China, had gone to Taiwan just ten days prior at President Richard Nixon's behest to show American support for the celebration of Taiwan's national day. He was impressed by the aging "old boy" of the island, Chiang Kai-shek, who remained sharp as a tack in his eighties.[1] Reagan, angry at what he saw as the unjust treatment of a U.S. partner and of an aged statesman whom he personally liked, felt he had to act. He picked up the phone and called the White House.

Speaking with the president, Reagan forcefully expressed his anger. The UN vote revealed the "moral bankruptcy of the organization" and was an "immoral act of political expediency." Reagan "was just sick" over it, and his "every instinct [said] just get the hell out of that kangaroo court and let it sink." However, he knew that was not politically possible and instead recommended a temporary recall of the American ambassador to the UN, George H. W. Bush, and then refuse to participate in any votes of the General Assembly after Bush returned.

57

Doing so would "put those bums in the perspective they belong." Nixon listened sympathetically—Reagan was an important conservative voice who would play a role in his reelection in 1972—but never seriously considered Reagan's advice. Instead, Nixon had Secretary of State William Rogers call the angry governor to calm him.

In his criticisms of the UN, Reagan singled out newly independent African nations for particular vitriol. No European nation had voted against the resolution, but Reagan did not speak against NATO allies like the United Kingdom and France. Canada likewise escaped Reagan's wrath. Instead, he expressed his shock and outrage at seeing on television representatives from African nations celebrating the vote. Reagan launched a racist attack (in private, but with a tape recorder running), saying he could not stand watching "those monkeys from African countries," who were "still uncomfortable wearing shoes," act in such a way. The shocking and offensive description reveals much about how Reagan saw the developing world. He believed the African nations needed to be grateful for their colonial experiences and that their votes indicated they were not truly ready for independence and self-rule. Though Reagan did not publicly use such language and there is no other known recording of him using it in private, his actions over the next two decades reflected his nostalgia for the colonial period and his sense that nations in Africa and in Latin and South America needed the West to guide them to the right beliefs and systems.

These perceptions stemmed from Reagan's own sense of American history and his reading of westerns and military novels. Legends of the frontier were central to how Reagan saw the world stage. In *The New American Militarism*, historian Andrew Bacevich argues that as a politician and leader Reagan "beguiled himself and his supporters" with a notion of "soldierly ideals," of which he had a "trove of instructive and inspiring anecdotes." His administration created a "sanitized version of U.S. military history and fostered a romanticized portrait" of those in the armed forces.[2] An idealized American frontier was central to this act of creation.

Throughout his political career, Reagan spoke in glowing terms of the American West of the post–Civil War era. He believed that the pioneers, settlers, and soldiers who extended federal control to the Pacific had embodied the best attributes of Americans. This sense did not come from the region's history, in which he would have found a more complicated story and a profoundly negative racial legacy—but rather adventure stories and westerns. Westerns of the 1950s built on the moral code Reagan took in from his "hero worship" of John Carter and shaped the future president's sense of how the United States should act globally.

Reagan also paired his western hagiographies with a romantic recollection of his youthful reading of imperialist literature. Rudyard Kipling's "Tommy" in Afghanistan and the Sudan became indistinguishable from American cavalrymen on the plains. Reagan mentally linked the actions of Britain in the late nineteenth century with those of the United States at the same time, seeing both assuming the "White Man's Burden" and bringing civilization to ungrateful peoples. His open embrace of this relationship as president led directly to American complicity in moral and physical tragedies.

GLIMMERING BADGES: REAGAN, L'AMOUR, AND THE WESTERN

Bloodied and battered, surrounded by the people he had saved, Marshal Kane did not look particularly relieved or happy to have killed the notorious criminal Frank Miller and his gang. The protagonist of *High Noon* instead looked on his soon-to-be-former townspeople with disgust. They preferred to see the marshal turn tail, flee, and allow criminals into their town rather than risk violence. Kane set out to defend the town alone. He had prevailed only because his new wife set aside her pacifist beliefs to help her husband, killing one gang member and distracting Miller long enough for Kane to draw down on him. With the town and its citizens safe, Kane could no longer stand to be in their presence. Glaring at the assemblage, he slowly removed the iconic five-pointed marshal's star from his chest and threw it into the dirt. He then silently boarded a wagon and set off with his wife to begin their life together. The film earned seven Oscar nominations and won four, including Best Actor for Gary Cooper for his portrayal of the embittered marshal.

Both the film and Cooper's performance left a powerful impression on Reagan. They became a touchstone for the president, and he frequently referred to it when discussing policy with his senior advisors.[3] He would refer to wanting a policy of the sort Kane would adopt, a phrase his staff recognized as a "code." Such a policy would see the United States "do what's right; deal with the risks; leave the recognition for others."[4] Like Marshal Kane, Reagan would fight for oppressed peoples whether they wanted U.S. help or not, and then ride off into the sunset. His administration would save reluctant townspeople from bandits and seek no acclaim after, content with the knowledge that the good guys had won.

High Noon was only one of many western tales that built this sensibility in Reagan. The books of Louis L'Amour were also collectively an important touchstone for the president. In the same ceremony in which he recognized Whittaker Chambers, he presented the Presidential Medal of Freedom to the western storyteller. Reagan declared that L'Amour "played a leading role in shaping our national identity" with novels that "portrayed the rugged individuals and the deep-seated values of the frontier." These stories, Reagan was sure, reminded Americans of their "potential as an exploring, pioneering, and free people."[5]

The ceremony was the second time Reagan honored L'Amour at the White House during his first four years in office. In 1982, Reagan awarded him the Congressional Gold Medal, making L'Amour the first novelist to receive the honor. He presented it at a rodeo-cowboy barbeque on the south lawn of the White House, praising L'Amour and the assembled cowboys for carrying on the legacy of "the men and women of the Old West," who had possessed a "certain integrity of character" that still appealed to Americans. His assembled audience represented the "great tradition of the American West" and, Reagan believed, played a crucial role in perpetuating a particular national identity.[6] Reagan's repeated references to western values in both ceremonies underlined the great importance he placed on the mythologized west in defining his values.

L'Amour was the most prominent western mythologizer of his time. Over a long career, he wrote more than a hundred books; nearly two hundred million were in circulation at his death in 1988.[7] He was born in South Dakota in 1908, four years before Reagan, and had an unconventional education. He left school at the age of fifteen and read works by H. G. Wells, Kipling, and George Bernard Shaw to fill in educational gaps. His fascination with the west began with family stories of the Sioux killing and scalping his grandfather in 1862. This interest grew as he listened to his maternal grandfather's stories of service in the Civil and Indian wars. Like Reagan, L'Amour discovered and devoured Burrough's John Carter stories. The adventurer of Barsoom inspired the moral codes of many of L'Amour's characters; Burroughs receives special mention both on L'Amour's official website and in his memoir *Education of a Wandering Man*, where he credits John Carter with sparking him to read science fiction and nonfiction.[8]

A young L'Amour paralleled Burroughs' own wanderings; he traveled widely and worked in ports, timber camps, mines, on freighters and compiled fifty-one wins as a professional boxer.[9] With the American entry into World War II, he attended Officer Candidate School at Camp Hood in Texas and received a commission in the army. He joined a contemporary equivalent of the cavalry, the tank destroyers, and landed at Normandy on D-Day. L'Amour would be awarded four Bronze Stars for his service in the European Theater. After the war he moved to Los Angeles and began to write, finding intermittent success selling short stories to pulp magazines.[10] His big break came in 1952, when *Collier's* published his story "The Gift of Cochise." The tale of an Apache warrior and of a slow-burning romance between a pioneer woman and a "lean angry man" drew the attention of one of Hollywood's biggest stars.[11] John Wayne purchased the rights to make a movie of it, to be titled *Hondo*. As part of the deal, L'Amour wrote a novelization of the film. Film and book were both wildly successful, and L'Amour's debut novel would receive praise from the Western Writers Association of America as one of the top twenty-five westerns ever written.[12]

Hondo takes place in Arizona amid rising tension between Apache tribes and settlers. The story's protagonist, Hondo, an army scout, encounters an isolated farmstead while escaping a group of Apache. There he meets Angie Lowe and her son Johnny. Seeing that the farm has fallen into disrepair, he begins the work, manual labor that would have been the duty of Angie's missing husband Ed. Upon his departure an Apache band led by Vittorio arrives; the warriors adopt young Johnny into the tribe after he tries to fight them. Hondo eventually returns, but only after having killed Ed Lowe, who ambushed him. He tells Angie of the death but initially hides that it had been at his own hands, enabling her to claim Hondo as her husband when Vittorio returns and tries to force her to marry a member of the tribe. Fighting breaks out between the Apache and settlers; Hondo and Angie try to remain neutral but eventually side with the army and help them defeat Vittorio. The novel and movie end with Hondo, Angie, and Johnny riding off together for Hondo's own farm in California.[13]

Throughout the book, Hondo acts according to a strict moral code. He helps out on the Lowe farm in the belief that it is what any good man would do, recognizing that the property reflected "good solid work that a man could be proud of."[14] Hondo returns to it because he feels compelled to protect Angie and her son, fearing for them as war looms. Usually straightforward and honest,

he recognizes that on occasion "a man has to lie if it makes it easier for someone."[15] This belief allows him to go along with Angie when she, having learned
that it was Hondo who had killed her husband, forbids him to tell Johnny the
truth of the matter. She convinces him that this lie would best serve Johnny
and allow the boy to see Hondo as his father in the future. L'Amour presents
both Hondo's desire at first to tell Johnny the truth and his eventual decision
to let the boy believe his father had died honorably as morally correct and that
each "good" choice has its reward. For the former, Hondo has the satisfaction
of being honest and supporting the cause of truth; in the latter he can marry
Angie and help raise Johnny, providing the masculine figure he believes both
need in their lives.

Protagonists who follow a code are staples of both L'Amour's work and of
westerns in general. These simple depictions of morality appealed to Reagan,
who often pined for an imagined west. In his autobiography he lauded the "brief
post–Civil War era when our blue-clad cavalry stayed on a wartime footing
against the plains and desert Indians" as rivaling Kipling's British Empire for
"color and romance."[16] This reimagining took the works of Kipling and westerns at face value without regard to, or intellectual curiosity about, historical
accuracy. He was happy to see Native Americans, Afghan tribesmen, and the
Mahdi's warriors portrayed as clearly uncivilized, albeit worthy, foes. These non-
White peoples deserved praise for their valor and adherence to their codes of
honor, but in Reagan's view simply did not understand what they fought against.
British soldiers and American cavalrymen knew best, in Reagan's estimation,
and were themselves elevated by risking their lives to expand civilization. This
ahistorical outlook erased the agency and histories of many and kept Reagan
from understanding why diverse groups of people would violently resist the
United States and its allies or feel drawn to different political ideologies.

Reagan's fascination with the period led him to attempt several times to
be cast in westerns, to no avail. He did become close friends with John Wayne,
who supported Reagan during the Hollywood strikes of the late 1940s. It was
almost certainly Wayne who introduced Reagan to the works of L'Amour.[17]
Reagan remained an avid fan in the White House, reading L'Amour's recently
released *Jubal Sackett* in the hospital recovering from cancer surgery in 1985.
His love of L'Amour's works was well known, and he frequently, and enthusiastically, received the author's books as presents.[18] At the presentation of the

Congressional Gold Medal to L'Amour, Reagan displayed his familiarity with his books. Unable at one point to find the author before realizing L'Amour was next to him, the president quipped that the writer had "sneaked up on [him] just like Bowdrie," a Texas Ranger featured in many of his short stories.[19] At the former president's death, Nancy Reagan donated all but five of Reagan's collected books to the Ronald Reagan Museum. The five she kept were all written by the same author; Nancy noted that she saved those for herself, "because Louis L'Amour was [her] husband's favorite author."[20]

Lifelong love of westerns and his use of the genre's tropes as shorthand for policy partially explains his administration's actions in Central America. In 1979, in Nicaragua, the Sandinistas, a communist guerrilla movement backed by the Soviets and Cuba, overthrew the regime of Anastasio Somoza Debayle. Historically the United States had supported the Somoza family despite its obvious corruption and violent methods of suppression. Only the brutal murder of ABC correspondent Bill Stewart in 1979 led the United States, during the Jimmy Carter administration, to cut off support, expediting the Sandinista victory.[21] Reagan immediately criticized Carter's response to the crisis as a repeat of the takeover of Cuba by communists in 1958.[22] He failed to empathize with Nicaraguans or seek to understand why Somoza and the United States were unpopular in the country. Instead, he viewed the conflict strictly in terms of monolithic communism, arguing in a speech that "Nicaragua is closer to Miami, New Orleans, San Antonio, Los Angeles, and Denver" than was Washington, DC.[23] In Reagan's view, Nicaragua was clearly the first step of a Soviet plan to apply pressure to the United States rather than a local response to a brutal, corrupt dictator. Rising leftist movements in El Salvador, which saw communists take power in 1979, in Honduras, and in Guatemala seemed to confirm his fears.

Reagan entered office determined to undo Carter's decision to keep the country uninvolved in the conflict, a policy Reagan saw as akin to appeasement. He amalgamated the conflict into a simplistic Cold War narrative despite analysis to the contrary from the State Department. A January 1981 issue paper prepared for the incoming administration assessed that the Soviets, knowing of Reagan's concern over their involvement in Central America, would "not gratuitously undertake provocative actions" there, it not being an area of significant national interest. The paper did allow that the Soviets were providing aid to insurgent groups and would "probe . . . U.S. tolerance of their political-military initiatives in the region" and likely support sympathetic regimes to the extent the United States would permit.[24] Any Soviet involvement at all, however, was beyond what Reagan and his advisors wanted to permit, and they began to seek ways to intervene.

One of Reagan's earliest meetings with the National Security Council (NSC) dealt with this topic. In it, Reagan reiterated his campaign criticism of Carter, expressing his determination to "change the attitude of our diplomatic corps" and his anger that his predecessor had been too quick to "throw out our friends because they can't pass the 'saliva test' on human rights." The president wanted to "see that stopped" and to increase support for regimes like Augusto Pinochet's in Chile, regardless of atrocities they had perpetuated.[25] Popular opinion and the legislative branch disagreed with this viewpoint. Congress attached and passed three amendments to other legislation, known collectively as the Boland Amendment, that limited the ability of the administration to support the Contras, a group seeking to overthrow the Sandinistas. Reagan and his advisors believed these measures removed any leverage they might have had over Nicaragua. They also believed these actions stemmed not from legitimate moral opposition but from antimilitary and anti-American sentiment.[26]

Reagan could not imagine why most Americans would not want to support the Contras. Though the group was connected to drug cartels and committed atrocities against civilians and Sandinistas, Reagan saw it as an important partner because of its anticommunism and felt the rest of the country should focus, with him, on the more important ideological battle. He became convinced that only a shadowy campaign backed by communists could explain domestic opposition to aid for, even intervention in support of, the murderous rebels. Writing to Victor Krulak, a retired Marine lieutenant general, he argued this subversive campaign was a "sophisticated lobbying job," a "well-funded operation" backed by the Sandinistas and possibly Moscow.[27] He was not the only one to see a conspiracy. Vice President George H. W. Bush's brother, Prescott Bush Jr., wrote the CIA director in 1984 to demand an investigation into Connecticut senator Chris Dodd, alleging that Dodd's relationship with Bianca Jagger, the ex-wife of Rolling Stones frontman Mick, was suspicious. Prescott Bush believed Jagger was "trained in Cuba by the Cuban equivalent of the KGB" to work with the Sandinistas and was "honeypotting" the senator. Only the "considerable amount of disinformation" from Bianca Jagger, a human-rights activist, could result in "Dodd's hand-ringing [sic] dovish attitude on the Salvadoran situation."[28] Casey responded to Bush that the matter was "somewhat out of our bailiwick" at the CIA and instead referred him to FBI director Bill Webster.[29]

Such conspiracy theories around the Boland Amendment ignored the real reasons for the restrictions. Congress feared executive actions that might lead to another Vietnam and was leery of getting involved with groups that flagrantly disregarded human rights. The absence of viable and acceptable partners in the region and a sense that the communist threat was overstated left many in Congress convinced that inaction was the best course regarding the Sandinistas and other leftist movements there. Reagan and his administration stridently disagreed and entered office determined to find a way around the will of Congress and the people.

Reagan agonized over how to bring down the Sandinistas. He confided to his diary after a 1981 National Security Policy Group meeting that the session "left [him] with the most profound decision [he had] ever had to make." He was convinced that Central America was the "world's next hotspot" and Sandinista Nicaragua nothing more than "an armed camp supplied by Cuba and threatening a communist takeover of the region."[30] Firm in his belief that communism represented an existential threat to freedom and intentionally oblivious to the evils of U.S.-backed groups in the region, Reagan chose to follow his code.

A month later, during an NSC meeting, he predicted that the United States would be unable to "solve this problem with Congress and public opinion being" against intervention. Reagan wanted to get involved but needed deniable options. He asked the NSC to provide such options, involving covert activity that "would be truly disabling and not just flea bites" against Nicaragua. He also made it clear to those in the room that he would not back down or accept defeat on the issue.[31] Given this resolution and the biases of his advisors, it should have been predictable that the president's feelings had turned to illegal action. Reagan's *High Noon* references signaled his staff to do whatever it took. John Poindexter, at one time Reagan's national security advisor as an active-duty vice admiral, later recalled the president "had very simple, straightforward principles" on which he based his guidance.[32] Allusions to westerns were a part of this guidance. They defined the simple principles and gave advisors like Poindexter a sense of what Reagan wanted.

As president, Reagan was often more concerned with vision than specifics. This meant that a story told in the context of a policy discussion might be all his staff received in terms of guidance. Indeed, Poindexter recalled that Reagan "put great trust and confidence in his staff to take care of the details."[33] In the case of Nicaragua, Reagan's broad framing of the issue and expressed desire to do something covertly, without stated or implied restrictions, that would hurt the Sandinistas paired with his oft-cited desire for Marshal Kane–type policies of doing the "right thing" regardless of outside support or opinion gave the NSC license. The council took Reagan's language as an imperative order to act and so illegally subverted the Boland Amendment to back the Contras. Public revelation of support to the Contras, funded by sales of weapons to Iran, then under embargo, shocked Americans. The resulting Iran-Contra scandal nearly brought down the entire administration and severely damaged the public's trust in Reagan.

National Security Advisors Robert McFarlane and John Poindexter had understood Reagan to have given them tacit approval to take whatever action they deemed necessary. They gained Reagan's approval to sell weapons to Iran ostensibly as a quid pro quo for pressuring its Hezbollah proxies to release hostages in Lebanon. In a rare moment of concurrence, Shultz and Weinberger both strongly advised Reagan even that the proposal was illegal but failed to dissuade him. Reagan directly approved trades of arms for hostages multiple times between 1984 and 1986. Weinberger would lament in his memoir that Reagan was "misled by some who had full access to him" and was following "advice that led him away from his sure instincts."[34] This was a generous reading of Reagan's intentions in the matter, considering that he defended the trades in frequent letters to supporters after the scandal broke. Reagan declared in his address to the nation on the scandal that although "my heart and my best intentions" told him it was true the United States did not trade arms for hostages, "the facts and the evidence tell me it is not."[35] The "facts and the evidence," however, pointed to his direct approval and private defense of the transactions: the statement was, though moving to many voters, a conscious lie to the American people.

By itself, the trade of weapons for hostages was illegal and a political scandal. Poindexter, CIA director William Casey, and Oliver North, a Marine lieutenant colonel assigned to the NSC, made it exponentially worse by pursuing their own policy objective, and what they assumed was Reagan's as well, of supporting the Contras. The men secretly sold the weapons to Iran at a markup, directing the proceeds to a slush fund through which they channeled money to the Contras. This directly subverted the Boland Amendment, and its public revelation turned the burgeoning scandal into a potential matter of impeachment. Testifying before Congress, Poindexter declared he "made a very deliberate decision not to ask the president" about the slush fund but was convinced Reagan would approve if he were asked to. The advisor had intended to "insulate [Reagan] from the decision" to prevent scandal.[36] Poindexter, knowing Reagan did not care for details, saw in the president's western references and moral proclamations authority to do whatever it took. That such senior advisors as the director of the CIA and the national security advisor believed they could approve such actions themselves, actively subverting congressional legislative intent, and not feel the need even to inform the president is a damning indictment of how Reagan led his staff. It shows the need to pair vision and imagination with concrete detail.

In his speech after the release of the report of the presidential Tower Commission (convened, with Senator John Tower of Texas in the chair, to review and assess the NSC's role in the episode), Reagan seemed to acknowledge this shortcoming. He refuted Poindexter's assertion that the buck for the scandal stopped with Poindexter, as national security advisor, and acknowledged that the president was the one "who is ultimately accountable to the American people." Reagan then outlined planned structural changes to the NSC and new appointments to important positions. He also declared that he would in the future be "informed and informed fully" about his administration's actions.[37] However, the reality proved difficult for Reagan; he was either unwilling or unable to change his leadership style. Colin Powell, brought in as deputy national security advisor in the wake of the scandal, later recalled how even after Iran-Contra, "the president's passive management style placed a tremendous burden" on his staff.[38] The general grew frustrated at Reagan's unwillingness to give firm decisions.

Reagan's inability to view the conflict in Nicaragua through a better lens than that of cowboy stories prevented him from looking at the situation with the empathy and curiosity he brought to European relations. Even as the Iran-Contra scandal unfolded, Reagan continued to assert, "You can't be against the Contras without being for the Communist government of Nicaragua."[39] He correctly viewed the Sandinista regime as autocratic and tied to Cuba—in his mind clear "black hats." However, the simple black-hat/white-hat morality of a western did not apply to Nicaragua; the Contras were morally no better than their foes. They engaged in terrorism, ran drugs, ignored human rights, and if victorious would likely create a regime no less corrupt and autocratic than those of the Sandinistas or Somoza. Reagan's policy throughout the region showed similar gaps in understanding. He supported authoritarian and violent regimes like that of Rios Montt in Guatemala, unwilling to see the inherent hypocrisy. Announcing the Reagan Doctrine in 1985, he declared the United States could "not break faith with those who are risking their lives . . . to defy Soviet-supported aggression and secure rights which have been ours from birth," but his administration's support for the Montts, Contras, and dictators of Central and South America effectively denied many those same rights.[40]

The prominence of *High Noon* in shaping Reagan's worldview incurred another major risk. He missed or chose to ignore the uncomfortable subtext of the movie. Carl Foreman, the screenwriter, had expected the film to be his last, because he had been summoned before HUAC. He wrote the movie as an allegory of what he considered the disgusting and fearful search for communists in Hollywood. Marshal Kane represents people like Foreman and Trumbo, the cowardly townspeople people like Reagan. Alternatively, Foreman might have seen Reagan as part of the Miller gang, but certainly not as the lawman. Reagan would be a *High Noon* black hat. Reagan's friend John Wayne recognized the subtext and declared the final scene of Kane angrily discarding his star "the most un-American thing" he had ever seen.[41]

The misinterpretation, or willful ignorance, of Foreman's allegory demonstrates the risk of using fiction as a shorthand. Reagan's usage of Bruce Springsteen's song "Born in the USA" is another case in point. The lyrics, which evoke a left-behind blue-collar man, could not have contrasted more strongly with the 1984 "Morning in America" rhetoric, yet Reagan's reelection campaign made prominent use of the song at rallies and events. Reagan's use of stories depended on everyone being familiar with and interpreting the source material in remarkably similar ways—specifically, his way. Misunderstanding and exploitation were possible. Longtime friends and advisors, like Thomas Reed, would recognize the intended message and act in good faith. Others did not. This was a source of David Stockman's critique in *The Triumph of Politics*. Reagan's reluctance to engage in nuanced policy discussion frustrated people outside his immediate circle, and, as we have seen, the lack of clear guidance allowed staffers to interpret his words and stories in ways most favorable to their own projects. Nevertheless, feelings Reagan imbued from stories played a significant role in the direction of his administration, and westerns were not the only genre that inculcated them in Reagan. Military stories and tales of courageous last stands also often exerted a powerful hold on the president's mind.

YOUNG, NOBLE, AND DAMNED:
HEROIC SACRIFICE AND MILITARY WORSHIP

It is the height of the war on the Korean Peninsula. A flight of F2 Banshees screams off the deck of the aircraft carrier USS *Savo Island*, leaving a trail of smoke as they race across the Sea of Japan to strike targets in North Korea. The pilots and carrier crew perform their duty nobly, giving no sign that less than a day before a popular jet pilot and a search-and-rescue crew had died during a mission to bomb bridges at Toko-Ri. The mission had been a success despite the cost, and Adm. George Tarrant, commander of the task force, could not but marvel at the men serving under him. Racked by grief himself at the loss of the pilot, a surrogate son replacing one lost in World War II, he stood watching the jets soar away and silently asked, "Where did we get such men?"—men who would risk their lives for so little recognition and with slight knowledge of what they fought for.[42]

The episode in James Michener's 1952 Korean War novella *The Bridges at Toko-Ri* left a permanent impression on Reagan. Tarrant's awe for those who served under him and the seeming impossibility of finding and being worthy of such men captured the way Reagan viewed military service. More importantly, it conveyed the attitude he wanted the American public to take toward those who wore the uniform. Reagan believed that service members were on the frontiers of freedom and were, like the cavalrymen of his romanticized westerns, heroes who would risk everything to save the lives of their fellow citizens and to advance freedom and civilization. Throughout his life, Reagan expressed curiosity about, and interest in stories about, life on the extreme edges of White, European civilization and those who self-righteously claimed to be carrying that banner westward or to the stars.

He also enjoyed stories of heroic last stands. The cavalrymen in his westerns often became martyrs to the cause of Western civilization and in their deaths exhorted their comrades to strive for greater things. Speaking to the 1981 graduating class at West Point, Reagan recounted a story by James Warner Bellah.

The writer was best known, though likely not to the cadets, as a screenwriter on the John Wayne films *Rio Grande*, *Fort Apache*, and *She Wore a Yellow Ribbon*. Also, he had worked with Reagan on a project titled *Battle Mountain* and had written an episode of the Reagan-hosted *General Electric Theater*.[43] However, in his speech Reagan was concerned with Bellah as an author of westerns.

The president called him "our Rudyard Kipling[,] because of his stories of our Army on the frontier." This comparison matched the idea in his autobiography that the post–Civil War period was America's version the British Empire of Kipling's stories. Reagan's speech recalled a Bellah story about a commander dying on the battlefield and passing on his responsibilities to a lieutenant. The "poignant scene" saw the fallen leader ordering his subordinate to "do the nasty job that has to be done . . . or forever after there will be the taste of ashes in your mouth." This moment represented a passing of the "torch of leadership" of the sort that his audience of graduating cadets were experiencing. In linking them Reagan sought to challenge the new lieutenants to live up to the standards of the American frontier of myth.[44]

Reagan's reference to Kipling too was important, as the president wanted the new officers to draw on the moral codes Kipling's work sought to impart. He idolized the British officers of the late 1800s as portrayed in the poems and short stories of Britain's archpoet. As with *That Printer of Udell's*, it was Nelle Reagan who had introduced her son to these works that would shape his outlook for decades. The poem "If" quickly became his favorite.[45] In it, Kipling offered advice on not only how to win "the Earth and everything in it" but also how to "be a Man," advice for which a young Ronald, with no good male role model, longed. "If" challenged its reader to "keep your head when all about you are losing theirs and blaming it on you" and to maintain self-confidence even "when all men doubt you," and to do what is right regardless of the cost and perceptions of others.[46] Kipling's code was the same that Reagan later found inspiring in westerns. It was the code he wanted military leaders to embody in the 1980s.

Intention and action were critical to Kipling. His work frequently put British soldiers in impossible positions and praised their nerve in continuing to perform. The striving toward civilization despite the likelihood of failure conferred on Britain, Kipling was sure, a national identity. The poet thought the same of the United States. In his 1899 "The White Man's Burden," he praised it for becoming an imperial power with its seizure of the Philippines from Spain the year before. The poem called on the rising great power to ignore the prospect that its colonial adventure would only yield "the blame of those ye better, the hate of those ye guard" and see "sloth and heathen folly" undo its hard work. The very act of trying to "civilize" a part of the world, however, would end America's "childish days" and show it worthy of the world stage.[47]

Speaking to administration officials in 1988, as he prepared to leave Washington, he told them that "what Kipling said of another time and place [was] true today for America." The nation stood "at the opening verse of the opening page of the chapter of endless possibilities."[48] However, Reagan took the quote somewhat out of context. In it, Kipling was, for once, celebrating not the British Empire but rather the age of flight.[49] Still, the quoted text spoke to how Reagan saw America's role. He continued to embrace the idea of a "White Man's Burden" long after its heyday.

Hannah Arendt's *Origins of Totalitarianism* argues Kipling was the "author of imperialist legend" and accurately accused his work of having little to do with the "realities of British Imperialism."[50] In her view, Kipling knowingly engaged in "hypocrisy or racism" in propagating works like the "White Man's Burden"; she was sure that "only those who had never been able to outgrow their boyhood ideals" would take him seriously.[51] Reagan never escaped his boyhood ideals. Though he would reappraise them at times in his life, he would on each occasion merely reaffirm the values he had taken from Burroughs, Kipling, and Wright. After all, he continued to seek out stories that were not only structured the same way as but also owed their inspiration to those early-twentieth-century books. Bellah, L'Amour, and others knowingly emulated Burroughs and Kipling and crafting their stories on the same lines. Since Reagan rarely read a different sort of story and certainly did not find a more diverse tale that resonated for him, he consistently preached the values of a ten-year-old in Illinois.

The narrowness of his reading also led him to adopt the racial undertones in Kipling, Burroughs, and westerns. The phone call to Nixon after Taiwan's expulsion from the UN revealed Reagan regarded the peoples in Africa as uncivilized. His views on the continent did not evolve. Throughout the 1970s on his radio program and in the 1980s as president, Reagan consistently sided with racist apartheid regimes out of fear that a majority-Black-ruled nation would be easy pickings for the communists. While he paid lip service to the idea of majority rule in Rhodesia and South Africa, he derided the idea of establishing it immediately: the "high voltage rhetoric by the left" would, if implemented, lead to failure.[52] The clear implication of his remarks was that he believed Black Rhodesians were not ready for the right to vote.

Reagan saw communists behind the nationalist movements in both Rhodesia and South Africa. He was correct that the Zimbabwe African National Union–Patriotic Front (ZANU-PF) in the former and the African National Congress in the latter had ties to communism and the Soviet Union, but Reagan grossly overestimated the extent of those connections and the influence Moscow had on the two movements. In a 1977 broadcast Reagan alleged that Robert Mugabe, leader of the ZANU-PF, could not win an election, because he "had no substantial following among Black Rhodesians" and had rejected "all conciliatory moves by the Ian Smith government" (Smith led the last White government of what would become Zimbabwe the next year) on, he charged, the orders of the Soviet Union.[53] The inaccurate perception of pervasive Soviet influence in the ZANU-PF made Reagan unable to realize why a majority of Rhodesians would reasonably doubt Smith's intentions and commitment to giving up power. Mugabe's coming four decades in power were in fact to expose him as a corrupt, vicious autocrat, but Reagan's opposition to his taking power was centered not on those traits but on the erroneous belief that Moscow would be the true power in Harare.

Reagan reacted similarly to demands to end apartheid in South Africa. He believed that Desmond Tutu, Bishop of Johannesburg and a leading anti-apartheid activist, was "naïve" to ask the United States to suspend aid to the racist state.[54] Fear of communism was again for Reagan the main factor. Reagan asked President Pieter Botha of South Africa to make concessions but also cautioned that the country "must not become a playing field for Soviet ambitions."[55] His letter expressed sympathy for Botha's position and promised official support and credit for any reforms.

In 1986, as Congress and the American public pushed for sanctions on South Africa, Reagan felt compelled to speak against them. He acknowledged that South Africa fell "terribly short on the scales of economic and social justice" but warned that imposition of sanctions would play into Soviet hands. Any immediate transition or revolutionary violence would bring in a communist government and grant the Soviets access to "vital minerals . . . for which the West has no other secure source of supply."[56] The speech swayed no one; Congress soon passed the Comprehensive Anti-Apartheid Act and overrode Reagan's veto. That the Republicans held the majority in the Senate at the time demonstrates how out of step Reagan was with his own party on the issue.

It is now clear that fear of Soviet influence in South Africa was not reasonable given the state of the USSR in 1986. It had little ability to project power beyond Europe and was actively pulling back from commitments elsewhere. It was also unreasonable of Reagan to expect Black South Africans to accept continuation of a racist, oppressive government to further American Cold War interests. He quite irrationally believed they would come to appreciate the role of the United States in preserving freedom broadly while they had little of their own. Reagan wanted Black Africans in Rhodesia and South Africa to wait—a sacrifice he would never have asked of Americans or Europeans. He wanted Central and South Americans to make the same sacrifice, to accept dictators in the name of a broader struggle in which they had no stake. In Reagan's view, the United States too would sacrifice resources and lives, and the good guys would win.

Reagan frequently spoke of sacrifice, employing in his speeches anecdotes of last stands and dying leaders. The Bellah story in his West Point speech and the fictional B-17 of his addresses to the Medal of Honor Society in 1983 and at the William Woods commencement in 1952 are prominent examples. The theme also featured in writings of his own as a young man. A short story he wrote while at Eureka College told of two Americans in the trenches of World War I. It was titled "Killed in Action," and its main characters were David Bering and James Edwards. Edwards sees no point in the conflict, but Bering insists that it is just; he has delayed attending Harvard and marrying his hometown sweetheart to fight. Edward is moved by Bering's "talk of sacrifice and glory." In that moment the trench erupts in combat; Bering saves Edwards' life before being wounded, and the two never see each other again.[57]

Years later, Edwards, now a successful businessman, reads of the death of his trench mate. Bering has lost his future because of his wound: he never went to Harvard, never married, and became a tramp, ending in a potter's field. Still, his heroism and conviction had saved and transformed Edwards' life. In Reagan's telling Bering was a hero, because, like his favorite protagonists, he did the right thing even knowing he could expect scant reward for his choices and in fact ended up suffering greatly for them.[58] The ending of "Killed in Action" and the attraction for Reagan of stories featuring military sacrifice are odd, in that Reagan typically disliked sad stories. However, loss and heroic sacrifice in military settings were for him happy endings. Those protagonists willingly laid down their lives to advance greater causes. Dying in the name of right was to be desired, even praiseworthy, for Reagan. The image tied in to his romantic reading of Kipling, Burroughs, and westerns. Michener's *The Bridges at Toko-Ri* offered a similar "happy" ending.

That novella, whose denouement was described above, tells of an aircraft carrier group in the Korean War that has just received a mission to destroy bridges located in "a deadly combination of mountains and narrow passes and festering gun emplacements." Though their destruction would not bring a major tactical gain, the force's commander, Admiral Tarrant (whose flagship is the carrier), believes it would send a powerful message and "convince the Reds we'll never stop . . . never give in . . . never weaken in our purpose." Such a psychological blow could hasten the end of the war.[59]

Lt. Harry Brubaker, a fighter pilot and the story's primary protagonist, is unconvinced. He is unhappy to be in the fleet at all, bitter at having been called up from the reserves and leaving behind a successful law practice and his wife and two daughters in Denver. He is the squadron's top pilot, however, despite his misgivings and belief that "in Denver nobody even knew there was a war on." He worries that his wife "couldn't take America anymore. . . . [W]e gave up our home, my job, the kids. Nobody else in Denver gave up anything." Tarrant chides Brubaker for these thoughts, asserting that "society is held together by the efforts . . . and sacrifices of only a few."[60]

His reconnaissance flight over the targeted bridges leaves Brubaker shaken. Only after a sleepless night spent writing to his wife can he control his fear and embark on the mission. The squadron succeeds in destroying the bridges, but Brubaker then goes after a secondary target and is shot down. He parachutes safely but once on the ground is surrounded and killed by communist forces. Only at the exact moment of his death, thinking of his daughters, does Brubaker come to understand "in some fragmentary way the purpose of his being in Korea."[61]

Tarrant's awe and wonder that the nation had found "such men" became a centerpiece of many of Reagan's speeches about the military. Awarding the Medal of Honor to MSgt. Roy Benavidez, U.S. Army, in February 1981, Reagan cited Michener. He described him as an author who "wrote movingly of the heroes who fought in the Korean conflict" and then posed Tarrant's question. Reagan admitted he had "asked that same question when our POWs were returned from savage captivity in Vietnam." However, unlike Tarrant, Reagan could answer the question. America got such men where it had "always found them, in our villages and towns, on our city streets, in our shops, and on our farms."[62]

The administration intended the event to set a new tone for the portrayal of the military in American society. Carter had approved Benavidez' medal in the waning days of his presidency, and his secretary of defense, Harold Brown, had planned to award it in a quiet ceremony without presidential involvement. The ceremony did not occur before Carter left office, and Reagan sought to elevate its profile. He would personally read the citation, a first for a president and turn the presentation into a showcase of the administration's support of the military and of his goal to bridge the civil-military divide exposed by the Vietnam War. Caspar Weinberger, the new defense secretary, wanted the event to show that "the American people as a whole . . . respected, honored, and appreciated the military."[63] (Benavidez himself would come to doubt this; in 1983, before the House Select Committee on Aging, he would speak out against the Reagan administration's planned cuts to disability payments. Benavidez would charge that "the Administration that put this medal around my neck is curtailing my benefits.")[64]

Reagan referenced Michener and Tarrant again in his speeches for Armed Forces Day in 1981 and 1982. In the latter he offered the same answer to the admiral's question.[65] A 1983 ceremony (three months after Benavidez' congressional testimony) to honor Hispanic Americans in the military saw Reagan again use the story, as well as others that explicitly celebrated Hispanics—notwithstanding their absence in Michener's novella.[66] The frequent recycling demonstrated the importance Reagan placed on what he saw as the core revelation of *The Bridges at Toko-Ri*—that a select group of Americans would always rise to their nation's call.

It is unsurprising that *The Bridges at Toko-Ri* appealed to Reagan. Like *Hondo*, it became a successful Hollywood film starring William Holden. Holden had been best man, and one of only two guests, at Ronald's and Nancy's wedding. However, Reagan always took care to cite Michener specifically when using the story, not the movie. This was in keeping with both how Reagan viewed the book and the role Michener played in the early Cold War.

Historian Christina Klein notes that Michener had "put his writing in service to the government" in the 1950s. He was outspoken in his support of U.S. policy and acted as a "paraphraser" who translated "Cold War rhetoric into popular narrative."[67] Michener's work brought fictional vignettes of American righteousness and might into the homes of millions of Americans, leading many to identify more closely with U.S. positions. Reagan was certainly one of these Americans. Another was Medal of Honor recipient Daniel Inouye, who while in the House of Representatives praised Michener as "one of most effective anti-Communist weapons in the worldwide struggle."[68] In Inouye's eyes, Michener's writing made large parts of Asia immune to the appeal of communism.

Michener's work also favorably portrayed the American military-industrial complex. It frequently depicted new military technology and highlighted the need for the newest and best weapons. Most Americans first heard of the now-venerable B-52 through his newspaper reporting.[69] In fiction, Michener presented technology as essential to saving American lives. Jet fighters, with their "singing beauty," speed "almost silently" in the "vast upper reaches of the world."[70] Their pilots can escape death and fly away from "savage, cheated mountains" that would claim a lesser plane.[71] If, by some chance, a jet crashes Michener reassured his audience that the latest in aviation technology could rescue its crew. In both media reporting and fiction, he praised helicopters that pulled pilots from frigid oceans "where exposure kills a man in less than twenty minutes."[72] One reading Michener during the Korean War could not doubt the "powerful assembly" that was a U.S. carrier group or help but imagine the vast potential such technology could provide the American military.[73]

Michener's work combined the high technology of John Carter and the moral code of Hondo. It also reinforced the racial stereotyping and gender norms found in those works. *The Bridges at Toko-Ri* does little to describe Koreans but does have a few Japanese characters—objects of sexual desire readily available to American sailors ashore, or as people saved from their savage ways by the United States. Brubaker takes leave in Japan with his family and meets a Japanese family in a bathhouse. All quite naked, they learn to interact, and Brubaker realizes that if in 1944 he had "hated the Japanese and had fought valiantly against them," over time "hatreds dissolved."[74] The moment revealed to Brubaker a part of the good the United States was doing in the world and why he needed to fight in Korea. It was this realization that would crystalize the instant the bullet entered his skull as he thought of the world he could give his daughters.

Women represented civilization in Michener's Korean War novella. The author argued through the character of Tarrant that a man fought to defend civilization, "comprised mainly of things that women and children want." The women of Michener's world were "invariably right": while it was "bright, lovely women" who wanted to end wars, they could also goad their husbands into fighting. For Michener, women understood peace in Augustinian terms, wanting "no more war . . . but no humiliation."[75] The peace must be a just one.

Reagan spoke of women in similar terms the year *The Bridges at Toko-Ri* came out. He reminded the graduating class (all women at the time) of William Woods College in Fulton, Missouri, that "boys your age [were] tonight standing in Korea." These were the boys the graduates were "going to marry": the ones who had remained in Fulton were unworthy. Reagan wanted his audience to "teach, heal, and mother" the children of those now fighting on the other side of the world. They would "push back against the darkness" through bearing children and nurturing families. Reagan depicted the highest calling of those women not as themselves wearing the uniform in which he took such pride but rather taking care of those who did. It was their responsibility to avoid the sort of "momism" that made many men "unable or unwilling to face the test of war on behalf of their country." His embrace of gender roles that were already rapidly going out of date and his diminishment of women's ability to contribute more than domestic tranquility encapsulated the role he felt his mother had played and of women in the stories he read.

The converse spoke to Reagan's belief in the transformative power of service. In Michener's story, Tarrant praises the "voluntary men" who fight and present a thin line against tyranny.[76] Michener used the phrase to describe his expectation that masculinity was a matter not of biology or age but of action. Reagan encountered similar sentiments in Kipling's "If," with its list of accomplishments required to become a "Man," with a capital *M*.[77] Westerns too shared this trope, defining masculine worthiness entirely in terms of adherence to a code. There is some irony in Michener's evocation of "voluntary men," given how large a percentage of the personnel in Korea were there not because of a voluntary trip to the recruiting station but by means of the local draft board. Tarrant's idea of voluntary men and Reagan's of the superior worthiness of men who served together presaged major changes in the civil-military relationship.

The role of the military expanded greatly after World War II, and the United States for the first time sought to maintain a large peacetime force. The relationship between that military and the state became an increasingly frequent topic of discussion. The year prior to Reagan's William Woods speech and the publication of Michener's *The Bridges at Toko-Ri*, Douglas MacArthur had brought the issue of civil control of the military to the forefront when he sought to override presidential authority and assert the autonomy he wanted to expand the Korean War into China. Truman rejected the likely disastrous strategy and fired the famed general, leading to a fervent, though short-lived, debate about the decision.

Questions about how deeply elected leaders should involve themselves in military affairs arose frequently in the literature of the time. Michener's work was part of a trend, one that would include serious political-science works like Samuel Huntington's 1957 *The Soldier and the State* and science fiction like Robert Heinlein's 1959 *Starship Troopers*. Both looked at the role of service, citizenship, and society. Both Heinlein and Huntington largely, and wrongly, were convinced that civilian control consisted of raising, training, equipping forces and then providing general guidance on what to fight, leaving the specifics to those with "military expertise." It is likely Reagan read both works while traveling to talk to General Electric plants and found himself in agreement with the idea of politicians exercising "objective control" but ceding significant autonomy to those in uniform. This approach also fit with his tendency to focus on vision rather than detail.

Michener, Huntington, and Heinlein also likely helped Reagan conclude that voluntary sacrifice was the mark of a true citizen and to support the idea of an all-volunteer force. At the height of the Vietnam War, as governor of California, Reagan appeared on the ABC show *Issues and Answers* and "questioned the whole business of the draft"; it would make the "uniform a symbol of servitude" and oppression rather than the mark of a true citizen he envisioned it to be.[78] He believed in the justness of the war but wanted Tarrant's "voluntary men" to fight it and to be elevated by and appreciated for their service.

He maintained this line in the 1970s after the United States abandoned the draft and created an all-volunteer force. Writing to Senator Mark Hatfield amid nationwide calls to reinstate the draft, Reagan stated that "only in the most severe national emergency does the government have a claim to the mandatory service of its young."[79] Reagan viewed the Cold War as a national imperative, but he felt volunteers would succeed in winning it. Bacevich argues that Reagan's vocal and consistent support of people in uniform displayed his belief that they were patriots, heroes, and idealists.[80] However, the reliance on volunteers did not excuse ordinary Americans from doing their parts as well.

As for women, Reagan clearly identified their role at William Woods to "teach, heal, and mother" the Korean War vets and their children.[81] He took up less emotional responsibilities of society in his 1979 article "Do Your Kids Belong to Uncle Sam?" In it he argued that American service members were poorly compensated for their sacrifices and that the fact made them "experts" in "understanding the cause and effects of inflation."[82] Reagan expressed belief that increasing pay and benefits would draw more into the military and yield a stronger force than the draft could produce. He also consistently pointed to an obligation on the part of the broader population to speak of the military in glowing terms. Bacevich finds that he established doing so as a "new standard of civic responsibility" most citizens would be happy to meet as it required no "sacrifice on the part of the average American."[83] This too-simple rhetoric about the civil-military relationship displayed Reagan's acceptance of Tarrant's belief that only a few stood in defense of civilization. Those "voluntary men" were all Reagan thought necessary; if equipped with the best weapons, they would prevail. Pairing the best of a free society with the best technology would ensure the good guys would win.

4

UP FROM
THE DEPTHS

The Means and the Will

J ust two months after surviving the assassination attempt, Reagan spoke at
two commencements, giving speeches that he hoped would establish a shared
understanding of what his administration sought to accomplish. The first, at
Notre Dame, focused on the domestic and moral, befitting its setting at the large
Catholic university. His second graduation speech addressed the military and foreign relations, issues that were arguably Reagan's top priorities, behind repairing
the economy. This speech too would have an ideal setting: he would address the
graduating class of the U.S. Military Academy in West Point, New York.

On that day Reagan assured the new lieutenants that America was experiencing a great revival. The president saw "hunger on the part of the people to
once again be proud of America," a hunger that created a "new spirit" and ended
"the era of self-doubt." The young men—and for just the second time in the
academy's history, women—in front of him were proof and cause of that spirit.
These volunteers were the "prime ingredient" in the protection of American freedom. Reagan drew on the Revolutionary War history of the site, telling his audience they were like the great chain that had once stretched across the Hudson,
charged with "holding back an evil force that would extinguish the light we've
been tending for 6,000 years."[1]

The president contended the previous decade had been a dark one in terms of military accomplishment and of how the nation viewed its servicemembers. Reagan accused past administrations of neglecting the military: by keeping pay low, diminishing G.I. Bill benefits, and not providing the equipment and guidance necessary to win the nation's wars. The public at large was guilty of "widespread lack of respect for the uniform" because of the Vietnam War and resulting tenseness in civil-military relations. These twin failures to uphold what Reagan viewed as a sacred obligation left too many of the "young men and women [who] volunteered for duty" to find their reward only in the "patriotism" of their fellow citizens, and "they were shortchanged" even in that small compensation. While their willingness to serve spoke highly of their moral character (and, in Reagan's private estimation, followed the best traditions of the American frontier and dime-store novels), those in uniform needed better from their fellow citizens.[2]

Over a brief five months, Reagan believed his administration began rectifying the imbalance. He listed with pride his young administration's accomplishments in raising pay, establishing a task force to expand the G.I. Bill, and increasing funding for the military across the board. Servicemembers now lived at "better than a bare subsistence level." As a result, more civilians were answering their nation's call. Reagan highlighted rising enlistment numbers and, more importantly, a "decided rise in quality" of those choosing to serve. Reagan did not take full credit for this, though: he believed Americans had "rediscovered how much there is to love in this blessed land." They were rejecting the moral equivalency advanced by popular culture and seeing their nation with fresh eyes. Reagan now charged the new officers to go forth and continue that movement, to "restore the sense of pride our men and women [were] entitled to have in wearing the uniform."[3]

The restoration of American military honor was a central goal of Reagan's first term. He believed rebuilding popular support for those in uniform was essential to his broader Cold War policy. Without it, his administration would be unlikely to take the broad, and expensive, actions he wanted to undertake to counter the Soviets. Over his first months in office Reagan took every opportunity to shore up popular support; the ceremony awarding Master Sergeant Benavidez the Medal of Honor was one, the address to the cadets at West Point was another. After the latter, Reagan observed in his diary that there were few things "more stirring than a West Point graduation" and recorded the pride he had felt as he "shook 900 hands."[4]

In the days before while writers were drafting the speech, Secretary of Defense Weinberger encouraged the president to use the opportunity to "increase the appreciation and honor the American people feel for the uniformed services." This was a topic the two had "discussed before"; both worried about the generally negative public image of the military. To counter it, the secretary suggested, Reagan should encourage Americans to engage in easy, cost-free patriotism, a commitment that required no sacrifice but left a good feeling. The speech should encourage citizens to do as their ancestors had in the Civil War and the world wars, to express "deep appreciation and honor" for the military in every way they could. Weinberger predicted that encouraging Americans to thank those in uniform for their service would augment the military's pay with an irreplaceable "psychic income."[5]

Weinberger's suggested phrasing did not "make the cut." However, Reagan did share the secretary's convictions. Both men felt as the administration entered office that Americans lacked the "will and spirit" to meet a challenging national security environment. Both were sure that without rebuilding national willpower they would be unable to increase the size, capability, and mission of the military. Popular will is an essential component of national power, and Reagan knew it would take more than his rhetoric to reverse negative perceptions that had set in over the previous two decades. Popular culture mattered as well. The depiction of the military in books and films shaped public attitudes toward the military and had a direct impact on the ability of the administration to implement its desired policy.

Early drafts of Reagan's West Point speech put this dynamic in stark language. They had the president declaring that the "ingratitude and lack of respect shown to those in a military uniform was a national disgrace" and that it was owing in part to "the film industry's pandering to this anti-American and antimilitary sentiment." Hollywood's actions and content were "reprehensible." On the margin of the draft were listed by hand the offending films: *Coming Home*, *The Deer Hunter*, and *Apocalypse Now*. Each received a Best Picture nomination at the Academy Awards, and each depicted the Vietnam War in a harshly negative light. Also, the films also presented military people as mentally deranged and morally compromised.[6]

That passage too failed to make the final cut, largely owing to reluctance of senior White House staffers to antagonize Hollywood.[7] However, that it was written and formally considered demonstrated how deep were the administration's concerns about popular culture in the United States. Staffers feared that the movie industry as a whole thought the Cold War "was an exaggerated concoction of a president halfway between stupid and crazy" and that it would push that narrative on the American public.[8] Speechwriter Dana Rohrabacher, for example, believed Reagan "felt personally about the movies," given his own background.[9] The president sensed the film industry had begun to portray the United States in an unfairly negative fashion after he left Hollywood for politics. In 1970 he had praised the producers of *Patton* for making a movie that would counter the "pernicious and constant degrading of the military."[10] Now in the White House, Reagan hoped to inspire more films like *Patton* and, in the words of historian Gil Troy, "resurrect the grandeur of the nation."[11] Achieving this meant presenting the military in ways, and in settings, that would cause audiences to feel compelled to cheer for servicemembers.

Sporting events were an obvious setting. The long relationship between organized sports and the U.S. military made arenas more than suitable. Many of these stadiums, such as the Coliseum in Los Angeles and Soldier Field in Chicago, were explicitly monuments to fallen soldiers. In 1982 a Reagan supporter who seized on the connection wrote Michael Deaver, the deputy chief of staff, to advocate using NFL games as "an informal structure to promote patriotism." If Reagan were to record a message of support, he proposed, NFL teams could play it at halftime and so link beloved local teams and the national "team," the military. The message should "encourage a standing ovation to the veterans," inviting the crowd to take part personally and physically in a display of gratitude.[12]

Deaver liked the idea but felt the NCAA would offer a better venue, the NFL season having been disrupted that year by a strike.[13] Over Veteran's Day weekend in 1982, accordingly, millions of college football fans heard Reagan proclaim that current servicemembers and veterans were "an elite group of men and women" who "even in times of peace keep the country secure from foreign threats." Continuing his practice of whitewashing the Vietnam experience, he equated service there with that in the world wars and Korea; all four had made the United States "safer and freer."[14] Stadiums across the country roared their approval.

Sporting events also became showcases for the latest in military technology. Flyovers and static displays reinforced Americans' certainty of the superiority of their weaponry and offered them a connection with the military that required little effort on their part. These displays helped Americans forget about the military failures of the 1970s and restore the faith of the 1950s that technology would carry the day. The link between sports and the military became strong, and events such as Super Bowl XXV, played in the wake of Operation Desert Storm in 1991, was to be a "multilayered patriotic display."[15] Increased television coverage grew the audience well beyond stadium capacity, bringing impressive images of high military technology into homes across the country.

The administration associated its positive narrative about the military in other forums as well, praising the work of authors and filmmakers who adopted patriotic themes. Allen Drury, the Pulitzer Prize–winning author of *Advise and Consent*, is one example. At its publication in 1959, *Advise and Consent*'s anticommunist message and conservative bent seemed to go against the tides of contemporary popular culture. Moonlighting as a reviewer for the *San Francisco Chronicle*, Weinberger wrote it a glowing review.[16] Shortly after Reagan's election, Drury sent the president-elect one of his novels; Reagan happily reported back that they had helped him in "learning how to be president."[17] Shortly after, Reagan appointed Drury to the first of two three-year terms on the National Council of Arts, which oversees the National Endowment for Arts.[18] The president hoped the author would steer endowments and grants toward art favorable to the administration and its policy goals. Drury, for his part, wanted to take an even more active role in cheerleading for Reagan.

In 1984, he wrote to Weinberger with an idea for a new novel that Drury felt the administration would want to support.[19] Titled *Pentagon*, the novel would show the "sickness in the building" caused by years of neglect and how important it was to turn it around.[20] Weinberger fully supported the idea and allowed Drury to shadow him for a day as he researched the book. The secretary also arranged for Drury over a month of unique access to the Pentagon.[21] However, the book, when it came out in 1986, was a critical and commercial flop. Worse, in the eyes of the administration, it did not cast the Department of Defense in the best of lights. Drury's support for the department was evident, but his conclusions were far too pessimistic. *Pentagon* concluded with an assessment that the defense bureaucracy was itself a "fundamental weakness" that prevented the department from capitalizing on "the greatest concentration of brains and ability in [the country] or anywhere." Drury also argued, "The Kremlin has two enormous advantages on its side—history's greatest arsenal and the innate weakness of [the Pentagon]."[22] Drury's view was out of step with Reagan's and his grim warning of overwhelming Soviet capacity was not the reality of 1986. In any case he was too late. In1984, another author emerged to take Drury's desired role as the president's favorite author. A debut novel from a Maryland insurance agent was about to capture the administration's imagination.

A NEEDLE IN THE OCEAN

Tom Clancy was an unlikely person to become a prominent voice in national security. After graduating from Loyola College in Baltimore with a degree in English he settled into a career working with his wife at a small insurance agency in Owings, Maryland.[23] Poor eyesight had dashed his dream of serving in the military, but he maintained a lifelong interest in it, particularly in hardware. His agency's location between Annapolis and Washington, DC, brought him a client list full of naval officers. Conversations with them gave Clancy a substantial understanding of how the service operated, which he refined through playing tabletop games like Larry Bond's "Harpoon." Clancy wrote to Bond, himself a former naval officer, to congratulate him on a well-designed game, confident that "after digesting" the rules it would be easy to explain the concepts of real naval war to anyone.[24]

Clancy was also a lifelong Republican and strong supporter of Reagan. Shortly after the election, he requested a signed photo of the president through his local congressman, William Broomfield, who forwarded the request with a note describing Clancy and another requestor as "faithful Republicans."[25] The White House sent the insurance salesman the photo. Writing a friend in early 1985, Clancy bragged of voting for Reagan four out of five times he could have. In the 1980 primary he had voted for G. H. W. Bush, for which he asked God's forgiveness, ruefully acknowledging "*nobody's* perfect."[26] These political views and his love for the military led to his wholesale embrace of Reagan's rhetoric that pairing restored military honor with the virtue of servicemembers would bring Cold War victory. Clancy consciously incorporated the themes into his first novel, on which he began to work in 1982: *The Hunt for Red October*.

The plot centers on the attempt of a Soviet submarine captain to defect and deliver the USSR's most advanced vessel to the United States. Clancy based his story on the actual 1975 mutiny on board the Soviet frigate *Storozhevoy*, then at its base on the Baltic.[27] The mutiny saw the ship's political officer and enlisted sailors take it over and attempt to sail it across the Baltic toward Sweden. Soviet aircraft quickly disabled the rudder, foiling the escape and leading to the capture of the mutineers. Moscow executed the political officer responsible.[28] Clancy recognized that setting the story on a submarine would increase the dramatic tension and create an opportunity for a compelling narrative of high-stakes hide-and-seek. This technique of taking contemporary events and technologies and tweaking them to raise fictional tension was a hallmark of Clancy's books and a major driver of their popularity.

Clancy had from the beginning grand plans for *The Hunt for Red October*; it would be the middle book of a trilogy featuring the character Jack Ryan. Clancy in fact began his project with outlines for the first and third, what would become *Patriot Games* and *The Cardinal of the Kremlin*. He also planned two books outside the Jack Ryan trilogy, the unfortunately titled *The Panache Procedure* and *The Pandora Process*. These would not see publication, but key plot elements would make their way into *Clear and Present Danger* and *The Sum of All Fears*, respectively. That over the course of 1982 Clancy completed the draft of *Red October*, chapters of *Patriot Games*, and the other drafts was a glimpse of his future prolific output as well as a suggestion of a quiet time in the insurance business.[29]

Clancy knew nothing about publishing. He had no literary agent and did not seek one, instead sending his manuscript directly to the Naval Institute Press. The publisher was best known for *The Bluejacket's Manual*, a book given, in many successive editions, to new sailors since 1902.[30] A branch of the private, nonprofit U.S. Naval Institute in Annapolis, it had never published original fiction. Clancy approached it first because another branch of the Naval Institute, the monthly *Proceedings*, had recently published one of his letters—the first time his words appeared in print. Clancy had hand-delivered it to the *Proceedings'* editorial office, an unorthodox approach that was successful for him.[31] He resolved to try it again, this time with the press editors. In a stroke of incredible fortune, they had recently decided to publish fiction, if it was "wet," and accepted *Red October* for their first outing.[32] To defray the costs, they sold the paperback rights in advance to Berkley Books, a division of Putnam, for $35,000, an amount the acquisition and subsidiary rights editor Deborah Grosvenor viewed as middling for a debut author.[33]

The Hunt for Red October first appeared on bookshelves in July 1984, mostly in Washington, DC, and New York City. Early sales seemed to suggest Clancy had been correct when he wrote a friend, "The odds of becoming the next Frederick Forsyth [*The Day of the Jackal, The Odessa File*, etc.] are . . . somewhere between merely exponential and astronomical—incredible." He was aware that "writers normally die poor" and was happy to have a "book-jacket with [his] name on it."[34] The initial run of 16,000 copies did sell out by mid-November, but interest in the book remained regional.[35] Reviews of the book seemed unlikely to propel it up the charts. The *Wall Street Journal* found Clancy's work "quite satisfactorily" entertaining and "great fun."[36] However, the *Los Angeles Times* took a dim view of it: Clancy could make "arcane information of U.S. and Soviet submarines approachable," but his "cardboard characters" left much to be desired.[37] Clancy was a success in the Northeast Corridor but certainly not on track to create a multimedia empire that would leave him a nearly hundred-million-dollar estate.[38] That, however, is exactly what it would do; after that December review the "astronomical—incredible" began to happen. Clancy would in fact find and win his biggest fan in the nation's highest office.

THE PERFECT YARN

Nancy Reynolds, at the time Reagan's assistant for electronic media, read the book on a trip to Argentina.[39] She had been well acquainted with Reagan as a reader since he was governor of California and she had been on his staff. Now she realized that Clancy's book had everything Reagan looked for in a story.[40] Reynolds gave the president a copy of the book for Christmas, and he inhaled it. Reagan read a third of it the day he received it and continued reading it throughout the week, often staying up far later than normal. By the end of the week, he confessed to staff that he had been tired during a meeting that day because he had been up until three in the morning devouring Clancy's submarine story.[41] Reagan took several opportunities to praise it publicly. He described it to *Time* magazine as "unputdownable," and, asked at a press conference what he was reading, his answer was *The Hunt for Red October*—"the perfect yarn."[42]

White House staff noticed the importance of the book to Reagan and began to search for the few unsold copies of the small first release so they could understand why it was special to him. Kenneth Adelman, a leading arms-control negotiator, located one, but only by discovering it shelved incorrectly as a non-fiction, technical work.[43] The efforts he and his staff went to in locating and then reading the book demonstrated the depth of their knowledge of how the president thought. Already familiar with how Reagan used *High Noon* and *Witness*, they sensed Clancy's book would become a similar resource. Kenneth deGraffenreid, the NSC senior director of intelligence programs from 1981 to 1987, inferred that reading Clancy reinforced "a lot of what we might assume was in Reagan's head."[44]

After Reagan's endorsement, not only "policy wonks" searched for copies. Fortunately for them, it was soon widely available. After the president praised it the book went into reprintings; in two months *The Hunt for Red October* sold an additional 75,000 copies. It became a *New York Times* best seller, and, in a hint of international intrigue, *Time* magazine noted the Soviet embassy in the District of Columbia had "reportedly bought several copies, presumably for shipment to Moscow."[45] In the midst of the media push, Clancy received an invitation to meet Reagan in the Oval Office: Reagan was bringing yet another creator of his heroes to the White House. Meeting Reagan left Clancy awe-struck—like Dorothy opening the door of "the wrecked house [in] Munchkin-land" and suddenly seeing in Technicolor. The president exuded charisma "an order of magnitude" more than he had expected; Reagan could, Clancy thought, "charm the fangs off a cobra" with his personality that "envelops you like a cloud." At the end of their brief meeting talking about Clancy's book, Reagan asked about the writer's next project. On learning it would be about World War III, he interestedly asked about who would win, to which Clancy responded, "The good guys."[46]

Reagan then rose, leaving to eat with Henry Kissinger (then in the private sector) and discuss what the ascension of Gorbachev to the general secretary-ship of the Central Committee of the Communist Party of the Soviet Union—the de facto leader of the USSR—meant for U.S.-Soviet relations.[47] Clancy meanwhile left the White House optimistic about future interactions between the superpower leaders, confident that Reagan would charm "Garbage-ov," in fact "probably drive him into the pavement."[48] The chat left the president and new author convinced they had read the other correctly. Reagan saw a writer who understood his administration's goals and would tell its story in a popular and memorable way. Clancy saw in Reagan a leader in whose goals he could, all the more, place his faith, and resolved to continue publicizing them. In a letter to Reagan afterward, Clancy wrote that their brief time together had been one of three things "more important than monetary success" that had come to him from the book. The other two were to have his son see his picture on the dust jacket and the third to receive the twin-dolphin badge of a submariner at the Pentagon. Clancy wanted Reagan to know "he would deem it a privilege" to undertake anything that could "ever be of the slightest service."[49] Though he never told Clancy, Reagan certainly viewed the writer and his work as of more than slight worth. He was impressed by the writer's personality, identified with Clancy's middle-class background, and delighted to see gallant American service men and women in the pages of his books. He became a lifelong fan and would frequently use Clancy's books in developing how he thought and spoke about strategy.[50] The existence of and public response to *The Hunt for Red October* also told him Americans were receiving his message about how the United States could win the Cold War. Technology and free men and women would lead the good guys to victory.

THE HUNT FOR RED OCTOBER

As the eponymous *Red October*, armed with ballistic missiles and the newest of a class of the largest submarines ever built, departs its home port on its maiden voyage, the captain, Marko Ramius, meets with his political officer. Ostensibly, the meeting is to open and discuss their boat's orders to test its nearly silent "caterpillar drive." Ramius, who has other plans, murders the commissar. He and his senior officers intend to defect to the United States and bring with them a potentially Cold War–changing technology. The escape should have been easy, but Ramius cannot leave without goading the Soviet naval leadership, which dispatches the entire Soviet navy (presumably the Northern Fleet) to find and destroy their wayward vessel.

The book's protagonist, CIA analyst and historian Jack Ryan, is on a flight to Washington, DC, from London when Ramius defects. He intends in Washington to share with Deputy Director James Greer photos of the *Red October* obtained by British intelligence and then pick up a skiing Barbie for his daughter's Christmas present. However, the naval movements spark a crisis, and war fears sweep Ryan into a White House meeting, where he persuades the principals that he has correctly deduced Ramius' intentions. The president then tasks him with working with the British and U.S. fleets in the North Atlantic to confirm his theory before war can erupt.

On the USS *Dallas*, a technologically advanced sonar system operated by a vastly overqualified sailor, establishes an identifying signature of the otherwise untraceable *Red October*. This allows Ryan to contact Ramius, and the two plan the defection. The Soviet sub fakes a radiation leak requiring its sailors to evacuate the boat with U.S. naval assistance in a rescue submarine; the officers remain to pretend to destroy the boat lest the Americans capture it. Ramius then welcomes Ryan and the commander of the *Dallas* on board to steer the ship into American waters and safe haven. Just before reaching safety, a protégé of Ramius now commanding an advanced submarine of the Alfa class finds his mentor's defecting boat and seeks to destroy it. Ramius rams and sinks the attacking submarine. As the book closes, the *Red October* and its advanced technology are safe in American hands and the Soviets are none the wiser. The United States scores an important victory in a secret battle of the Cold War.[51]

REAGAN'S READING OF *THE HUNT FOR RED OCTOBER*

Nancy Reynolds had displayed a strong understanding of Reagan's taste in selecting the book for him. Clancy's work was as if tailor-made for the president. Jack Ryan fit easily in the mold of John Carter or any number of reluctant heroes in westerns. He embodies a strong moral code and does not seek reward. Despite working for an intelligence agency, he hates deception in itself, even apologizing to an admiral for wearing a Navy uniform to maintain his cover—he does not "like pretending to be what [he is] not."[52] Ryan also eschews laurels. Instead of meeting with the president after his success, he boards a flight back to London and falls asleep holding his daughter's Christmas present. This ending effectively channeled Reagan's interpretation of *High Noon*, a hero who rises to an incredible challenge but then chooses to return to the life he had planned for himself rather than take the higher positions and rewards now available.

The book's depictions of sex and violence also fit Reagan's preferences. Approximately two hundred people die in the book, but Clancy does not portray the violence in graphic detail. He does describe how "a quart of blood had poured down the front of the flight suit" of a wounded pilot, in a scene intended to establish the rising tension and danger of war.[53] This scene would in concept be familiar to Reagan, as it is a standard storytelling trope to kill or grievously wound an otherwise anonymous good guy to spur heroes to greater action. As for sex, *The Hunt for Red October* has none. Its most explicit comment is a reference to a supporting character's "zest for life" as represented by his many children.[54] The *Wall Street Journal* noticed the absence, quipping that the only positive trait of Ryan's not discussed was "his undoubtedly impressive technique in bed."[55] This is true of most Clancy books, though he did consider writing a romance novel, believing the genre was "where the real money was."[56] Fortunately, it never came to pass, and readers were spared sex scenes occurring amid detailed descriptions of military hardware.

The relatively clean nature of *The Hunt for Red October* increased its appeal to Reagan, who disliked the increasingly explicit portrayals of sex and violence in popular culture. In 1970 he lamented that "good and inspirational stories . . . are too often tarnished by dialogue laced with profanities and vulgarities" and that the "inevitable bedroom scenes," which left "little to the imagination," were distractions.[57] His reaction to *An Officer and a Gentlemen* is a case in point. The movie showcased the military in a mostly positive light. Andrew Bacevich feels it showed that "service in uniform . . . was a worthy aspiration" and that joining the military "offered a way to be *somebody*."[58] This was the message of Reagan's West Point address and much of his public rhetoric. However, Reagan hated the film, calling it "a good story spoiled by nudity, language, and sex."[59]

Violence, however, was more acceptable in storytelling to Reagan. He viewed *Rambo: First Blood Part II* shortly after its release and recorded that everyone watching it "had a good time."[60] He likely appreciated the film's portrayal of Vietnam vets as capable fighters wronged by their country. Reagan also joked afterward he would "know what to do" the next time there was a hostage crisis.[61] Sylvester Stallone's work in the Rocky and Rambo franchises evoked the muscular patriotism Reagan was promoting and earned the actor multiple invitations to the White House.[62] Compared to a Stallone film, the violence in *Red October* was nonexistent and easily in the range of what Reagan found comfortable.

Clancy modeled his fictional president after what he knew or sensed of Reagan, something that likely increased Reagan's enjoyment of the book.[63] The fictional president had "dazzling charm" that could "turn on and off like a spot-light," something Clancy would find true of Reagan in their meeting.[64] Clancy's "president" also has the wary respect of the Soviets in the story, who see him as someone whose friendly face makes it "easy to underestimate him" and hides a calculating, brilliant mind that was "always ready to seize the advantage."[65] Gor-bachev frequently complained of Reagan that he would "pocket concessions" and give nothing in return.[66] After meeting Reagan, Clancy was convinced he modeled his character correctly. The president had indeed the "twitchy alert-ness of a fox," belying his "soft voice" and very relaxed manner."[67] The film char-acter even nods to Reagan. In the penultimate scene a triumphant president snacks on jelly beans, Reagan's favorite candy, silently basking in the presence of the defeated and dejected Soviet ambassador.[68]

These features made Reagan like the book. Its message, pairing virtuous servicemembers and civilians in government service with technology to defeat the Soviets, is the reason Reagan quickly began to praise it publicly, overcoming for once his "reader's conceit that books were secret personal treasures."[69] He believed that in expanding Clancy's audience he was growing his own and help-ing to build a supportive climate in popular culture for his policy ambitions. *The Hunt for Red October* showed Reagan that his first term was successful in pushing back moral equivalency and that there was space to push further.

REFIGHTING VIETNAM

Reagan intended his commencement speech at West Point to "declare the Vietnam syndrome was over" and personally drafted most of it to make sure it would convey how gallant he perceived the military to be.[70] He wanted to share his vision of U.S. servicemembers as romantic, chivalric, and brave, like the cavalry troopers of his imagined west and Kipling's British soldiers on the edge of empire. This speech built on the vision he had conveyed in his inau-gural address, where he had criticized those who insist "there are no heroes," accusing them of not knowing "where to look."[71] He encouraged his audience to find heroes in uniform and engage in the kind of simple hero worship he had throughout his life.[72]

Toward the end of the address, Reagan referred to Martin Treptow, a doughboy who had died during World War I. Treptow had left behind a pledge in his diary promising to work, save, and sacrifice "as if the issue of the whole struggle depended on me alone." Reagan, unwilling as ever to ask Americans to sacrifice, noted the situation they faced today would not require nearly as much of them. Americans simply had to "believe in our capacity to perform great deeds," and their renewed patriotism and optimism would lead soldiers like Treptow to accomplish great things. Reagan in effect asked Americans to be routinely complimentary about the military and those in it; his administration, he assured the country, would take care of the rest.[73]

That meant, in part, expecting Americans to view Vietnam in as heroic terms as they did World War II and other wars in which America had been victorious. He linked Vietnam directly to both world wars and Korea in his inaugural and Veteran's Day messages. During the presentation of the Medal of Honor to Master Sergeant Benavidez, Reagan went further and actively sought to rewrite the narrative of the conflict. He lambasted the Carter administration for not awarding the medal itself, accusing his predecessor of leaving it "overlooked or buried for several years." This was disappointing to Reagan, who believed Vietnam demonstrated the "incurable humanitarianism of our troops." His speech highlighted the construction by soldiers in 1969 of "1,253 schools and 597 hospitals and dispensaries" and their contribution of "over $300,000 from their own pockets" to give to the Vietnamese. In combat they had "fought as bravely and as well as any Americans" in history. That they "came home without a victory" was not because of their failures "but because they'd been denied permission to win."[74]

This explanation presaged the character of Rambo in *First Blood Part II* asking if "we get to win this time." Reagan sought to create a new narrative of the war that cast American servicemembers as unambiguously moral and as superior in every way to the soldiers of the North Vietnamese Army and Viet Cong. This was a "Lost Cause" school of thought for the 1980s, one that blamed "a failure to commit fully to the war" as the reason the United States lost.[75] While campaigning Reagan stated he felt it was time Americans "recognized that ours was, in truth, a noble cause" in Vietnam.[76] He believed that by changing how Americans talked about the disaster in Vietnam he could change how they spoke of the military. If it more publicly cast the war in the simplistic white-hat/black-hat dynamics of Reagan's preferred Cold War narrative, then his administration would enjoy a freer hand in responding to communist threats throughout the world.

However, there is no historical basis for Reagan's "Lost Cause" approach to the Vietnam War. American soldiers did not win every engagement, and the moral basis of the conflict was anything but simple. Reagan also purposefully refused to believe that the atrocities committed by American soldiers against the Vietnamese population reflected on the nation. Writing in 1971 about the March 1968 My Lai Massacre, Reagan termed "the Calley affair" (Lt. William Calley Jr.'s infantry platoon and others had slaughtered several hundred unarmed men, women, and children) as "one of the most complex problems we [that is, the nation] had." In a mind-blowing understatement, Reagan admitted the officer "did wrong" in ordering his men to shoot unarmed civilians. However, to Reagan this simply meant that society "must accept that some men become brutalized by war." He also sought to emphasize that the enemy "had a different standard than ours," comparing the Vietnamese to Native Americans fighting the U.S. cavalry in the Indian Wars. The press, he charged, had failed to expose "the savagery and atrocities" the enemy inflicted on civilians and U.S. military personnel. Reagan believed this context made Calley's actions "more understandable" and showed that he should not be "treated as just a wanton criminal."[77]

The disturbing letter and its callous attempt to dismiss Calley's war crimes reveals much about how Reagan viewed the Vietnam War and Cold War. He continued to employ frontier imagery when discussing the conflict and cast non-White people as savage. This rhetoric fit his response to the UN vote on Taiwan's status and further demonstrates Reagan was incapable of empathizing with people of color in the global South. In his mind, they existed to be civilized by the United States in fulfillment of the mission Burroughs and Kipling assigned the country nearly a century before. The civilizing effort would in turn elevate the moral worthiness of Americans and put it on display, facilitating the demise of communism. The letter also placed in stark relief Reagan's belief that the United States could do no wrong in fighting communism. Atrocities, whether few or (in the case of Vietnam) many, did not reflect on the nation or its moral rightness. In fact, they were the fault of the victims as they, or their neighbors, had degraded the otherwise pure American soldiers. Reagan believed Calley "probably could have gone through life without committing a single crime until we exposed him to the brutalizing force of war."[78] These beliefs built on the worst racial stereotypes of the imperialism-promoting authors of

Reagan's childhood reading and created in Reagan a willingness to accept and yet dismiss horrific actions that undermined the cause he cared for most.

The letter also showed the way Reagan wanted Americans to view their country and military. He wanted nothing short of the "hero worship" he professed. The civil-military relationship should be an uncomplicated one where average Americans proudly declared their support for the troops, the government funded them lavishly, and no one seriously questioned what they did in combat; the inherent morality of the United States and of service in its armed forces would ensure success. Clancy's *The Hunt for Red October* captured Reagan's preferred relationship perfectly. All the Americans in it are smart, willing to sacrifice, and morally unimpeachable. Though Jack Ryan is no longer in the military, he had served as a Marine and even left a lucrative career as a stockbroker for one with the CIA: he was "bored with making money" and valued service more.[79]

Clancy lavishes praise on his fictional naval officers. The commander of the USS *Dallas*, Bart Mancuso, is "one of the youngest submarine commanders in the U.S. Navy" and got there through his intelligence, instincts, and willingness to listen to subordinates.[80] Adm. James Greer, the CIA director, managed to stay in the Navy "past retirement age . . . through brute competence." Clancy compares him directly to Adm. Hyman Rickover—though Greer considers himself "a far easier man to work for" than the controversially demanding and confrontational father of the nuclear Navy.[81] The Greer character also draws on Adm. Bobby Inman, a former director of the National Security Agency (NSA) who was the deputy director of the CIA as Clancy began drafting the novel.[82] Like Greer and Mancuso, carrier group commander Adm. Joshua Painter is "a gifted tactician and man of puritanical integrity."[83] Only Adm. Charles Davenport has a negative trait, that he is "supposed to be a bastard to work for"— hardly an indictment given how well he performs his duties.[84] Enlisted sailors share their superiors' positive traits. SM2 Ronald Jones, who detects the *Red October*, had to drop out of the California Institute of Technology because of a prank gone awry. Soviets who later encounter him express shock at the trust his superiors place in him, implying the superiority of even the lowest U.S. servicemember to the highest in the Soviet Union.

Veterans too are worthy role models in Clancy's work—Ryan, of course, but also Skip Taylor, a former officer whose career was cut short by an accident.

Poised to command a submarine, he had been hit by a drunk driver and lost a leg. He remains "naval adjacent," teaching at the U.S. Naval Academy, and now he plays an important role in searching for the *Red October*. Like Ryan, he turns down any reward for his work; offered reinstatement on the list of officers eligible for command, Taylor declines, knowing he would "just be taking someone's slot."[85] The admiral who offered the opportunity had known Taylor would do so but laments privately the unfairness of someone with Taylor's potential being no longer able to serve. Taylor's willingness to forego, in the name of the service's interest, his own advancement exemplifies the ideal of self-sacrifice Reagan admired in the military. Taylor was the sort of character Reagan wanted Americans to think of when reading about fictional veterans.

The Hunt for Red October tapped into the "new appreciation for men and women in military service" that Reagan saw across the country. Speaking at Annapolis in 1985, he argued the country now had renewed faith in naval officers to "make [their] judgement and move forward" in environments where "issues [would] not be black and white." Enlistments were up and, Reagan claimed, the quality of people in uniform continued to improve, as citizens joined to "share their time, energy, and talent to keep America strong, safe, and free."[86] Reflecting in his diary after the speech, Reagan recalled it as "a stirring day" and the midshipmen's spirit "something to behold."[87]

Clancy's work built on Reagan's efforts to restore public confidence in the FBI and CIA as well. As he entered office, the intelligence community was still reeling from the Church Committee investigations starting in 1975. The committee uncovered wide-reaching abuses of power by the FBI, CIA, and NSA; its findings resulted in significant new oversight for the agencies, which Shultz advisor Charles Hill believed "pretty much devastated the CIA."[88] The shocking illegal actions, paired with a lackluster record of accomplishments, had left the agency diminished in the eyes of Americans. Popular culture reflected this. Movies like *All the President's Men* (1975) and books like Robert Ludlum's 1980 *The Bourne Identity* showed an FBI and a CIA run by cynical, power-hungry men who routinely ordered illegal and immoral actions.

Reagan now wanted Americans to extend the same moral support to employees of the CIA and FBI that he asked them to show military service-members. Speaking in 1982 outside the CIA headquarters in Langley, Virginia, to its members, he promised Americans that "the days of such abuses" as revealed by the Church Committee were past and assured them that the agency now performed in "a way that is lawful, constitutional, and in keeping with the traditions of our way of life." That this public declaration ran counter to his NSC's active subversion in the next few years of the Boland Amendments suggests cynicism on Reagan's part and a hope that Americans would settle for platitudes and not ask questions. His remarks on this occasion seem to support that view. Reagan praised the CIA employees for their "intellect and integrity," declaring that these traits as well as "wit and intuition" constituted that on which "the fate of freedom rests for millions." Those before him were "heroes of a grim twilight struggle," a phrase he would repeat in a closed-door session with the CIA's Directorate of Operations. Reagan condemned "nearly a decade of neglect and sometimes overzealous criticism," stating that people who served as heroically as Nathan Hale in the Revolutionary War and the operatives of the OSS in World War II deserved better.[89]

Reagan viewed his campaign to rebuild confidence in the CIA and the broader intelligence community as a "companion piece" to his analogous effort with the military. He viewed intelligence collection and analysis as critical policy tools, "part and parcel of defending American constitutional values."[90] Reagan liked to link the intelligence community of the present day, as he did the military, with predecessors of World War II and the Revolutionary War. This allowed him to build on the language of grievance and advance narratives that Americans were failing those who protected them. Reagan was more than willing to bury serious questions about the CIA's conduct as matters of mismanagement and the difficulties of operating in shadowy, savage environments, just as he did those arising about American soldiers in Vietnam.

The Hunt for Red October meshed with this view; it directly attacked the oversight mechanisms put into place following the Church Committee. The novel's CIA analysts correctly deduce what is happening with the *Red October* and Soviet navy and act both heroically and ethically to bring about a key U.S. victory. FBI agents conduct a successful counterintelligence investigation after a CIA source in the USSR is executed, his name having been leaked. They identify a Soviet spy on the staff of the chair of the Senate Select Committee on Intelligence, set up in 1976 to oversee the actions of the CIA. They use the knowledge not only to misdirect the Soviets but also to force the retirement of a senator noted for his hostility to both the FBI and CIA.[91] The gratuitous episode does little for the plot of the book but does advance the argument that it is elected officials and their staffs and not misbehaving spies who are the real national security threat.

Clancy's fictional version of the national security establishment took Reagan's rhetoric at face value and translated it into a compelling story enjoyed by millions. Reagan undoubtedly was reassured as he read the book and saw it atop best-sellers lists. The former actor remained deeply sensitive to the currents of popular culture and celebrated having found a story where the good guys won a clean and moral victory. Equally important was Clancy's portrayal of the stakes of the conflict. Reagan and his staff were convinced that the "Cold War was profoundly serious" and worried that many stories consumed by Americans argued the opposite.[92] They happily embraced Clancy as a "comrade in arms" who could help them rebuild American belief in their own rightness and the moral imperative of their cause.

Throughout his first term in office, Reagan embarked on what Ambassador Dobrynin viewed as an "uncompromising new ideological offensive."[93] The longtime Soviet diplomat immediately began expressing concern at the president's tone. At a private function in March 1981 he cornered Weinberger and made sure the secretary understood he was "really quite concerned about the perceived strength of the anti-Soviet position."[94] Just one year into the administration, Dobrynin had ample rhetoric to which to point.

Beginning with his inaugural address, Reagan used the presidential "bully pulpit" to advance his belief that the Americans were the white hats of the Cold War. In this first address as president Reagan claimed no other nation had a weapon more powerful than "the will and courage of free men and women"; America's "adversaries in the world [did] not have" them.[95] Reagan built on this message in his May 1981 commencement address at Notre Dame explicitly intended to contrast "an imperial Soviet Union" that was "hostile to human rights and economically ruinous" with an America that demonstrated respect for self-determination and rule of law. The language would "swing the President's full weight behind key ideas" of a "fresh and coherent national strategy" that was "struggling to penetrate the bureaucracy" and the American public.[96]

Though Reagan did not mention the USSR by name in the speech, frequent allusions to communism and totalitarianism left little doubt who he was talking about. He declared the "West won't contain communism, it will transcend communism," leaving it a "bizarre chapter in human history," the "last pages" of which the United States would write. Communist nations projected only a "façade of strength" with their "ideology and war machines," which the people of the free world would vanquish.[97] (The line did not elaborate on why Reagan believed U.S. ideology and war machines, which he planned to expand, were not a façade.) He also quoted with approval Pope John Paul II's recent encyclical against communism and "liberation theology," terming them nothing but a "distortion of justice."[98] Reagan agreed with the pope that the ideologies left people "stripped of fundamental human rights" in the name of a failed ideology.[99] That he used Pope John Paul's message at one of the nation's largest catholic universities signaled how much importance Reagan assigned religion in the fight against communism and hinted at an administration hope of enlisting the Vatican's help.

Despite Dobrynin's protests, Reagan continued his rhetorical attacks. In June of 1982 as he spoke to the British Parliament at Westminster, he echoed themes from his speech at Notre Dame the previous year, pledging to leave "Marxism-Leninism on the ash-heap of history." A "crusade for freedom" was being planned to ensure the victory of the West over communism.[100] The direct, combative language came at a time of rising tension and put the two speeches among Reagan's best remembered and most quoted. However, they were continuations of decades of such rhetoric and parts of Reagan's consistent effort to frame the Cold War in moral terms favorable to the United States. They reflected a conscious choice and were directed beyond their audiences not just to the Soviets but also to Americans and the West in general. Reagan believed he needed to build, along with military capacity, popular support and will to fight.[101]

The Hunt for Red October fit neatly into this messaging. Clancy uses religion to account for Ramius' defection, writing into the character's backstory secret baptism as a Catholic. Ramius' religion fades as he advances in the Soviet navy but enabled him to commit "the gravest sin in the Communist pantheon," becoming "individual in his thinking."[102] After a surgeon botches a procedure on Ramius' wife, she develops an infection that should be treatable. However, the hospital's antibiotics vials have been filled instead with water—by factory workers who chose to "meet" their quota rather than confess there was not enough medicine—leading to her death. Standing over her grave, Ramius realizes that the Soviet Union "robbed him of a means to assuage his grief with prayer" and deprived him of "the hope—if only an illusion—of ever seeing his wife again."[103] He inwardly breaks with the USSR on the spot and begins planning his defection.

The reason for Ramius' rejection of the USSR would have brought Whittaker Chambers to Reagan's mind. He frequently quoted how Chambers broke from communism after realizing the ideology was incompatible with humanity "at the level of unconscious life."[104] Ramius' defection becomes a return to life from Hades and a fulfillment of Reagan's 1950 promise that "you too can be free men again."[105] Clancy's depiction of individual Russians as people with whom Reagan could identify built on the empathy Reagan had long felt for those living in the Eastern Bloc.

Clancy's work portrays the Soviet system as remorselessly evil. References to "gulags," prison camps, abound, and his Soviet characters are fatalistic about their state and how it treats them. The Politburo (the Political Bureau of the party's Central Committee, effectively the seat of power) is self-interested and power-hungry, ordering and sanctioning violence with the slightest provocation. But the state pays a price for this cruelty and inhumanity: in *Red October* one day a veteran of the Great Patriotic War (World War II's Eastern Front) now working in a mailroom, having met his quota declines to process the waiting stack of mail, in which is a letter from Ramius declaring his defection. The worker, who has unknowingly bought the submarine an extra day's head start, jokes as he leaves, "As long as the bosses pretend to pay us [i.e., with a nearly worthless currency], we pretend to work," a variation of one of Reagan's favorite jibes about the Soviet Union.[106]

Clancy's framing of the ideological aspects of the Cold War matched Reagan's public remarks over decades. His *Red October* rewards individual thinking and freedom and penalizes autocracy; the Cold War battle plays out exactly as Reagan always said such a battle would. Andrew Bacevich attributes this to Clancy being one of a group of "market-savvy writers" who "discerned the changing mood."[107] But whatever can be said of other writers, Clancy had no "market savvy" at all when he began the book. His not having a literary agent and approaching a press that had never published fiction demonstrate this. Instead, the novel was a product of his earnest belief in Reagan and his policies. That *Red October* succeeded was the result of the American public's increasing acceptance of Reagan's view. Clancy's editor, Deborah Grosvenor, saw the book as a product of its era and thought his timing incredibly fortunate.[108] However,

Reagan wanted to do more than change how Americans viewed the Cold War: administration also wanted to transform the equipment and forces the United States used to fight it.

PERFECT WEAPONS FOR VIRTUOUS MEN

"Technology, plus freedom, equals opportunity and progress." Reagan's message to graduating cadets of the U.S. Air Force Academy succinctly captured the core of his strategic vision. The boundless creativity of Americans living in a free society paired with innovative marvels of the future would bring world peace. Reagan looked to history to confirm this, arguing that despite the two millennia separating them, "the armies of Napoleon had not moved across Europe any faster than Caesar's legions—and neither army worried about air cover."[109] The United States had changed this: inventions by Americans brought mankind from horseback to "open cockpits to lunar landings" in Reagan's lifetime. The rockets of science fiction had become reality. As this technology evolved, the United States rose to new heights globally, proving to Reagan the capacity of Americans.

However, as the administration entered office, it feared that Americans were not being provided the technology needed to prevail, to achieve "peace through strength." National Security Decision Directive (NSDD-32) of May 20, 1982, acknowledged a large gap "between strategy and capabilities." The U.S. military was coming out of the 1970s in no shape to "deter military attack by the USSR" and certainly not to "contain and reverse" the growth of communism.[110] The policy document called for immediate enhancement of conventional (nonnuclear) forces stationed in Europe and development of new, more lethal weapons to overcome a perceived Soviet advantage.

Other planning documents from Reagan's first years in office tell the same story. A 1981 study by the State Department's Policy Planning Staff termed "U.S. conventional and [European] theater nuclear force posture weaknesses" a "priority problem" that severely limited strategic flexibility in Europe.[111] Laurence Eagleburger, the assistant secretary of state for European affairs, agreed. He wrote the secretary, Alexander Haig, that "Soviet power has grown enormously" over the past decade while American ability to counter the communists decayed. If the United States was going to achieve "serious, equitable arms control," it would need to embark rapidly on the "development of adequate military capabilities."[112] As late as 1983, despite massive increases in military spending, the administration still worried the U.S. military was not measuring up. A new national security decisions document, NSDD-75, posited that the country still needed to "modernize its military forces" significantly to ensure "Soviet calculations of possible war outcomes" were so unfavorable to the USSR as to deter it from aggressive action.[113]

In 1984, this narrative shifted. Amid his reelection campaign, Reagan spoke optimistically about American technical capability. In an Air Force Academy commencement, he declared the service was "the best darn air force in the world," because of both the people joining and investment in new airframes, ordinance, and training.[114] This was more than campaign rhetoric. Internal administration documents said the same. A National Security Council study from May 1984 trumpeted that "America's strength has been revitalized" by aggressive investment in the military. Improvements in personnel and new weapon systems had greatly "improved U.S. military strength" and would provide the administration the tools it needed to achieve broader strategic goals in its second term.[115] A reelected Reagan had reason to feel optimistic as he settled in to read *The Hunt for Red October* that Christmas. He believed the United States was now set to deliver on the vision he had shared with Air Force cadets of free people and technology winning the Cold War. Clancy's story gave him a way to do exactly that.

Technology, of course, was a central theme of Clancy's work. Reagan was particularly impressed with the author's accuracy in intricate technical details and asked Clancy about that in the Oval Office. Clancy claimed that was the easy part, that the real challenge was the characters' dialogue—something with which his reviewers certainly agreed.[116] The author did strive for technical realism, though, and was justifiably proud of the handling of detail in his books. As part of the prepublication process, the Naval Institute Press submitted the manuscript of *The Hunt for Red October* to two active-duty submariners. The first cleared the book; the other declared it unpublishable because it contained classified information but withdrew the objection when Clancy detailed the publicly available sources he had used.[117] The latter reader would not be the only one to think Clancy had access to sensitive material. Secretary of the Navy John Lehman confided to this author his first response to the book was to demand to know "who the hell cleared this?"[118]

The Hunt for Red October, in fact, uses technology as its "MacGuffin." The *Red October*'s "caterpillar drive" fuels the narrative. It represents a grave threat to American technological superiority; specifically, it would allow the Soviets to evade the U.S. Navy's new, advanced attack submarines and thus position their nuclear-armed submarines along the eastern seaboard. Fortunately, it is the only area in which the Soviets possess an edge, and significantly, it is the only piece of hardware in the book that is fictional. The rest, being actual, serves to demonstrate the real-life superiority of American technology in every area. Throughout the novel, the Soviets are unable to surprise their American counterparts; U.S. radar and sonar tracks their movements perfectly. A Soviet pilot chastises his "intelligence officer for telling him he could sneak up" on U.S. planes, which instead have surprised and intercepted him.[119]

The book's Soviet commanders do not enjoy the same advanced warning. Their carrier, the *Kirov*, only receives sixty seconds' notice before a squadron of A-10s, flown from the continental United States, arrives to stage a mock attack in the North Atlantic. Clancy's American commanders use the simulated attack to send a message that if they "were serious [the Soviets] would all be dead now." The Soviet admiral takes the point and orders his fleet to be as "meek as mice" from that point forward.[120] He also forbids any response to further American prodding lest U.S. sensors learn sensitive information about how the Soviet equipment works. The scene is a fictionalized "enactment" of a concept expressed in NSDD-75 of using technology to force the USSR to change its strategic calculus. American technology in the book does indeed make the cost of engagement unacceptably high for the Soviets, who significantly moderate their behavior as a result.

Longtime Reagan speechwriter Dana Rohrabacher has no doubt that Clancy's work influenced Reagan.[121] The president, of course, was grateful to see a work of popular fiction depict his policies so favorably, but the book offered him more than that. It provided a way for Reagan personally to visualize intricate military matters. It also contributed to his belief that his first term was a success. Without high-level access, Clancy had written a narrative that advanced the same message Reagan was reading in policy documents and hearing in meetings. *The Hunt for Red October* was a valuable tool for Reagan for thinking about the state of the Cold War and seeing the impact his messaging was having on contemporary American culture. Reagan was also far from the only person in his administration to use Clancy's work in this manner. The author took on surprising importance as others sought to capitalize on his relationship with the president for their own agendas.

In the summer of 1985, the British *Times Literary Supplement* asked Caspar Weinberger to review some work of fiction that deserved "to be better known."[122] The secretary of defense had reviewed books for the *San Francisco Chronicle* for several decades and happily agreed. Kay Liesz, his longtime personal secretary, suggested he review *The Hunt for Red October*, having "it on good authority that our big boss across the river thoroughly enjoyed it" and was "almost singlehandedly responsible for its zoom to the top of the best-sellers list."[123] Weinberger took his secretary's advice and produced a remarkably favorable review of Clancy's book, praising its "vast and accurate" portrayal of U.S. technical capabilities and declaring that the book held "many lessons" for "those who want to keep the peace."[124] Two years later Weinberger would have similar praise for Clancy's third book, *Patriot Games*, for the *Wall Street Journal*. That new book, he said, depicted technology with an accuracy "up to the limit of declassified information," that lent it "authenticity, and hence believability" and, in turn, importance and value.[125]

In reviewing *The Hunt for Red October*, Weinberger was seeking to do more than curry favor with Reagan. He was deeply concerned about the depiction in fiction of the United States and particularly sensitive to how stories portrayed the military and intelligence communities. In another *Wall Street Journal* review he savaged Robert Ludlum's *The Bourne Supremacy*, which has the State Department and CIA engaged in such illegal and immoral activities as abduction, blackmail, and assassination.[126] Weinberger felt Ludlum was intentionally seeking to tear down the image of the United States: "the required LeCarre [*sic*] syndrome" (the characters and settings of John le Carré's hugely famous Cold War espionage novels are antiheroic, bleak, and morally ambiguous) had been given "full rein," and Ludlum had taken pains to show "those on our side are also guilty." He worried that people reading Ludlum would "really think this [was] the way the government's business [was] done" and so felt compelled to go on the record against the book.[127]

Clancy had many fans in the Pentagon beyond Weinberger. The Navy quickly realized the value for it of narratives like *The Hunt for Red October*. Vice Adm. Nils R. "Ron" Thunman, the service's senior submariner, hosted a lunch in Clancy's honor at the Pentagon and presented him a large plaque and the submariner's uniform device, a brass badge with dolphins flanking a submarine. Five other admirals attended as well, including the Vice Chief of Naval Operations. Clancy happily answered their questions and took the opportunity to ask if the Navy would support a film version of his book; the answer was "a qualified yes."[128] A few years later the Navy did in fact support the filming of *Red October*, in large part because Clancy insisted as part of his contract with the filmmaker that the finished movie could not depict the Navy negatively in any way.[129]

Staffers in the White House also latched on to Clancy's book. After his meeting with Reagan, Clancy attended a luncheon organized by Deputy Chief of Staff Michael Deaver. There he engaged in a "lively and erudite" discussion of "arcana of naval warfare and strategy" with Lehman.[130] He also discussed the prospect of winning a nuclear war with once-and-future national security advisor Brent Scowcroft. The former Air Force general believed the United States could win such a war; the author disagreed. Later in the month of March 1985 Clancy received an invitation to a state dinner. There he met Bud MacFarlane, then Reagan's national security advisor. MacFarlane liked Clancy's book but wanted to stress that he personally was not like his fictional counterpart. Clancy gamely agreed and then shared a plot idea on "sea-power and mobility" he claimed the NSA liked. Later in the evening, a photographer confided to Clancy that "*every-one* [Clancy's emphasis] in the White House" had read and liked his book.[131] By March 1985, then, the author knew he had high-ranking support. The unanimous verdict of the Reagan administration was that his novel was entertaining and could change how the broader public thought about the U.S. military.

The Hunt for Red October was in fact part of a significant shift in the portrayal of American power in popular culture. If Reagan entered office deeply concerned about the output of Hollywood, as he began his second term the movie business was a source of optimism. Each of the top three films of 1985 took Reagan's rhetoric seriously and brought it to a wide audience. Two Stallone films, *Rambo First Blood Part II* and *Rocky IV*, occupied the second and third positions, each earning over $100 million. They had Soviet villains and patriotic American protagonists. *Rambo* took up the conservative alternative history of Vietnam; its title character returns to Vietnam with the assurance he can "win this time."[132] His mission to rescue abandoned POWs drew on an unsubstantiated but prominent Republican accusation that American soldiers were still being held in Vietnam.[133] *Rocky IV* embraced Reagan's Cold War moral framework, casting Rocky and by extension the United States as an underdog against the chemically enhanced specimen Ivan Drago. Rocky's heart and his willingness to work hard win over the Soviet spectators at a revenge bout in Moscow on Christmas Day, and they cheer him as he vanquishes the Russian. He then delivers an eloquent speech: "If I can change, and you can change, everybody can change," and the Cold War can end.[134] The change that actually came, though, was the Soviet state coming to embrace certain basic human freedoms and allowing its people more liberty.

The top film of 1985 was *Back to the Future* (amassing more than $200 million). Its depiction of suburban life in the 1950s and 1980s conformed to Reagan's evocation of what living in America should be. Early in the movie there occurs an attack by "Libyan terrorists," drawing on contemporary events (the Libyan leader Muammar Gaddafi was sponsoring attacks and allowing host terrorist training camps).[135] A few real-life military engagements between American and Libyan forces in the 1980s made these villains recognizable to Americans, in line with Reagan's policies. Clancy's third book, *Patriot Games*, employs Libya as the enemy as well, in a manner that earned praise from Weinberger.

In 1986, good cultural news for the administration continued. *Top Gun* dominated the box office. The iconic fighter-pilot movie received significant support from the Navy and was an effective two-hour-long recruitment video. For its production the Navy made available the services of two aircraft carriers and modified jet fighters.[136] Its story involves a nameless communist state, but the dramatic tension comes from competition among the Navy pilots in a training program for the most highly skilled.[137] The film advances the Reagan notion that superior technology plus committed, free men yields victory. It also helped establish a notion in its viewing audience that war could essentially be a video game. *Top Gun* started in pop culture the "nintendoization" of conflict that would erupt in the military itself with Operation Desert Storm. Its narrative and that of similar films promised Americans that their military would use its technology to win quickly and decisively, and all they had to do was watch and cheer for the good guys.

TECHNO-THRILLER RISING

How to Win the War

Margaret Thatcher was angry with Reagan. In October 1986 Reagan and Gorbachev stunned most of the world by nearly agreeing to eliminate all nuclear weapons within a ten-year window. Thatcher did not share the near-global disappointment that the two leaders had not come to a final agreement. Unconsulted and caught off guard, she cabled Reagan the day after the summit to let him know that the "prospective agreement to eliminate all long-range nuclear missiles . . . caused [her] considerable concern." Thatcher feared it showed a reluctance of the United States to back NATO and would "cause even more difficulties for Western unity." She advised the president in future to negotiate "along the lines we have discussed" and avoid undermining the security of Western Europe.[1]

She phoned Reagan the next day to reemphasize her displeasure. Thatcher "repeatedly stressed the importance of nuclear deterrence in the face of the imbalance of conventional forces in Europe."[2] Reagan was unmoved and replied that NATO "could have a strategy" to address the issue. Reagan then "strongly commended" to her Tom Clancy's *Red Storm Rising*, which had come out two months earlier, as "an excellent picture of the Soviet Union's intentions and strategy." A memo of their conversation records that Reagan "had clearly been much impressed by the book."[3] The recommendation confused Thatcher, to whom her private secretary had to explain the reference.[4] While she likely did not take up Reagan's reading suggestion, the call did leave her convinced he would not abandon his position on abolition and in fact "showed considerable pride in it."[5]

Thatcher was not the only person Reagan told about *Red Storm Rising* and how it affected his thinking. On the way to Reykjavík on board Air Force One to meet with Gorbachev, he had talked with his staff not about preparations for the summit but of things his staff viewed as trivial.[6] They were used to this; Reagan typically did not "feel the need to have things fully staffed out before meetings" and relied instead on his negotiating skills and charisma.[7] What Reagan spoke with the staffers about was *Red Storm Rising*, which he called his "research" for the coming talks.[8] The negotiating team thought he was joking—part of the story takes place in Iceland.[9] The president was not joking. Clancy's book in fact played an important role in Reagan's decision that the United States could abolish nuclear weapons. Its narrative told Reagan a story he found convincing of American soldiers with advanced weapons and NATO allies defeating the Soviet Union decisively and conventionally— without resort to nuclear weapons, which would presumably lead to all-out nuclear warfare.

Before departing Iceland after the summit Reagan addressed American servicemembers and their families stationed there. He told them of the "hard and tough" negotiations just ended and lamented that the delegations had come close to "the most far-reaching arms control proposal in history" but ultimately had been unable to agree. The United States could safely make such a proposal because of the men and women, like those before him, who served on "NATO's frontline," "strengthened world peace," and ensured "the prevention of war." They were America's "secret weapon" and guaranteed that the "flame of freedom" would "spread its light throughout the world."[10]

These remarks built on Reagan's first-term rhetoric of the military as "gallant and brave," language designed to shape the way the American public viewed those in uniform.[11] It also evoked his strategic principle of "peace through strength," to which he had been devoted for decades. Yet at the summit, to the astonishment of many, Reagan had told Gorbachev "it would be fine with him if we eliminated all nuclear weapons," to which the Soviet leader had replied, "Let's do it."[12] Only Reagan's refusal to confine research on the "Strategic Defense Initiative" (SDI, a proposed interceptor and radar system to protect the United States from ballistic-missile attack) to laboratories for a decade (i.e., not actually to build such a system) prevented agreement. The president's supporters and U.S. allies saw the new development as a sudden and dangerous shift and were confused by Reagan's seeming willingness to throw away one of his first term's major accomplishments.

The bafflement was understandable, as Reagan provided little indication of his "abolitionist" dream. One of his administration's early initiatives sought to increase American strategic capability with a five-point program to modernize the U.S. "nuclear triad" of long-range bombers, submarine-launched ballistic missiles, and ground-launched intercontinental ballistic missiles (ICBMs). The program resulted in a new missile design, revival of B-1 bomber development, modernization of the rest of the bomber force, improvements to submarine-launched Trident missiles, and more robust command and control.[13] Reagan had also decided to grow the number of nuclear weapons in the U.S. arsenal to over 17,000 by 1987.[14] After such a major emphasis on expanding and improving nuclear deterrence over his first five years in office it hardly seemed likely that Reagan would spend his last three seeking to dismantle it.

One of the first geopolitical challenges the Reagan administration had faced centered on the deployment of "intermediate-range," "nuclear-capable" Pershing II missiles in Europe, from where they could strike not only attacking Soviet forces but targets well inside the USSR. The issue was a holdover from the Carter administration, which agreed in 1979 to base Pershing IIs on NATO territory in response to the Soviet 1977 deployment of the SS-20, an equivalent missile posing a reciprocal threat to Europe. Once in office, Reagan and his advisors fully backed the idea. Jack Matlock of the NSC, later argued that the 1977 Soviet action "changed the nuclear balance in Europe" by replacing an old system (known as the SS-4 and SS-5) with "a substantially larger number of the more capable weapon."[15] Weinberger saw the Soviet decision as a "politically and militarily threatening change" in the continental balance of power.[16] Charles Hill was even more gloomy, convinced that if the United States did not deploy new missiles it would have to capitulate to Soviet domination of Europe.[17] Such views were embodied in the NATO Double-Track Decision of December 1979, which—failing Warsaw Pact agreement to elimination of such missiles on both sides—called for a strong response to prevent "Soviet superiority in theater nuclear systems."[18]

Reagan vocally supported deployment of the Pershing II despite mounting opposition both at home and abroad. He noted in 1981 that the United States had no missile comparable to the SS-20 (the existing Pershing I had much shorter range, and the new missile would not be in service until 1983) and even "dismantled the last such missile in Europe over 15 years ago" (the Jupiter, retired in the early 1960s).[19] Bringing the capability back to Europe could be avoided only if the Soviets agreed to dismantle not only the SS-20 but also the SS-4 and SS-5—that is, responding to one of the NATO decision's "tracks." Moscow had no intention of doing so, and NATO implemented the other track: by 1986, the United States placed 143 Pershing IIs in Europe. Little about Reagan's rhetoric and action here suggested an antinuclear stance.

Neither had Reagan given any indication while a campaigning. He railed against the proposed SALT II (Strategic Arms Limitation Talks held in 1979 to extend the 1972 SALT I Treaty) framework as a "serious blow to our security."[20] The deal (Carter and Leonid Brezhnev, then the Soviet leader, had signed it in Vienna, but the Senate would ultimately reject the formal treaty), he thought, must have resulted in "purring sounds from the Kremlin."[21] On his weekly radio show, Reagan called for new classes of bomb, specifically a "neutron bomb," designed for maximum radiation but relatively low blast effect. He viewed it as "truly akin to the science fiction death-ray," an image speaking to both his love of the genre and poor grasp of technical specifics.[22] Reagan seemed to think the weapon would only kill people but leave property and countryside intact, likely unaware that a neutron bomb detonation would still be a nuclear blast, albeit a smaller one than the Lance missile fielded by NATO at the time.

Reagan's rhetoric throughout the 1970s and actions early in his presidency convinced many that he not only accepted stability enforced by the threat of "mutually assured destruction" but might even be happy to push the nuclear button.[23] A 1984 open-mic gaffe allowed Americans to hear Reagan declare he was "outlawing Russia forever" and beginning a bombing campaign in five minutes.[24] The incident certainly did nothing to alleviate fears of many Americans that the president was leading them to war. Popular culture increasingly reflected this sense; films like *Wargames* in 1983 sought to show the futility of nuclear conflict and the real danger of one occurring.

Comic books too captured these rising fears. Alan Moore's graphic novel *Watchmen*, acclaimed by *Time* as one of the top hundred novels since 1925, makes frequent reference to the Bulletin of Atomic Scientists and its "Doomsday Clock" to instill a sense of impending doom. In it, fear of nuclear war between the United States and the USSR drives former heroes to mass murder.[25] Frank Miller's critically acclaimed and commercially successful *The Dark Knight Returns* of 1986 featured an amiable Reagan blundering into nuclear war over an island like Grenada (which he had ordered invaded in 1983). A panel shows him clad in a radiation suit, informing the American public that the Soviets are "pretty bad losers"—and then an iconic sequence shows Superman being struck by a nuclear missile. Miller subverts Cold War propaganda by first placing Superman, emblematic of truth, justice, and the American Way, in the path of the warhead clearly poised to turn it like he would a normal bullet but then left withered and zombie-like by the detonation, barely alive—a clear foreshadowing of the potential fate of his adopted home.[26]

Not even readers of Dr. Seuss could escape the arms race. In 1984, the beloved children's author published *The Better Butter Battle*. It featured two societies, differing only in how they butter their bread, engaging in an arms race with increasingly advanced technology from "the boys in the back room." As it ends, both populations are living underground, their guards atop a wall preparing to annihilate each other.[27] Reviewers found it "not a funny book" and Seuss' most "thinly-veiled allegory."[28] The *New York Times* thanked the former political cartoonist for "trying to find a way to tell children the nuclear facts of life" but also hoped for a "colorful sequel" in which the two societies learned to coexist.[29]

A 1983 made-for-television movie, *The Day After*, may be the most famous example. It is a depressing movie of life in a small Kansas town following World War III. Critics saw it as, although "terrible" in terms of writing and acting, an "effective primer on the horror of thermonuclear war."[30] Many found in it a "rallying cry" for the "nuclear freeze" movement;[31] that possibility sufficiently worried the administration, which previewed the film, to request the network to air immediately afterward a "town hall" with George Shultz. Eventually the White House decided that commercial breaks and poor editing reduced the film's impact.[32]

Many historians point to the film as sparking a change in Reagan's outlook, but this is inaccurate. Reagan's diary does record that the film left him "greatly depressed" but also castigates it as "anti-nuke propaganda" and pledges that the administration would do everything it could to "take over" its message. Specifically, *The Day After*'s visuals left him resolved to "do all we can to have a deterrent" that would prevent a Soviet launch.[33] He had already spoken of that antinuclear vision nine months previously in announcing SDI, and nothing about this film changed his perspective. Another science-fiction film, though, did influence Reagan's views on nuclear weapons. The 1951 classic *The Day the Earth Stood Still* challenged common narratives of American Cold War power and left a lasting impression on Reagan.[34] In it, an advanced alien tells the peoples of the earth that they need to set aside their warlike ways or risk their planet being "reduced to a burned-out cinder." If they did not abandon their atomic weapons, they could not join advanced societies in the stars but instead would simply destroy one another. The alien, Klaatu, tells Earth's leaders that security for all "does not mean giving up any freedom, except the freedom to act irresponsibly."[35] Reagan shared Klaatu's definition of freedom, frequently declaring that "with freedom comes responsibility" and linking it to arms control.[36] Colin Powell, Reagan's national security advisor between 1987 and 1989, believed that Reagan's conception of arms control and antinuclearism stemmed in part from *The Day the Earth Stood Still.*[37] It also seems likely that the film's internationalist bent inspired, at least in part, Reagan's desire to share SDI broadly despite his distrust of the Soviet Union.

Paul Lettow, however, convincingly argues that Reagan "held audacious unorthodox views regarding nuclear weapons" long before he became president.[38] Some of his earliest political activity was in protest against the atomic bomb; he was to have led a rally against the bomb in December 1945, but Warner Brothers intervened.[39] He also frequently railed against the idea of mutually assured destruction. In 1968, campaigning for the Republican nomination for president, he drew on cowboy stories to describe the notion, abbreviated as "MAD," as "two westerners standing in a saloon aiming their guns to each other's head—permanently." His longtime counselor Ed Meese was sure Reagan viewed the concept as "politically and diplomatically, militarily, and morally flawed."[40] This attitude was apparent as well to Reagan's arms-control negotiators, who understood how strongly the president's "hatred for nuclear weapons" affected both his strategy and his talks with the Soviets.[41]

As can be seen in reactions to his famous near-abolition of the weapons at Reykjavík, these feelings seemed at odds with his investment in them. Historian

James Graham Wilson holds Reagan was "torn between a crusade for freedom and peace through strength," that although nuclear abolition conflicted with the eradication of communism, he was unwilling to abandon either goal.[42] Still, the ideas of "peace through strength" and a "crusade for freedom" are not as diametrically opposed as they might seem, or at least not to Reagan. This is because of how Reagan discovered and then adopted both phrases during the period of his political formation in the 1950s and 1960s.

He adopted the language of "peace through strength" while campaigning for Barry Goldwater in 1964. Reagan's televised speech for the campaign argued that strength meant having the "courage to say to our enemies, there is a price we will not pay, there is a point beyond which they must not advance."[43] This formulation extended the notion of strength to include societal will, an understanding that one of his political mentors, Dwight Eisenhower, may have shaped. The view reflects the Clausewitzian maxim that winning a war "requires the product of two factors which cannot be separated, namely the sum of available means and the strength of the will."[44] While Reagan is very unlikely to have read *On War*, conversations in the 1960s with Eisenhower and active-duty military figures contributed to his grasp of this tenet of the work. His emphasis during his first term on both aspects of Clausewitz's equation further underscores recognition of the link between a nation's will and its means to fight.

Reagan had already adopted the language of "crusade for freedom." It came directly from Eisenhower who, then a private citizen, lead a Radio Free Europe fundraising drive in which Reagan took part. "Ike" called on Americans to meet the communist "threat with courage and firmness" and to aid the peoples behind the Iron Curtain with "access to truth." They would be leveraging America's "most formidable weapon," its moral superiority.[45] Reagan adopted this language in a commercial he made for the campaign, pleading for donations to "pierce the Iron Curtain with truth" and portraying the Crusade for Freedom as "your chance and mine to fight communism."[46] Decades later he would return to the rhetoric in a speech to Parliament in London, declaring that democracy would leave "Marxism-Leninism on the ash-heap of history" by means of a "major effort" to support a "crusade for freedom that [would] engage the faith and fortitude of the next generation."[47] The *New York Times* at the time recognized the Eisenhower reference and described the speech as "full of echoes of the cold war of the 1950s." Though the term "crusade" had military connotations, Reagan meant it as "a peaceful struggle for ideological supremacy."[48] Practically, his crusade took the form of the National Endowment for Democracy, which funded nongovernmental groups promoting democracy abroad.[49] In this context, Reagan's "crusade for freedom" nested under the notion of "peace through strength" as a nonmilitary way to build global will.

The seeming disconnects between Reagan's antinuclear feelings and his push to build more weapons stems not from ideological dissonance but rather his perception that the West had neither the means nor the will to contain a Soviet assault into Western Europe (the most likely flashpoint for a nuclear war) without them. Military doctrine painted the same picture. The prevailing doctrine of "Active Defense," developed in 1976, warned military leaders they "must prepare . . . units to fight outnumbered and to win." The only way to do that would be to substitute "firepower for manpower."[50] In this context, the firepower would almost certainly need to be nuclear. The doctrine was also unlikely to work; it required, as critics noted, nearly perfect intelligence to mass assets at the right places.[51] In 1982, the United States moved to the doctrine of AirLand Battle, which relied more on technology to enable NATO forces to disrupt advancing armies into the depth of their formations. However, the new doctrine still explicitly treated an "integrated tactical [i.e., short-range] nuclear-conventional response" to Soviet invasion "as mandatory."[52] Only in that way could large Soviet formations be prevented from moving efficiently and smaller NATO ones defeat them in detail. In effect, military planners did not believe they could win a war without nuclear weapons.

As usual in such cases, the Reagan administration blamed its predecessors for the situation. Admiral Poindexter believed the "Carter administration had not done enough to keep the Defense Department funded, pointing to "lack of maintenance and overreliance on dated weapons platforms.[53] As a result, in his view, the United States lacked the readiness to execute NATO doctrine, putting the alliance in a poor position with regard to the Soviets. Carter's secretary of defense, Harold Brown agreed, to a point. While in office he wrote that then–national security advisor Zbigniew Brzezinski was "too optimistic" about the state of U.S. conventional forces. If the United States did not greatly increase spending it would "slide behind rapidly in military capabilities across the board" and be unable to fulfill its strategic obligations.[54] Though the Carter administration did take steps over its last years in office to remedy the situation, its measures did not go nearly as far as the Reaganites wanted.

Early policy documents reflected the new administration's conviction that it faced a conventional-forces "gap." Within a month of Reagan's taking office, the State Department's Policy Planning Staff began a study to "identify conventional and theatre posture weaknesses" that prevented the United States from competing "effectively with the Soviet Union in Europe," so as to "correct the growing imbalance in U.S.-Soviet military power" in the face of "increasingly aggressive behavior."[55] NSDD-32 of 1982 would institutionalize these concerns, positing the "loss of U.S. strategic superiority" and the "overwhelming growth of Soviet conventional forces capabilities" as established facts.[56]

Reagan brought this message to the American people in a commencement address at his alma mater, Eureka College. The Soviets, he declared, were maintaining despite their economic and social difficulties the "largest armed force in the world," a serious threat. This meant there was no "sound East-West military balance," a balance that Reagan saw as "absolutely essential" to peace. He referred to a recently released NATO study that made clear that the Soviets had "built up their forces across the board" over the past decade while United States and NATO defense spending "declined" in real terms.[57] The study was the first publicly released by NATO that painted so a grim picture.[58] NATO's secretary general, Joseph Luns, argued in the foreword that over the previous twenty years "the numerical balance of forces . . . [had] moved slowly but steadily in favor of the Warsaw Pact." NATO's technological advantages had declined. Between them the shifts had put at risk the ability of the alliance to overcome the numerical superiority of Warsaw Pact forces.[59]

Reagan agreed fully with these assessments and concluded that any arms-control deal at the time would lock the United States and its allies into an unfavorable position permanently. At a 1981 meeting he told the NSC that the United States required "positive movement on modernization before we go into negotiations."[60] This was his public stance as well. He often acknowledged the concerns of the nuclear-freeze movement but dismissed its demands as untenable in the current environment. Freezing production of nuclear weaponry would be possible only once there was no U.S.-Soviet "gap" in either conventional or nuclear weapons.[61] Ultimately, Reagan declared, his "goal [was] to reduce nuclear weapons dramatically," but he believed it would not be possible until the United States could fight and win outnumbered—as would necessarily be the case in Europe—without them.[62]

By 1986, however, Reagan was confident that the United States had achieved that position and that accordingly it would be the Soviets who would be disadvantaged by the elimination of nuclear weapons. He was one of the few people, if not the only one, in his administration who believed this at the time. Reagan was aware of that opposition and took advantage of it at Reykjavík, pleading with Gorbachev that if the two men were indeed to eliminate nuclear weapons he needed to keep SDI to make the deal politically palatable at home. Reagan argued that "the most out-spoken of the critics of the Soviet Union over the years, the so-called right wing," were already "kicking his brains out" for considering limitations on, let alone abolition of, nuclear weapons.[63] Gorbachev, though likely struck at Reagan's not counting himself among the Soviet Union's "most outspoken critics," was unmoved, and the deal ultimately collapsed.

In the meantime, as Reagan expected, opposition to the proposal was furious. Poindexter wrote immediately after the summit that it would return the strategic environment to that of the 1950s, when the United States had had only a chance of stopping a conventional assault.[64] He suggested banning all land-based missiles but keeping the submarine-based ones.[65] The idea nakedly favored Washington, and Moscow (whose strategic arsenal was primarily land-based) would never have agreed to it. During a December meeting each member of the Joint Chiefs of Staff argued the ten-year framework the two leaders had envisaged would severely damage the strategic balance in Europe; it would take a politically impossible level of spending to build enough conventional deterrent power in the intervening decade.[66] When the White House issued a new national security decision document reiterating Reagan's desire to eliminate missiles and directing the Pentagon to develop a strategy not involving intercontinental ballistic missiles, Weinberger replied that it was impossible.[67] The Soviets did not accept the framework themselves, and so the United States needed to ensure its "national security planning and military programming remain[ed] unaltered."[68]

Reagan also faced domestic opposition beyond the White House and Pentagon. Nixon and Kissinger cowrote a piece in the *National Review* that the proposal would reopen the recently closed "gap in deterrence."[69] Brent Scowcroft (not then in government) called the framework an "absolute disaster" and insisted the weapons would be necessary for decades.[70] Opposition was bipartisan: the chair of the House Armed Services Committee, Les Aspin, a Democrat, also took to the *National Review* predicting it would take ten more divisions in Europe to achieve conventional deterrence and there was no way to fund such expansion.[71]

Leaders in Western Europe feared the prospect of abolition. The framework "amazed" European media outlets and raised old fears of "an America strategically decoupled from Europe."[72] Even before the summit took place, the French had expressed concerns about concessions the Americans might make that could force them to make up their own gap in deterrence.[73] West Germany too expressed significant reservations, Chancellor Helmut Kohl calling the proposal "breathtaking" but unrealistic, as it would leave a "conventional imbalance in Europe" still not "properly addressed."[74] The United Kingdom was caught completely off guard and even after Thatcher's conversations with Reagan continued to urge the administration to walk back its position. Sir Anthony Acland, the ambassador to the United States from the United Kingdom, met with Shultz to relay London's views on the conventional imbalance. However, Shultz held firm; he believed "longer term" fears of Warsaw Pact superiority were not "wholly justified."[75] The ambassador next held a meeting with Poindexter, which also went poorly, despite Poindexter's own reservations about the framework. What Acland termed "an unsatisfactory discussion" gave the British only "confused" and "contradictory" answers.[76]

What the ambassador heard from the president's closest advisors could only have been "confused" and "contradictory": Reagan himself viewed conventional security in Europe completely differently than they did, or than did most of his other supporters and allies. Despite their concerted efforts to sway him, he remained committed to the idea of massive nuclear-arms reduction and ideally abolition. Reagan thought the United States and NATO could win a conventional fight, if not in 1986 then before the ten years of the Reykjavík framework expired. He sought to get the Soviets to agree to large successive reductions, estimating that they mistakenly believed they were negotiating from strength. The result would be a long-term environment favorable to the West and potentially an end to the Cold War on American terms. The firmness of this belief came in no small part from his reading of *Red Storm Rising* just two months before the summit.

RED STORM RISING AND THE PRESIDENT

Reagan must have loved being told by Clancy in the Oval Office that the winners of his then-upcoming book would be "the good guys." He loved the ending even more once the book was published. *Red Storm Rising* (on which Larry Bond collaborated with Clancy as coauthor) not only built on the pairing of technology and virtuous American servicemembers (from *The Hunt for Red October*), but also reinforced the president's thinking about the strength of NATO versus that of the Warsaw Pact and about the feelings of the Soviet people toward their state. It also translated the relatively new AirLand Battle doctrine into a narrative form digestible to him. It provided a realistic-enough vision of World War III to Reagan, and the news from the conflict was good.

Clancy kept his promise to the president about the victors, though he did let the Soviets take NATO by surprise. The book opens with a terrorist attack on a Soviet refinery that creates an energy crisis in an already economically struggling Soviet Union. The Politburo determines that Iran's oil fields must be seized but that to do so the USSR must first "eliminate NATO as a political and military force." Certain the alliance is "divided and soft" and will quickly fold, the Soviets concoct a casus belli by staging a terrorist attack against children visiting the Kremlin.[77] The Soviet Army invades West Germany and makes fast territorial gains. The Soviets also seize Iceland, in a surprise amphibious assault, cutting NATO's supply lines. The prospects look grim. However, thanks to the technical superiority of its systems NATO eventually holds on the continent, retakes Iceland, and forces its supply lanes back open. Fresh troops from the United States arrive in Europe making a conventional victory impossible for the Warsaw Pact. A Soviet general then refuses to employ nuclear weapons, stages a coup, and ends the war. The book ends with the hint of a democratic future for the USSR.

How NATO wins in *Red Storm Rising* was critical to why Reagan latched on to the story so strongly. It was neither the first "techno-thriller" on a NATO–Warsaw Pact conflict to appear nor the first that Reagan read. A major one had appeared in 1978, Gen. Sir John Hackett's *The Third World War: August 1985*. The recently retired British general, consulting other flag and general officers, had wanted to publish a popular book that would raise alarm over the weakness of NATO. An early draft even had the Soviets win the war, capitalizing on the "damage of the locust years of the 1970s."[78] However, his colleagues convinced

Reagan family Christmas card circa 1916–17. Reagan recalled his first public performance during this time, reading an article on the Preparedness Day Bombing in San Francisco. *Courtesy Ronald Reagan Library*

Reagan began his career as a sports
broadcaster. Working in the theater of
the mind honed his storytelling abilities.
Courtesy Ronald Reagan Library

Reagan, then head of the Screen
Actors Guild, testifying before the
House Un-American Activities Com-
mittee in 1947 as a friendly witness.
Courtesy Ronald Reagan Library

Reagan confers on Louis L'Amour the Congressional Gold Medal. The western author was one of Reagan's favorites, and the genre strongly influenced his approach to foreign policy. *Courtesy Ronald Reagan Library*

Reagan meets with advisors, including Robert McFarlane, John Poindexter, and Oliver North, to discuss policy toward Central America. Reagan's tendency to avoid policy specifics and use fiction as shorthand contributed to the Iran–Contra crisis. *Courtesy Ronald Reagan Library*

Reagan presents the Medal of Honor to MSgt. Roy Benavidez, U.S. Army, in February 1981. The administration intended the ceremony to shift public discussion of the military. *Courtesy Ronald Regan Library*

Tom Clancy submitted his unsolicited first book to the Naval Institute Press because the Naval Institute had previously published two of his submissions in its monthly *Proceedings* magazine. Fortunately for the writer, the publisher had just decided to release original fiction—as long as it was "wet." *U.S. Naval Institute photo archive*

Reagan meeting with Tom and Wanda Clancy in the White House in March 1985. Reagan asked him who would win in Clancy's next novel, to which the author replied, "The good guys." *Courtesy Ronald Reagan Library*

The Reagans with Sylvester Stallone and Brigitte Nielsen in October 1985. The actors starred in November 1985's *Rocky IV*, one of several movies that year that embraced Reagan's rhetoric. *Courtesy Ronald Reagan Library*

Reagan delivers his "Tear Down This Wall" speech in front of the Brandenburg Gate. He battled with his advisors to keep the line, intending it to show his support for the people of Germany. *Courtesy Ronald Reagan Library*

Reagan with Suzanne Massie, an author who through her books and meetings with Reagan helped him differentiate between the Soviet system and the Soviet peoples. *Courtesy Ronald Reagan Library*

Reagan meeting with Gorbachev at Reykjavík. During the summit the two leaders nearly agreed to eliminate their nuclear arsenals, but Reagan's attachment to the Strategic Defense Initiative ended hopes for a deal. *Courtesy Ronald Reagan Library*

Hackett that such an ending would "cause more harm than good" in terms of its intended message, and he changed the outcome to a NATO victory.[79]

Historian Adam Seipp believes it is "difficult to overstate the impact" of Hackett's book in allowing "readers to focus on [Hackett's] presentation of their country and his visionary battle scenes." By the early 1980s it was "the most talked about and frequently referenced scenario for a global military conflict."[80] It was a smash hit as a paperback. The book debuted in the ninth position on the *New York Times* list in June 1980, and its success likely contributed to the decision of its publisher, Berkley Books, to secure the paperback rights of *The Hunt for Red October*.[81] *The Third World War* had provided Clancy with a basic template to work with for *Red Storm Rising*, and the two have much in common. Both put major emphasis on the battle of the Atlantic and importance of supply lines, demonstrate the importance of technology, and end with coups in the USSR. Finally, Hackett's concluding argument that "if the crisis of 1985 had occurred in 1977" it would be "scarcely conceivable the Soviet plan . . . could have failed" and his calls for increases in military spending also seem tailor-made for Reagan to jump on and use.[82] But he did not. The president added the work to a June 1984 list of books he was reading and never publicly referred to it again.[83]

Why not? Part of the reason was readability. Clancy's storytelling is superior to Hackett's, and his characters are more dynamic. *The Third World War* has no central narrative or protagonist, making it difficult for the president to project himself into the story. Both authors deployed heavy technical detail, but Clancy was better able to render the arcane intelligible. The most important difference, though, is how the war ends in each. Hackett's book depicts a limited nuclear strike, each side destroying one major city. The starkness of this embrace of the logic of mutually assured destruction and the amorality with which Hackett's NATO leaders select their nuclear target likely negated the book's importance to Reagan. It did not tell the story the way he wanted to experience it. Clancy's Soviet general choosing humanity and leading a coup marked a narrative that fit perfectly with how Reagan wanted to think about the people living under Soviet rule and about the moral superiority of the West.

Red Storm Rising effectively channeled Reagan's idea of "peace through strength." In his address at Eureka College Reagan identified five points on which a just peace would rest. Foremost was "a sound East-West military balance."

That, in combination with the other four—"economic security, regional stability, arms reductions, and dialogue"—made a road map by which to "seek peace with the Soviet Union."[84] All five feature in *Red Storm Rising*. The presence of these themes, used in the way he had himself outlined, made the book for Reagan a realistic, relevant, and worthy reference point for thinking about the next decade.

BALANCING THE SCALES

Achieving conventional parity with the Soviets was one of the main goals of Reagan's first term in office, and once reelected he expected to continue emphasizing it. As a December 1985 NSC review emphasized, "lower levels of nuclear forces" necessitated "increasing contribution" from "primarily non-nuclear systems."[85] NATO could not simply match the Warsaw Pact soldier for soldier. While Reagan was fond of mentioning that the alliance's combined population and gross domestic product were greater than those of the Eastern Bloc, these advantages could not be useful in practice. Neither the American populace nor that of Western Europe would accept the long-scale, permanent mobilization implied, on one hand; on the other, if a British interlocutor might happily agree with Ken Adelman that Bulgaria spent nearly four times what the United Kingdom did on defense, he would add that he and his countrymen had no desire to live as Bulgarians did.[86] Instead, the West would need to be vastly superior *technologically* on the battlefield.

Historian Odd Arne Westad argues that "technology was a main reason for the durability of the Cold War as an international system."[87] The rapid advancement of military and other technologies following World War II allowed both the United States and Soviet Union to build and maintain global influence. These advancements enabled the employment of coercive power at speeds and on scales impossible in previous eras. However, by the Reagan years the Soviets lagged significantly. The consumer society of the West spurred innovation and competitiveness in ways unrivaled by the communist nation. Powerful demand for personal computers had strengthened norms of individual freedom, open markets, and access to information. Much of the technology developed had dual military and civil application. If Soviet weaponry had always been known for durability and reliability, NATO equivalents quickly became more sophisticated and precise. It was also expensive, prohibitively so for the Soviets. In the early 1980s the U.S. military alone had over twenty thousand computers and processors, significantly more than in the entire USSR. As the United States entered the digital age, Soviet planners still tracked production on instruments from the 1950s.[88] As they prepared for Reykjavík, Soviet leaders were aware they "could not afford massive new investments in science and technology in order to catch up."[89]

Contemporary American assessments recognized the advantage. In 1987 the CIA reported that while the Warsaw Pact retained its quantitative advantage over the previous ten years, it had broadly failed in "pushing the state of the art in designing its weapons." Instead, it utilized an "evolutionary design process" focused on incremental improvements and upgrades. The agency concluded that by 1986 "only a small share of Soviet [weapon system] inventories" were advanced designs.[90] The United States had made "better use of emerging technologies," the NSC assessed; the increased lethality and survivability of its systems would offset the Warsaw Pact's greater numbers.[91] This advantage was the result of significant increases of spending from 1977 to 1987. NATO nations spent over 40 percent more over that period than their adversaries, a reversal from the previous decade.[92]

Most of this spending went into military modernization. The first Reagan administration expanded late Carter-era programs. It worked with Congress to build thirty-four warships, field over four thousand Abrams main battle tanks, and develop the Bradley Fighting Vehicle and Light Amphibious Vehicle. It also accelerated the development of the Apache attack helicopter, the Blackhawk support helicopter, precision munitions, and stealth aircraft. The new systems and improvements in training methods and doctrine led the Joint Chiefs to conclude unanimously that by 1985 the United States was more ready for combat "by every measure of common sense" than it had been in 1980.[93] Gen. John W. Vessey Jr., U.S. Army, Chairman of the Joint Chiefs of Staff, pointed out the American "lead in high technology" and how it could help overcome the USSR's "greater military and industrial base."[94]

Clancy's new book provided Reagan a narrative by which to visualize this new state of affairs. The *New York Times* review of the novel sang that it was "particularly good news . . . for Defense Secretary Caspar Weinberger." In *Red Storm Rising* "American technology works—spy satellites, stealth aircraft, advanced tanks and sonar, the lot." The result was a novel giving "an oddly comforting version of World War III." Reagan certainly took comfort in it. The reviewer did criticize the book for its "Victorian boys' book level" and its "undistinguished prose" but acknowledged that it put "good men in tight spots" to create a "rattling good yarn." This and the novel's "comforting certainty that our side will win" made it perfect for Reagan.[95] It was a throwback to the books of his youth, a recognizable friend that happened to capture perfectly the high-level meetings of his adulthood. The immersive narrative spoke to Reagan directly and greatly enhanced his thinking about the balance of conventional forces in Europe.

As the *New York Times* review noted, Clancy placed American technology on full display in *Red Storm Rising*. Whenever the situation appears most dire, a new system, a deus ex machina, delivers a critical NATO victory. In the air, the Soviets are unable to detect American stealth aircraft, a still-classified capability at the time, allowing NATO to strike deep in the rear areas of Soviet formations, disrupting logistics and force movements. Its inability to detect these aircraft leaves the Soviet Army confused and frustrated, as well as massively depleted in combat power. In contrast, large radar-surveillance and control planes provide near-perfect tactical intelligence that allows NATO to move its own airframes rapidly to where they are most needed. In ground combat, superior intelligence collection gives Abrams tanks a decisive edge: in an early engagement just ten of the new systems defeat over a hundred T-72s, the first-line Soviet tanks of that era. The superior American main battle tanks also benefit from "air integration," by which they can quickly bring in A-10 "Warthogs," which Soviet troops come to know as the "Devil's Cross," for its resemblance to the Orthodox cross and its "murderous" effectiveness.[96] The novel reads like a fictionalized version of AirLand Battle doctrine, which sought to leverage technological advantages into superior positioning of forces and achieve close integration of ground and air systems.[97] Clancy's book effectively argues between the lines that not only was the complicated doctrine feasible but that NATO could already execute it. Direct reference to AirLand Battle was a conscious choice by Clancy and Bond to increase the appeal of the book to military professionals. They intentionally excluded the doctrine's provisions for nuclear and chemical weapons, sharing Reagan's abhorrence of such weapons and his belief that they were no longer necessary.[98]

Technology was only half the equation for Reagan, however. Speaking at the Air Force Academy, he observed that "the pace of change, once orderly and evolutionary, [had become] frantic and revolutionary." Personal computers, significant growth in the use of transistors, fiber optics, and other marvels were pouring into modern life in a "cataclysmic rush." The language hints at the ominous potential of technology, the possibility that in the wrong hands it could shape the world in negative ways. Reagan again drew on his mythologized west to exhort the cadets to embrace the rush but preserve the future. Just as "the brave men and women of the west" did not "let the unknowns and dangers overwhelm" them, so must those of the U.S. military "accept the challenge of space" and recognize that their only limitation was their "own courage and imagination." Reagan believed American exceptionalism would be rejuvenated by technology, but only if both people in uniform and the broader public embraced their destiny.[99] In his mind the United States was again on the frontier and needed to rise to the challenge. Reagan was optimistic that it would meet the challenge; linkage of free people and high technology was part of what Shultz termed Reagan's "instinctive vision of the future."[100] *Red Storm Rising* shared it. The title of its *New York Times* review, "Virtuous Men and Perfect Weapons," captured perfectly the core message of the novel, not least for Reagan.

Reagan gushed in his diary about the combination. He had spent part of a day with the Joint Chiefs, where reorganization and personnel matters were discussed but "the real kicker [was] a report on new weaponry." It left the president convinced that while "we can't match the Soviets tank for tank" the United States had used its "technology and come up with a weapon that nullifies their superior numbers." Details about "top secret and brand new" aircraft excited the president.[101] Reagan was confident these weapons in the hands of American military personnel would guarantee victory in Europe if it came to war. This view was likely overoptimistic in 1986 and 1987—*Red Storm Rising* notwithstanding—but prevailing trends in the Soviet economy and military suggested that by the mid-1990s, Reagan's vision of how war would unfold in Europe would be realistic.

At Reykjavík, accordingly, Reagan was willing to pursue what he felt was an opportunity to establish a permanent American advantage at a time the Soviets believed it was they who had the upper hand. For it to work, there could be no war over the ten-year period of progressive disarmament. However, neither Reagan nor his advisors believed one was likely, that the "Soviet leadership was smart, intelligent, and not crazy," and whatever their ideological delusions would not pursue the destruction of the world.[102] It was this dynamic that led Reagan well beyond expectations at the summit: he sought "to reel the Soviets in."[103] *Red Storm Rising* helped Reagan identify what he believed was a narrow window between NATO's achievement of a conventional advantage and Soviet recognition of it—an interval in which he could exploit a strategic advantage of which his opponent was unaware. As a negotiator, he sought to use this to maximum advantage in pursuit of a lifelong vision.

KNOW YOUR ENEMY: THE PEOPLE VERSUS THE SYSTEM

In 1983, war between the United States and Soviet Union seemed perpetually imminent. Reagan's "uncompromising ideological offensive" left Soviet leaders deeply concerned that the United States was not just prepared for a fight but might actually provoke one. The double provocations in March—declaring the USSR an "Evil Empire" and announcing the Strategic Defense Initiative— created in Moscow an impression that the American president would go to any length to eliminate the USSR, even into space. In June, Yuri Andropov, who had succeeded Brezhnev as the general secretary, told the highly respected former diplomat Averell Harriman that he "had no confidence in the present administration" and that since "mistrust and enmity have heated up" war was increasingly likely.[104] The Soviets would not stand idly by and were preparing for the apocalypse. Over the summer, Andropov became increasingly convinced the United States was seeking to launch a first strike. The Politburo sent "urgent and detailed instructions" to KGB operatives in the United States to collect evidence of American war preparation.[105] This alert coincided with the deployment of Pershing II missiles, which was ample evidence in itself.

The Soviets contributed to the tension as well. In September 1983 they scrambled fighters to intercept a plane that had intruded into their airspace. The interceptors' pilots identified it as a U.S. spy plane and shot it down. In actuality, it was a civilian airliner. The destruction of Korean Airlines Flight 007 killed 269 people, including an American congressman. The Soviet leadership immediately sought to hide its involvement, but its denials were embarrassingly exposed on the floor of the United Nations when the American ambassador, Jeane Kirkpatrick, played audio recordings of the incident. The tapes revealed the Soviet pilots had had visual contact with KAL 007 for over twenty minutes and yet made no attempt to communicate with the plane before firing. Kirkpatrick accused the Soviets of "shocking disregard for human life and international norms" in an incident making obvious that "violence and lies [were] regular instruments of Soviet policy."[106] Reagan seized on the moment to further his attacks on the USSR. The president argued there was no way to mistake the profile of the Korean Airlines' Boeing 747 for that of an American reconnaissance plane. No one, he said, should "be surprised by the inhuman brutality" of the Soviet Union, particularly given its suppression of the 1956 Hungarian uprising, the 1968 "Prague Spring," and its ongoing actions in Poland and Afghanistan.[107]

In this environment of high tension, NATO conducted its annual large-scale Autumn Forge and Reforger exercises, as well as a "command-post exercise," Able Archer. A good military readiness exercise by necessity looks similar to actual war preparation, and these were no exceptions. For them the United States deployed an additional 16,000 troops to Europe and increased the readiness of its forces globally.[108] These U.S. deployments were intended—as was, in part, the annual NATO exercise series itself—to show "US resolve and the ability to defend Europe."[109] Senior Soviet military leadership and the Politburo nevertheless viewed that year's exercise as a "most dangerous" provocation, given its realism.[110]

Fortunately, there were Soviet operational leaders and senior advisors who had a more sanguine view. Alert levels did increase at Soviet air bases in Eastern Europe and at some missile sites. However, from the perspective of Vladen Smirnoff, the deputy head of intelligence for the Northern Fleet, "Able Archer was just a typical exercise[;] . . . there was nothing outstanding about it."[111] This clear-sightedness among Soviet military professionals proved to be important. During the exercise, Soviet early-warning satellites erroneously reported the launch of five U.S. nuclear missiles.[112] Stanislav Petrov, duty officer in a Soviet air-defense command center, recognized NATO was not postured for war and would almost certainly employ more than five missiles in a first strike.[113] He chose to wait, contrary to his orders, for confirmation from ground radar before passing news of launch to Moscow. No confirmation came, as the United States had not launched any missiles; the satellites had detected sunlight reflecting off the surface of the Atlantic.

Following the exercise, U.S. intelligence agencies were conflicted about the gravity of Soviet war fears. One initial review suggested the Soviets never seriously thought that war was in prospect, that they were "just rattling their pots and pans."[114] A more comprehensive review in 1990 concluded, however, the USSR had had in 1983 "a genuine belief" the United States and NATO planned to attack.[115] It does seem likely that in 1983 the Soviets believed war was more probable than it had been in previous crises, though this does not mean they actually expected it. Orders to the KGB to "collect on" U.S. preparations were prudent responses to Reagan's rhetoric and his administration's spending priorities. Whatever the case had actually been, however, the idea that Moscow seriously believed NATO would start a war shook Reagan. In his 1990 memoir he wrote that then, after three years on the job, he learned "many people at the top of the Soviet hierarchy were genuinely afraid of America and Americans."[116] This matched a June 1984 diary entry in which he had mused, "Maybe they are scared of us and think we are a threat."[117] These flashes of empathy were essential to the shifts to come in Reagan's rhetoric and his resolution to calm global fears that the Americans and Soviets would soon unleash their arsenals.

As early as the next year Reagan reflected on the tension just past. In a January 1984 speech he acknowledged that charged high rhetoric had "led some to speak of heightened uncertainty and an increased danger of conflict." That they had done so was "understandable" but "profoundly mistaken." Reagan then defended his administration's rhetoric and spending as calculated to create "less danger," by making the USSR less apt to "underestimate [U.S.] strength or question [American] resolve." So far, his words seemed to ignore that, as Reagan now realized, it was the Soviets who had found fearsome his typical talking points and that the Soviets worried Reagan was seeking war. However, he then struck a more conciliatory tone. Reagan spoke of a "gap in American and Soviet perceptions and policy" that prevented the sides from understanding each other. Both governments needed to find mechanisms by which to display good intentions and cooperate. "Strength and dialogue" needed to exist in equal measure, ideology could not be allowed to stop negotiation. But the most memorable passage of the speech was to come.[118]

Reagan asked his audience to imagine two couples, one American and the other Soviet (Anya and Ivan), seeking mutual shelter from a storm. Somehow able to communicate, the president asserted, they would disdain adversarial posturing over "differences in governmental structure and philosophy." Instead, they would find "common interests" in "the things of everyday life." They would talk about "ambitions and hobbies, and what they wanted for their children."

Most importantly, they would leave the shelter as friends. Reagan concluded, "People don't make wars"; they just want the freedom "to raise their children in a world without fear and without war" and work that "gives them satisfaction and a sense of worth."[119] The short, memorable story demonstrated Reagan's proclivity for parables; he had added it to the speech personally.[120]

However, the story was less conciliatory to the Soviets than it appears at first glance. Reagan implied that the ability of Anya and Ivan to pursue "common interests" was restricted, while the American couple was free to do as they willed. The absence of individual choice in the USSR was a frequent Reagan talking point. He even often joked about it. A favorite involved a businessman traveling to New York and to Moscow. In each city he rides in a taxi driven by a young college student and he asks each what he wants to do after graduation. The American cabbie responds that he has not decided yet, the Soviet that they have not told him yet. The joke captured Reagan's view of the key difference in the two nations, the ability of individuals, or the absence of it, to "work at some trade, craft, or profession that gives them satisfaction and a sense of worth."[121]

Reagan closed his speech with a veiled threat: "If the Soviet government wants peace, then there will be peace."[122] The statement placed the onus for the Cold War in general and the recent rise in tension entirely on Moscow. Reagan here seemingly lost touch with his flash of empathy with the Soviet Union and certainly overlooked American complicity in the origins of the conflict and responsibility for its current state. It is difficult to argue the speech reflected a fundamental shift in Reagan's perception about the stakes and morality of the Cold War. However, it did reflect an important subtlety in how Reagan saw the USSR. His sympathetic portrayal of a Russian couple showed his belief that it was its ideology and system, not its people, that were America's enemies. Ordinary citizens of the USSR were victims and deserving of liberation.[123] Reagan also afforded Soviet citizens an agency he denied people in Central and South America and Africa.

This empathy and agency stemmed from a concerted effort by Reagan and those around him to understand what life was for the Soviets. Jack Matlock, taking over from Richard Pipes as the NSC senior director for East European and Soviet Affairs, sought to humanize the people of the USSR for Reagan.[124] He did this with stories in which Reagan could see himself. A favorite technique was to give the president fictional memos such as, he suggested, might be submitted by Anatoly Chernyaev, a Soviet foreign policy advisor, to Gorbachev. These papers framed geopolitical issues from the Soviet perspective and allowed Reagan to imagine himself in his counterpart's shoes. Having in mind whom he was writing for, Matlock filled the missives with "jokes and anecdotes," framing issues in a way Reagan would find recognizable and memorable.[125] "Chernyaev" opens one memo with an admission of "getting soused at Igor's" before "playing around" with the "three most luscious secretaries in the Central Committee." It notes that Reagan is enjoying in the United States a "wave of popularity Franklin Roosevelt would envy" and laments that only someone with "a half liter of vodka in his belly" would believe the Soviet Union could outflank him.[126]

Also, Matlock brought in academics and outside scholars. Suzanne Massie, a specialist in Russian history and daughter of a diplomat, proved particularly effective in this role. Reagan met her the first time on the day of his "Anya and Ivan" speech and thereafter relied on her for insight into Russian life. Reagan asked her about religion in Russia, likely recalling the experience of Chambers and how faith could become a wedge between an individual and communism. Massie's assurance that the Orthodox Church continued to be important to Russian identity sparked Reagan's curiosity.[127] On a later occasion she gave Reagan a painted egg she had purchased on a recent trip to the Soviet Union—an image of Mary with the infant Jesus and the text, "We will not permit the world to be blown up." Massie offered it to the president as a "talisman" for his upcoming summit with Gorbachev. Both the egg and its message will have appealed greatly to Reagan as an indication of the strength of religious belief among the Russian people and of support there for his nuclear-abolition views.[128]

Massie's book *Land of the Firebird: The Beauty of Old Russia* also assisted Reagan's preparations for the summit. Reading it in September 1985, Reagan had found compelling its portrayal of the life of the common people in tsarist Russia. During preparatory "mock" summits in the White House, Reagan would occasionally interrupt to ask Shultz and others what would have happened to the nineteenth-century residents of St. Petersburg he had read about in Massie's book.[129] Here again is clear evidence of Reagan's interest in, and sympathy for, the everyday Russian, an empathy that contributed to his desire to negotiate a just peace and end the Cold War. His willingness to separate person from ideology made space for personal connections during negotiations and was a powerful tool at Reagan's disposal.

Reagan found in *Red Storm Rising* a similarly sympathetic depiction of ordinary Russians, whom he could link to Massie's nineteenth-century St. Petersburg merchants and people residing there in the 1980s. Clancy and Bond took pains to highlight Russian culture and portray most Russians in a positive light.[130] They agreed with Reagan that the Russians were victims of their government and if given the chance would adopt Western ideals. The two main Soviet characters frequently express revulsion toward their callous and immoral government. Ordered to employ nuclear weapons, they refuse and overthrow the regime, setting the stage for a democratic Russia. When faced with an ultimatum, the Clancy's fictional Russians choose humanity over ideology.

The Politburo members in the book are scheming and power hungry. Frequent references to death sentences, gulags, and human-rights abuses reflect the writers' sense of the fundamental corruption and violence of the Soviet system. A conspicuous exception to the generally positive portrayal of individual Russian is the brutal gang rape of a pregnant Icelandic woman by Soviet paratroopers. This scene was likely intended to show the brutality of Soviet occupation and as a reminder of the mass rape of at least a million Eastern European and German women by Red Army soldiers and other Soviet personnel in the last months of World War II, with at least the tacit approval of Soviet leadership. Clancy and Bond invite readers to infer the atrocity was state-approved and characteristic of communism's systematic brutality.[131]

Otherwise, references to Russian culture abound in *Red Storm Rising*. In an early episode analysts ponder why Soviet state television is showing the famous 1925 movie *Battleship* Potemkin—a film that glorifies Russian nationalism, something they thought the Soviets were "trying to get away from."[132] The Supreme Allied Commander Europe (SACEUR), "General Robinson," also perceives a gap between nationalism an ideology. The American general, fluent in Russian, converses with his Soviet counterpart about the late-nineteenth-century Russian writer and playwright Anton Chekhov, known for works that speak directly to Russian identity. His final play, "The Cherry Orchard," focused on conflict between Russian values and the Marxism then surging in Russian society.[133] The Soviet general playfully accuses Robinson of just trying to learn more about his enemy, but the American is genuinely interested; the book's readers are to infer that there is significant worth in Russian culture. That Clancy and Bond chose to highlight prerevolution material rather than

Soviet-era literature, such as *Doctor Zhivago*, implicitly encourages Americans to look to Russia's past for the common ground necessary for peaceful coexistence.

Red Storm Rising portrayed Russians in the same way Reagan thought about them. Neither Reagan's nor Clancy's view acknowledges that Russians were not the only people in the Soviet Union with a distinct history and culture, but the nuance of distinguishing between population and governmental system was uncommon in American popular culture and largely unreflective of how Americans thought about the Soviet Union. Their collective distrust of Russians dated back to the earliest days of the Cold War, when the government insisted that all Russians were communists and that all communists were dangerous ideologues bent on destroying everything that made America free. Popular culture shifted narratives in the 1960s but not to themes of peace-loving Soviets. Instead, works by Graham Greene, Kurt Vonnegut, and John le Carré argued that the United States was not a moral paragon either. The America of these authors often eagerly employed the immoral, coercive, and violent means of its rival. They saw the two superpowers as morally equivalent and equally deserving of scorn.

That was what Reagan's "Ivan and Anya" speech sought to change. *Red Storm Rising* was only one work that helped him do so; Hollywood too adopted the theme. The brutal Russian soldiers of the 1984 Russian-invasion action movie *Red Dawn* gave way to Rocky winning over a hostile crowd in Moscow. Reagan's obvious rapport with Gorbachev aided the shift. If someone with Reagan's history of staunch anticommunism could establish a relationship with a Soviet leader then it would be hard for an average American to view the Russian people as necessarily enemies of the United States. The Reagan-Gorbachev encounter was reminiscent of Richard Nixon's 1972 trip to China, in which he had met with Mao Zedong. Reagan's biography, like Nixon's, made a drastic shift in relations broadly palatable "back home." While defense hawks strongly objected in both cases, most Americans embraced the moves and promise of peace they implied.

Gorbachev's own celebrity during his visits to the United States exemplifies the evolution of American perceptions of the Soviets. The warm, even rapturous reception by Americans of the Soviet leader and his wife Raisa stands in stark contrast to those given Nikita Khrushchev in 1959 and Brezhnev in 1973.

At one point during a visit to Washington, DC, in 1987 Gorbachev waded into an excited crowd outside the Soviet embassy and clearly enjoyed the encounter. His experience was comparable with that of Chinese leader Deng Xiaoping, who during his 1979 visit had shown a human side—even donning a cowboy hat—to which Americans responded well and that increased the standing of his country in the eyes of many.[134] While popular culture and Reagan's more friendly language and warmer relationship with Gorbachev were not entirely responsible for the broader shift, they did play major roles.

During his visit to Moscow in 1988 it was Reagan's turn to display empathy. Speaking at Moscow State University beneath a giant bust of Lenin, he described how freedom is acted out at the community level and influences things like media, schools, courts, and small businesses. Reagan referred to a Soviet song, "Do the Russians Want War?," to show his confidence in his audience's good intentions. The song spoke of the silence of trees planted on soldiers' graves: no one desired war. The president promised that Americans felt the same and expressed a hope that the two nations' diplomats would one day find themselves not dealing with arms-control and military issues but "grappling with the problem of trade disputes between American and a growing, exuberant, exporting Soviet Union." He closed by evoking another tree and a different grave: he hoped that freedom would blossom in Russian like the "fresh green sapling planted over Tolstoy's grave."[135] The reference to the world-famous author Leo Tolstoy conveyed Reagan's confidence that a free Russia could produce more stories worthy of global acclaim, as it could not in the Soviet era.[136]

FRIENDS AT YOUR BACK

On a warm June day in 1987 Reagan stood in front of the historic Brandenburg Gate, at the Berlin Wall the communists had erected in 1961 to keep East Berliners from escaping to freedom. Speaking to a crowd of West Berliners, he would again blame the Soviet Union for the Cold War and challenge its leaders to move toward peace. Reagan returned to the theme of his 1984 "Anya and Ivan" speech, rhetorically telling Gorbachev, "If you seek peace, if you seek prosperity for the Soviet Union and Eastern Europe, if you seek liberalization," he should come to the Brandenburg Gate as indisputable proof that his policy of "openness" was genuine. Come to the divided city, Reagan thundered, and if he wanted peace, then "tear down this wall."[137]

The moment is an iconic one in Reagan's presidency. Delivered before a carefully chosen backdrop rich in symbolism for German and European history, his call to destroy the most visible symbol of the Cold War stands out as one of Reagan's most dramatic acts. Everything about the speech had been hotly debated in Washington, Bonn (the capital of West Germany), and Berlin prior to its delivery. Municipal leaders in West Berlin and the Kohl government feared the site was too laden, that such an address there would undermine their efforts to improve relations with East Germany (DDR, in the German acronym).[138] Similarly, Reagan's advisors thought the tone of the speech too provocative, given the strong working relationship now established between the American and Soviet leaders. Calling on Gorbachev at this point to tear down the Berlin Wall struck many in the administration as needless and potentially damaging. The final decision rested with Reagan, who, after considering the draft, said "I think we'll leave it in."[139] Reagan wanted to demonstrate American support for Western Europe and use the impressive backdrop to remind Europeans of whom he felt they should blame for the Cold War. A dramatic speech in front of a globally known symbol of oppression fit the bill perfectly.

Reagan's conception of "peace through strength," however, required steadfast allies. He did not expect the United States alone to deter the Soviet Union conventionally. The administration sought firm and lasting commitments from all partner states, West Germany and Britain in particular. They also doubted that the Soviets could truly count on their own "allies." The Warsaw Pact was not an alliance of choice, and many of its member states resented that the Soviets planned to fight World War III on their territories. Matlock believed, in fact, that Soviet military planners would need to think through where they placed Warsaw Pact formations, amounting to a choice of whether to risk betrayal on the flank or from the rear.[140] However, American planners doubted the willingness of other NATO countries to share the burden of deterrence. The Reagan administration had expressed grave doubt on that score when it entered office. "Political and economic retrenchment" seemed the order of the day on the continent. These feelings and specifically the growth there of the antinuclear movement led the NSC to urge Reagan to combat "Europessimism" through speeches that would restore the will of Europeans to engage in the Cold War.[141]

Thatcher's 1979 ascension to the prime ministership in the United Kingdom and Kohl's assumption of the West German chancellorship in 1982 helped bring the alliance closer. In each Reagan found a partner who supported his hard-line stance, and he built strong relationships with both. It was Thatcher who first gave Reagan a sense that Gorbachev was a different sort of Soviet leader. She had met him in 1984 prior to his elevation to the general secretaryship and had come away convinced they could "do business together."[142] Thatcher expressed as much to Reagan, and he kept it in mind as he prepared to meet Gorbachev for the first time in Geneva. There, although the two did not see eye to eye on all issues, particularly on "Star Wars" (as SDI was known in the American press) and the U.S. invasion of Grenada, these disagreements never threatened their relationship.[143]

For Reagan the importance of these relationships followed from that of the Cold War itself. This view led him to support allies at political risk to himself and created moments that exposed his inability to understand the moral ambiguities of the Cold War. Preparing to visit West Germany in 1985, he agreed to a request from Kohl to visit a cemetery in Bitburg and there commemorate the fortieth anniversary of the end of European Theatre of World War II. Reagan agreed, thinking to celebrate "forty years of peace between erstwhile enemies" and support an important ally in Europe.[144] However, the chosen cemetery contained the graves of several members of the Waffen-SS, notorious for its enthusiastic participation in the Holocaust.

News of Reagan's planned visit set off a firestorm of controversy in the United States. The Holocaust survivor and Nobel Prize winner Elie Wiesel, even while receiving the Congressional Gold Medal in the White House, pleaded with the president that Bitburg "is not your place." Reagan needed instead to "stand with the victims of the SS," as a matter of "not politics, but good and evil."[145] The plea resonated with Reagan's notion of morality but left him still resolved to go and convinced that it was the "morally right thing."[146] Reagan visited the graveyard as planned.

Reagan did so because Kohl was "a good friend and solid ally" who backed him on the deployment of Pershing II missiles.[147] As anger over the proposed visit exploded in the United States Kohl warned the president that he could either go to Bitburg or "see the Kohl government fall."[148] Reagan prioritized the needs of an important Cold War partner over the desires of victims of atrocity. As when he supported the Contras and the apartheid regime in South Africa, he was unable to frame the issue outside of his Cold War views; he felt that visiting a site with the graves of monsters was morally just if done in the name of defeating communism. Once again, Reagan was unfairly asking a victimized group to subordinate its feelings and needs to his crusade.

Such political fallout was a measure of the importance of NATO to Reagan. The alliance would be critical to reshaping the Cold War environment in a way favorable to the United States. In addition to military commitments, the Reagan administration counted on economic support as well. It expected NATO countries not only to provide markets and trade for the United States but also to avoid "subsidiz[ing] the Soviet economy" by trading with it and to keep high technology away from the Soviet Union.[149] Finally, Reagan expected member nations to present a unified front diplomatically.

NATO plays an analogously critical role in *Red Storm Rising*. In the battle for the Atlantic sea-lanes a combined British and American fleet retakes Iceland. It can do so only after a British and Norwegian air raid destroys a key Soviet radar site.[150] On the land front, West German forces work closely with American counterparts to guard NATO's flank, and at a critical moment West German fighter aircraft destroy Soviet attack helicopters closing in on alliance armored formations.[151] Clancy and Bond make it clear through their narrative that the United States needed strong partners and allies to win.

In contrast, as Clancy and Bond tell it, the Warsaw Pact is detrimental to the Soviet war effort. Prior to the war, East German forces intentionally misdirect a Soviet officer trying to follow members of a military liaison mission; it is common, a NATO advisor notes, for the Eastern-Zone Germans to refuse to assist their "allies" in finding their way in the country. During the war, the DDR refuses to allow the Soviets to employ chemical weapons as had been planned, and the leader of East Germany is aware that Moscow would view "even a united, *socialist* Germany" as a grave strategic threat.[152] The inclusion of DDR perspectives in the book is calculated to argue that the Soviets saw its partners as client states from which to extract resources, not as socialist allies. No Warsaw Pact nation contributes to the combat in *Red Storm Rising*. In desperate need of more troops, the Politburo elects to mobilize armies from Kazan, far to the east in the Tatar Autonomous Soviet Socialist Republic, instead of asking, or telling, an Eastern European nation to assist.

This portrayal was a conscious choice by Bond and Clancy. They wanted to show the Warsaw Pact as an unproductive and unstable alliance—as, ironically, what Politburo leaders thought NATO was.[153] Their version of the Warsaw Pact matched the viewpoint of the Reagan administration, where officials were optimistic that the Soviets had no reliable allies and would find their client states unwilling to underwrite a war that would see massive destruction in their countries.[154] This was another way that *Red Storm Rising* took the most favorable reading possible of American power and placed it in a narrative for Reagan in a way that allowed him to imagine what the world would look like over the next decade. Though an actual war would certainly not unfold with the same relative ease, neither was the book's depiction a pure flight of fancy. The attention the authors paid to researching fine details made the book's conclusions plausible, if unlikely.

WARFARE IN MINIATURE

All the material in *The Hunt for Red October* came from unclassified sources, but that would not be so in future Clancy novels. In them he sought out details, in hopes that precise descriptions of hardware would prevent experts from questioning the backbones of his stories.[155] The technical expertise and research skills Clancy showed in his first novel, paired with its friendliness to the Pentagon, made the author a favorite in military circles, someone with whom the Pentagon would cooperate. In writing *Red Storm Rising*, the author admitted he inferred "secrets about operational capabilities such as the stealth bomber" that would remain classified for another two years after the book's release. Clancy felt that revealing classified U.S. military capabilities in this way was helpful, arguing, "If everything we do is secret [the Soviets] won't even know enough to be afraid." Doing so also certainly helped the books sell better. In any case, the Pentagon offered few complaints; Lehman himself argued in the books' support and noted how they showed the dangers of selling technology to the Soviets.[156]

The success of *The Hunt for Red October*, as has been mentioned, had opened doors for Clancy. At events in the White House, the Pentagon, and CIA headquarters he spoke of the technical detail of his work and its importance to the story. At a luncheon attended by both the CIA's deputy and future director and Secretary of Defense Robert Gates his topic was how to "convey complex technical matters to the lay reader."[157] An event at the Pentagon was similarly well attended, with both the Deputy Chief of Naval Operations and Vice Adm. Nils R. "Ron" Thunman, the service's most senior submariner, in attendance. The support of high-ranking officials throughout the defense establishment greatly facilitated the research of *Red Storm Rising*.

That book's coauthors, Clancy and Bond, received special access to military bases. They discussed joint operations with NATO personnel stationed at Supreme Allied Command Atlantic in Norfolk, Virginia. Clancy particularly enjoyed speaking with British officers there, finding they spoke about tactics "a little more freely" than American officers.[158] The writers also had access to the Soviet defector Arkady Shevchenko, whose book *Breaking with Moscow* Clancy found to be "pure dynamite" for its starkly negative portrayal of Soviet leaders.[159] Conversations with the former Soviet diplomat strongly informed the depiction of *Red Storm Rising's* Politburo.[160] During the research, Clancy also had an opportunity to spend a week on a Navy frigate, drive an M1 tank, and get hands-on experience with a variety of military systems, all of which would feature in the novel.

Pentagon leaders saw in Clancy an ally and sought to uphold and enhance his credibility, even when he diverged from the military's preferred narrative. During hearings on the 1990 National Defense Authorization Act (NDAA), Vice Adm. Daniel Cooper faced questions about a recent article by Clancy arguing the British training model was superior to the American one for naval officers. In framing the question, Representative Norman Sisisky observed that Clancy had "a big following as a big naval expert," implying that his opinion merited a response from the admiral. Cooper disagreed with Clancy's view but praised him as a "fine individual" and a "real patriot." The criticism did hurt, as Cooper "love[d] Tom Clancy," but the author "did a lot for the submarine force." Representative Duncan Hunter added that Clancy helped "the Navy immensely." Cooper's careful responses and his fulsome praise show how sensitive the Navy was to Clancy's reputation and how importantly it viewed its institutional relationship with the writer.[161]

Clancy's books were seen as important not just because of their technical detail but also because they showed systems in action, how new technology would work and help defeat the Soviets. They provided context to a wide audience unlikely to listen to or care about congressional testimony or technical white papers. Clancy sought to make sure that even implausible episodes were at least technically possible. In *The Hunt for Red October*, Clancy realized he had written himself into a corner with regard to the ending. The submarine lacked the manpower (having evacuated most of the crew with U.S. assistance using a rescue submarine) to fight its pursuer effectively and could not use its torpedoes. Clancy then realized from scale models of the two classes of submarine involved, the double-hulled Typhoon was much larger than the Alfa attack boat: the *Red October* could ram the *Konovalov*, sink it, and survive. While an unorthodox maneuver, it would likely work in the real world. Similarly, in *Red Storm Rising* Clancy and Bond needed the Soviets to move forces to Iceland undetected. Rather than employ military transport, the authors' fictional Soviets load a regiment on the civilian containership MV *Julius Fucik*. They used the real-world measurements of the ship to determine that it both could carry the appropriate tonnage and had the deck space to act as a base of operations for the airborne regiment. Few, if any, war plans call for the use of a civilian ship in this manner, but the research into technical detail added realism to the work.[162]

Wargaming too was essential to the development of *Red Storm Rising*. While serving in the Navy, Bond had disliked the wargame the service used in training. Its classified mechanics meant officers could only play in special settings. To fix the problem, Bond made his own game: he developed and released *Harpoon* through *Dungeons and Dragons* cofounder Dave Arneson's Adventure Games. Clancy purchased a copy while working on *The Hunt for Red October* and wrote Bond to praise it. After they met and played the game together, Clancy invited Bond to collaborate on his next novel. *Harpoon* offered a form of fact-checking for *Red Storm Rising*; the writers would use it to verify the feasibility of plot events. The game's contribution was most prominent in the sea battle depicted in the chapter "The Dance of the Vampires," whose intricate sea and air movements Bond and Clancy wanted to make as realistic as possible.[163]

The book also drew on official wargames. After leaving the Navy, Bond had taken a job with the Center for Naval Analyses (CNA), a federally funded research and development center with close ties to the Navy. There he assisted in the development and execution of games that focused on maintaining sealanes in the Atlantic in the event of war in Europe. Such games addressed one of the most important operational threats to NATO's ability to fight on the continent: the possibility that men and material from the United States might be prevented from actually reaching the war. The games had inspired Bond to produce an expansion to *Harpoon* called *Convoy*.[164] Clancy told him it "would make a good book," and the concept became the impetus for *Red Storm Rising*.

Longtime CNA wargamer Peter Perla believes that part of the novel's appeal, especially to professionals, was how it took core findings from wargames conducted by the think tank and tabletop gamers and packaged them as a digestible narrative.[165] *Red Storm Rising* far exceeded the scope of these games, but their realistic examinations of strategic issues greatly enhanced the work's credibility.

Wargaming does not identify what will happen in a situation; rather, it identifies possibilities to analyze and plan against. The issues raised in wargames allow military planners to adjust plans, allocate resources, change force structures, and think through responses to successes or failures. A good wargame significantly, and invaluably, reduces the possibility of surprise in the event. Additionally, as Perla notes, wargames can have an outsize influence in that they carry a "greater emotional impact" than simply discussing operational designs.[166] The players become personally invested; they see their decisions have measurable impacts. By participating in the events, they are more likely to remember their choices and results and have it guide future behavior and choice. Novels and other narratives can do the same. A well-written story forces emotional investment from its reader, creating memorable and lasting connections. Reagan's recognition of this effect—one to which he was eminently susceptible himself—guided his communication in office. He found in *Red Storm Rising* a realistic portrayal of a future World War III and used it as a strategist might use a wargame. The work of Clancy and Bond supported Reagan's thinking about conventional war in Europe and helped set the stage for his stunning offer at Reykjavík.

Reagan was not the only one in government to use *Red Storm Rising* in this way. Its portrayal of the effectiveness of new technology made it a popular reference in Congress to draw attention to favored programs. Just a week after the book's release, a future Speaker of the House, Newt Gingrich, referred to it during a floor debate on the 1987 NDAA. Gingrich called it the "best single illustration of how a major conflict would work in the real world."[167] He was particularly drawn to Clancy's depiction of antisatellite weapons (ASATs). The only female combatant in the book shoots down several Soviet reconnaissance satellites from her F-5.[168] She succeeds despite the ASAT program's lack of funding, a problem Clancy incorporated to draw attention to and raise concern about the state of the ASAT program. Gingrich seized on this episode as suggesting that "opposition to antisatellite technology may well be the most irrational position on the [political] left this week." He quoted Clancy but went further, complaining that the lack of funding showed the "peculiarly twisted logic on the left" that "killing 800 pounds of electronics is terrible but shooting down an airplane to save 20,000 lives is acceptable." Gingrich concluded his partisan attack by accusing opponents of the program of being in league with the Soviets and happy to risk American lives.[169]

Thomas Downey, a Democrat from New York, called Gingrich's speech a "remarkable argument, based on fiction." He was unsure if it was a matter of "life imitating art or fiction imitating reality" but argued there was no "clearer example" of how arms control helped the United States than ASAT. He argued a limited ASAT capability would disincentivize the Soviets from militarizing space, leaving the United States with a massive strategic advantage given its greater reliance on satellites. Anything further would risk an expensive arms race and place the advantage at risk.[170] Importantly, while the congressmen disagreed about the program, they both accepted Clancy's depiction as realistic and something that needed reckoning with.

Red Storm Rising's ASAT references also made it into the Senate. During a 1987 debate on military funding future vice president Dan Quayle held aloft his copy of the book and demanded to know if his colleagues had read it. Quayle was certain that if they read Clancy they would realize "ASAT technology is what wins the war."[171] No Democrats were convinced about the technology's merits, but they did remember his reference. When Quayle was added to the 1988 Republican presidential ticket, Democratic staffers publicized the exchange in an effort to damage his candidacy, implying to Americans that Quayle was not a serious thinker; for one unnamed aide, it meant that "at least . . . we know he can read."[172] The attack did not deter Quayle, who continued to mention the book on the campaign trail. In September 1988 he diverged from prepared remarks on national security to use the novel once again to explain why Americans should support ASAT. Confronted afterward by embarrassed aides who felt Quayle should stick to the script, he told them his version was more exciting.[173]

Gingrich, for his part, viewed the book as more than a vehicle for political attacks and public rhetoric. Shortly after its release, he invited Clancy and Bond to lunch at the Capitol, where the coauthors discussed defense policy with members of Congress. Bond was struck to see Dick Cheney, then a representative from Wyoming, studiously taking notes of his response to a question from Cheney about Soviet naval capabilities. The luncheon left Bond convinced that many on Capitol Hill took his and Clancy's fiction seriously.[174] It was also an example of the widespread use of narrative in policy. Experiences like Bond's are common. Discussions of fiction take place daily in such settings; that they are often forgotten and unrecorded does not mean they are unimportant. This documented instance underlines how water-cooler talk and seemingly light entertainment can impact policy, creating what political scientists Paul Musgrave and J. Furman Daniel term "synthetic experiences" that "encode information in ways that affect judgement." Stories can "prompt the inward experience of a fictional reality" that informs responses in the real world.[175]

The military treated Clancy's work seriously enough to feature it in professional military education. All officers attending the Navy's course for prospective submarine commanders received a copy of *The Hunt for Red October* to read.[176] The Naval War College, in Newport, Rhode Island, immediately added *Red Storm Rising* to its curriculum, calling it a "very true to life story" in a syllabus.[177] Its value to the course was for the importance of NATO, the impact of technology, and the roles of politics and diplomacy in war; the curriculum for which the book was required reading was intended to introduce "officers to various maritime, national, and alliance strategies," showcase the importance of "joint and combined operations," and finally to "evaluate military decisions."[178] Using *Red Storm Rising* in this way shows both the seriousness with which the Navy took the book and its recognition that some lessons are better taught through fiction. Another aspect of its appeal for teaching was that it finessed issues of foreign disclosure. Its classified material (which American officers could gloss over as fictional speculation) could be usefully shared with the college's many international students without restriction. It is possible also that Clancy's book could offer a more realistic depiction of American capabilities than could a government-produced scenario, which would be subject to security review. The accessibility of the novel made it an ideal tool for use in a joint, international schoolhouse.

Finally, *Red Storm Rising* was a massive pop-culture success. It debuted in second place on the *New York Times* best-sellers list and within a month overtook Danielle Steele's *Wanderlust* for first place.[179] Only Stephen King's *IT* sold more copies in 1986.[180] For the remainder of the decade a new Clancy novel would occupy one of the top two positions in annual sales. The pay-television network HBO purchased the rights to *Red Storm Rising* and planned a miniseries. That project eventually fell apart because of cost, but related ventures in computer gaming were more successful. Sid Meier, of *Civilization* fame, created a PC game based on the book. Its success led to the creation of Red Storm Entertainment and the beginning of a video-game empire that has brought the Clancy brand to computers and consoles ever since.[181]

CREATIVE SPACES

Red Storm Rising is not "why" Reagan and Gorbachev almost abolished nuclear weapons. Many factors contributed to the near deal. Gorbachev needed an agreement to reduce the strain the weapons caused for the Soviet economy. He feared the Americans would otherwise try "keeping the negotiations machine running idle," to continue to exacerbate economic impacts.[182] Soviet leaders knew they could not afford new investment to counter SDI and distrusted Reagan's promise to share SDI technology.[183] These factors left them willing to negotiate and to agree to historic changes.

American policy makers too increasingly believed the time for serious agreements was at hand. Shultz perceived the increased willingness of Soviets to make concessions and wanted Reagan to move quickly to "reel the Soviets in."[184] The success of Reagan's "peace through strength" policies had created they believed an environment that would allow changes to nuclear postures without endangering American interests throughout the world.[185] Matlock believed in the sincerity of Soviet offers and similarly "felt optimistic that U.S.-Soviet relations might be on the verge of a sudden turn for the better."[186] These factors made the summit one with immense potential. American attitudes toward nuclear weapons heightened this potential.

Popular opinion ran strongly against nuclear weapons. The nuclear-freeze movement remained widespread and drew moral support from the Vatican. Popular culture furthered these views. Films like *Wargames* showed the potential of accidental nuclear war, and others like *The Day After* demonstrated its potential aftermath. Eliminating "nukes" even became central to the plot of the (terrible) *Superman IV: The Quest for Peace*. Consistent starkly negative views of nuclear weapons from Hollywood stood out within the film industry's embrace of Reagan's nationalism.

All of this buttressed Reagan's own nuclear abolitionism. Unable to pursue it seriously during his first term owing to the state of U.S. conventional forces, Reagan took the opportunity to do so in his second. *Red Storm Rising* helped the president recognize the moment. The book was a personal, cognitive wargame for the president and granted him the "synthetic experience" that policy memos and NSC meetings could not. Convinced by the book and other sources that NATO could defeat conventionally a Soviet invasion of Western Europe, he no longer considered nuclear weapons a necessary evil for the sake of stability. They now became an apocalyptic threat to individual freedom, a threat to be destroyed. Part of Reagan's plan to destroy them was the Strategic Defense Initiative. Far more than a bargaining chip, Reagan believed that "Star Wars" would be the guarantor of freedom should arms control fail. His unwillingness to give it up torpedoed the Reykjavík hope of freedom from nuclear weapons entirely and baffled allies, advisors, and popular culture alike.

PEBBLES FROM SPACE

SDI, Cultural Division, and Strategic Success

March 1983 changed the dynamics of the Cold War. Reagan continued his rhetorical offensive against the Soviet Union in his clearest terms to date, labeling it an "Evil Empire." He also announced an initiative that would divide opinion both domestically and abroad and generate significant concern in Moscow about its ability to counter it. The announcement caught many of his closest defense advisors and the military off guard, leading to a chaotic internal response and fractures in the administration. It had its roots in the president's imagined future. Reagan believed no one could be free who lived in dread of nuclear annihilation. He wanted to guarantee individual liberty by protecting all from that scourge. The Strategic Defense Initiative was his answer.

The speech announcing the program began in ordinary fashion. Reagan spoke of familiar themes, the growth of Soviet military strength and the expansion of communism in Africa and Central and South America. These realities meant Americans needed to accept continued high defense spending, whatever the administration's attempts at fiscal conservatism. Calls to cut the defense budget "came in nice simple arithmetic" but in Reagan's eyes were invitations to a dereliction of duty similar to the decisions of France and Britain to "neglect their defenses in the 1930s." Aggressive action by the Soviets and Cuba in Grenada,

El Salvador, Costa Rica, Honduras, Ethiopia, and Angola showed the threat. The ongoing Soviet war in Afghanistan and its support of martial law in Poland offered further evidence. Reagan argued that despite the vast growth in U.S. military capability the United States still had much to do to deter communist aggression globally. His listeners had heard all of this before from Reagan; they might have thought it odd that the administration would preempt broadcasts in prime time for it.[1]

Reagan was saving the most important part of the speech for the end: he wanted to share "a vision of the future" with the world. In his imagined world "free people could live secure in the knowledge that their security did not rest upon the threat of instant American retaliation to deter [*sic*] a Soviet attack." Instead, should Soviet missiles be launched, the United States would simply swat them out of the sky. If Americans put their faith in technology and their ingenuity as a free people, then American scientists would begin to develop a system to render "nuclear weapons impotent and obsolete." The immoral calculus of mutually assured destruction would no longer add up. Reagan's Strategic Defense Initiative would ensure that citizens of the world could live in peace.[2]

Shock greeted Reagan's address. The proposal violated the Anti-Ballistic Missile Treaty (ABM) signed in 1972 and might provoke military preemption if the technology showed signs of progressing. A day prior to the address the deputy national security advisor, Robert McFarlane, pleaded with his boss, Bill Clark, to get Reagan to drop the idea. Members of the NSC had "expressed [to him] their most extreme concern" about the initiative's likely reception at home and abroad. McFarlane also knew the Pentagon was unprepared for the announcement and wanted Reagan to speak with Weinberger and General Vessey "to solicit their views." Clark ignored the memorandum and supported the announcement.[3]

The State Department too was in the dark about Reagan's intentions until very late. Shultz learned of the plan only two days before the scheduled address—and from one of his undersecretaries rather than the president. Lawrence Eagleburger had received word that the president was moving forward with it on the basis of enthusiastic support from the Joint Chiefs.[4] However, Eagleburger misunderstood the Pentagon's view. The chiefs held serious reservations about the feasibility of the project and feared that investment in a defensive system would take funds away from their preferred projects.[5]

The confused and scrambling reaction in the NSC, State, and Defense illustrate the perils of Reagan's tendency to lead by vision. Reagan chose to include in the address, less than a week before its delivery, a program that had not emerged from a traditional interagency process.[6] The seemingly ad hoc manner in which Reagan raised it to global attention left individuals and agencies in the government trying on their own to interpret what he meant. Reagan did this before, announcing the "Crusade for Freedom" at Westminster and leaving the NSC to scramble to produce a policy to fit the president's rhetoric. In that case, the creation of a relatively minor agency to oversee endowments met the need. With SDI Reagan had something grander in mind, but what it was he never expressed effectively to those around them, simply assuming they shared his vision for the program. As a result, administration figures held a variety of views about the importance of SDI and what it would look like. Many incorrectly assumed it was simply to be a bargaining chip in arms-control negotiations. Those who thought it substantive responded in a way Poindexter characterized as "very negative."[7] Either way, the feedback did not deter Reagan, who would unflinchingly support the program throughout his remaining five years in office.

Public reception of the idea was no better than the internal one. A week after the speech, *Time* insisted it was best for all sides to be defenseless: "In the nuclear age it may be safer when each side has only spears." The magazine's editors criticized Reagan's "faith in technology as the solution to the country's military problems," believing it was "both forgetful about the past and short-sighted toward the future." After all, the Soviets had overcome technological gaps before and often in surprisingly rapid fashion; they had developed an atomic bomb just four years after the United States had done so. *Time* also feared that development of SDI would incentivize a Soviet first strike to avoid being left "permanently at America's mercy."[8]

Newsweek called SDI a "nuclear heresy." It called on Reagan to accept the recommendations of the recently completed commission on strategic forces.[9] The panel, chaired by Brent Scowcroft (between his two tours as national security advisor), recommended deployment of then-developmental "MX" ICBMs in the near term with a plan to replace them gradually with smaller "Midgetman" missiles. The replacements would each carry only a single warhead instead of the ten "multiple independent reentry vehicles" of the MX design.[10] Scowcroft's

commission felt its plan would enhance short-term deterrence and create a sur-
vivable "second-strike capability" (i.e., with which a response to a surprise "first
strike" could be launched). *Newsweek* argued that with the Scowcroft recommendation in place "Americans may feel somewhat more secure without making Moscow feel less so." Pursuit of SDI, in contrast, would "require enormous
diplomatic skill" to head off a new arms race, something the magazine found
lacking in the Reagan administration.[11]

The primary criticisms of *Time* and *Newsweek* only mattered if the program was technically and economically feasible, and there was fierce debate
over both. A *New York Times* editorial accused Reagan of pressing forward
without "firm scientific basis and political examination" and doubted the president's plan used theoretically sound physics.[12] A review from Congress' Office
of Technology Assessment (OTA) supported the *Times*, finding the prospects
of successful fielding the technology remote.[13] It quickly became common to
charge that the core of the administration's vision was science fiction. *Newsweek*
compared the proposed technology with the shields of the USS *Enterprise* of
the *Star Trek* television series and movie franchise; a *New York Times* editorial,
under the headline "Nuclear Facts, Science Fiction," called SDI a "pipe dream,"
a "projection of fantasy into policy."[14] Most famously, Senator Edward Kennedy
referred to the speech as "misleading Red-scare tactics and reckless *Star Wars*
schemes."[15] The reference to the popular science-fiction franchise stuck, and
"Star Wars" became the program's shorthand.

Reagan intensely disliked the nickname; he would "bristle every time our
media friends (?) call it 'Star Wars.'"[16] While the president was more a fan of
Star Trek (which had first appeared, on television, eleven years before the movie
Star Wars), it was not "brand loyalty" that caused his ire but rather the implication that his vision was unserious. Science fiction did in fact help Reagan
conceptualize the impact of technology, a technique he saw as perfectly reasonable. Edmund Morris, his official biographer, argues in *Dutch* that the John
Carter novels played a role in Reagan's desire for SDI.[17] While this overstates
the direct importance of Burroughs for the program, the books did affect, as we
have already seen, how Reagan thought about the future. In his speech at the
Air Force Academy, Reagan reflected that though only fifty-two years separated
his own graduation from his audience's, it seemed like ten times that. In that
period, "a new future was discovered and quickly rediscovered."[18]

It seemed natural to Reagan to take inspiration from imagined futures and to ignore the critics. This near-religious faith in the ability of American scientists to create new and awe-inspiring technology reverberated beyond the District of Columbia. It lent legitimacy to a literary genre from which he took inspiration and reopened previously settled debates. Throughout the public arguments over SDI, science fiction was front and center. It provided a spark for the idea and then turned into a cultural battleground on which the program's feasibility was fought out. Legendary authors in the genre fiercely advocated for and against Star Wars and inserted themselves into the public debate. They found policy makers receptive to their various opinions and often found themselves useful to people in government and news media who wanted to amplify their reach. The ability of science-fiction writers to translate arcane detail into compelling visions of the future lent them credibility and made them an important part of a national conversation.

CITIZENS' ACTION

Shortly after Reagan's election in 1980, a group of scientists, writers, military personnel, and others personally invested in space gathered in Tarzana, California. The suburb was named for Edgar Rice Burroughs' most famous fictional character (from one of his several non-Martian series). Calling itself the Citizens' Advisory Council on National Space Policy, the group looked to provide advice to the incoming administration. It was the brainchild of science-fiction writer Jerry Pournelle, who, convinced Reagan would win the election, had organized it to capitalize on his connections with people likely to rank high in the next White House.[19] During the 1970s, Pournelle had collaborated with Hoover Institution fellow Stefan Possony on a book titled *Strategy of Technology*. Possony was a mentor to Richard Allen, who would become Reagan's first national security advisor, and introduced Pournelle to him. Throughout the late 1970s Pournelle and Allen discussed policy, and the writer came to believe that he could use Allen as a channel through which to influence Reagan's thinking.[20]

Pournelle began his career working in aerospace for Boeing in the 1950s. Eventually he worked on Project Thor, which proposed using inert tungsten rods released from satellites to destroy targets on the ground with effectively the explosive power of a small-yield nuclear bomb. Its nonnuclear nature exempted

Project Thor from the restrictions of the ABM or the United Nations Outer Space treaties. The project led him to the world-famous theoretical physicist and Nobel laureate Edward Teller, with whom he and Possony worked on issues of space defense, proposing an innovative approach called "Brilliant Pebbles" that was canceled with the end of the Cold War. At the same time, he became involved with the Republican Party, serving as the San Bernardino County chairman for Goldwater's campaign in 1964. He first met Reagan in this capacity, after inviting the actor to give a speech and having dinner afterward. By the late 1960s, Pournelle had left Boeing and was pursuing a career as an author; he published his first book in 1969 and became head of the Science Fiction and Fantasy Writers of America, the genre's guild.[21]

Pournelle's political, military, science, and writing connections allowed him to assemble an eclectic group for the Citizen's Advisory Council's first meeting, which Larry Niven hosted, because of the size of his house and his wife's cooking talent.[22] Among the attendees were Lowell Wood (filling in for the ill Edward Teller), Buzz Aldrin, Robert Heinlein, Poul Anderson, and a number of senior military officers, active-duty and retired. The group would meet three times before the inauguration and produce a two-hundred-page document covering a wide array of space-related issues the members hoped the Reagan administration would address.[23]

Strategic defense was the centerpiece of their agenda. However, finding consensus in the group was challenging, as some attendees, represented factions that had for years pushed their own variations of the concept. Supporters of one idea would attack the technological underpinnings of another, producing a "fratricidal" environment where the chances of achieving a goal accepted by all were diminished by lesser divisions between camps. At the first meeting, attendees agreed to the "Treaty of Tarzana," which pledged them all to advocate for the general concept rather than particular methods of pursuing it. Science-fiction writers Heinlein, Pournelle, Niven, and Anderson, lacking expertise, largely abstained from the initial in-depth discussions. However, they played a crucial role in the final product; it was they who translated scientific jargon into language that "made it more interesting."[24] Their efforts bore fruit: Reagan reportedly read the entire document rather than just the executive summary. The document's favorable reception by the incoming president led Allen to ask the group for periodic recommendations on a variety of space issues.[25]

The group influenced Reagan's March 1983 announcement of the Strategic Defense Initiative. The speech's primary writer, Dana Rohrabacher, was in contact with the science-fiction community as he drafted it and was aware that "a lot of creativity" was available to the administration on space issues.[26] One of the most memorable moments from Reagan's speech came when he asked Americans, "Wouldn't it be better to save lives than to avenge them?"—language from the Citizens' Advisory Council paper.[27] Following the speech, the group worked to stir up public support for SDI. It enlisted Bjo Trimble, best known for leading the fan letter–writing campaign that had won *Star Trek* a third season on television, to organize a flood of letters to the White House praising the program. These letters provided a counter to the largely negative reception to the program in other arenas.[28]

Reagan's speech, however, sparked a schism in science fiction. As Pournelle would recall, the proposal "damn near split science fiction in America in half."[29] Debate about SDI's potential to cause the militarization of space, about its technical feasibility and its cost, and the risk of its prompting a Soviet strike played out in genre magazines, novels, and op-eds. Authors felt compelled to wrestle with Star Wars and addressed it in both fiction and nonfiction. Pournelle was the most active voice in favor, going as far as to publish a book, *Mutual Assured Survival*, that was simply a fictionalized version of the Citizens' Advisory Council paper.[30] The book's cover declared, "ICBMs Will Soon Be Obsolete" and carried a blurb from Reagan praising the council's work.[31] Reagan had written the group thanking its members for their work and for "addressing with verve and vision the challenges to peace and to our national security."[32] The letter highlighted the importance of the prose of science-fiction writers to the development of policy ideas.

Pournelle and Niven leaned into this idea with their 1985 book *Footfall*, which topped the *New York Times* best-sellers list. In it science-fiction writers directly advise the president about how to respond to an alien invasion.[33] The fictional advisors are thinly veiled stand-ins for Pournelle, Niven, and Heinlein.[34] Pournelle acknowledged inspiration from working on the council's paper, though Niven rejected the notion.[35] *Footfall* argued, in effect, in favor of the militarization of space and deployment of nuclear weapons on satellites to defend the planet. Overall, the book received favorable reviews, though some noted that writing themselves into the story only served to allow "the authors to score some points against fuzzy-minded liberals."[36] The reviewer inferred the intention correctly: Pournelle and Niven wanted the book to build support for a more robust military role in space. It was impossible for the authors to separate their personal beliefs from their writing; after all, as Niven observed of "sci-fi" writers, "We teach, we can't help it."[37]

Meanwhile, the debate over SDI drew in the authors commonly regarded as the "Big Three" of science fiction: Heinlein, Arthur Clarke, and Isaac Asimov. Clarke, author of *2001: A Space Odyssey*, wrote a short story for the Pentagon's *Defense Science Board Newsletter*. Titled "On Golden Seas," its protagonist was the nation's first woman president, a scion of the Kennedy family. Facing a debt crisis, "President Kennedy" surprises her staff by announcing a "Budget Defense Initiative." "A great reader of historical fiction," she has encountered in a book a way to extract gold from seawater. The proposal infuriates the Soviets, and though she offers to share the technology with Moscow, "nobody [there] believed her." "On Golden Seas" identifies a host of technological questions about the program and at the end the United States and Soviet Union seem to be on the verge of an arms race, both seeking to drain the world's oceans as quickly as possible.[38]

Reagan is highly unlikely to have read Clarke's story and even less likely to have enjoyed it had he done so. The inclusion of a Kennedy would read to Reagan as an intentional slight, and he would dislike the lack of seriousness with which Clarke treated SDI. However, the story did circulate through the Pentagon and the White House. Its explicit assertion that fiction can influence policy makers suggests why Clarke spent time on a story with no commercial prospects—to mirror Reagan's own use of stories in speeches and public comments. It was a short, memorable parable for administration officials.

Clarke in fact testified against SDI before Congress, calling it a "technological obscenity" and advocating greater cooperation with the USSR. These themes matched those of Clarke's novels, often involving utopian societies and fruitful exploration. Technology to Clarke was not something to destroy but rather a device by which to elevate societies and their citizens. Heinlein, however, viewed Clarke's testimony as a betrayal. Confronting his fellow legend at a 1985 meeting of the Citizens' Advisory Council, Heinlein demanded to know why Clarke, an Englishman, felt he could comment on American politics and insisted that Clarke's doubts about the technical feasibility of space defenses were "outrageously misplaced." The attack "really was vicious," Clarke reasonably felt, and it left him deeply hurt.[39] Clarke did ultimately reassess his views on strategic defense, later acknowledging that there were "certain aspects of SDI that made sense."[40] Those aspects did not include technological feasibility but rather the concept's fit as a strategy. That is, as he wrote in the *Bulletin of the Atomic Scientists* in 1992, Soviet scientists would know SDI was impossible but the program probably "scared the hell out of some of [their] countrymen with more medals than brains." Nevertheless, Clarke now felt his opposing SDI "may have done an involuntary disservice to peace."[41] Still, the rift between himself and Heinlein never closed.

Heinlein, who in 1959 published *Starship Troopers*, also feuded with Asimov, again ending a longtime friendship. They had worked together during World War II at the Naval Air Experimental Station in Philadelphia, where Heinlein secured Asimov a position.[42] Their relationship began to sour in the 1950s as Heinlein's politics became more right-wing and libertarian. Asimov accused Heinlein of having been a "flaming liberal" during the war and then turning into a "far-right conservative immediately afterward." In his autobiography Asimov blamed this rightward shift on Heinlein's second marriage. Reagan too, he inaccurately believed, had moved to the right after his marriage, to Nancy—not that he could "explain Heinlein in that way at all," Reagan having simply been "brainless." Notwithstanding the disclaimer, the close proximity of the two cases in the memoir implied strongly that Asimov had come to doubt the now-deceased Heinlein's mental capacity. He concluded his reminiscence of his former friend by attributing to him a "meanness of spirit."[43]

Asimov opposed SDI on the grounds that it was neither technically feasible nor economically viable. Writing for the advocacy group Americans for Democratic Action, he argued the program was "only Hollywood science fiction, and like almost all Hollywood science fiction, it is bad."[44] Asimov saw SDI as liable to create "a John Wayne standoff," in that, he felt, it would bankrupt both nations.[45] This view ironically echoed Reagan's own belief about the concept he meant SDI to render obsolete, mutually assured destruction. Asimov took his opposition directly to science-fiction fans. Writing in *The Magazine of Fantasy and Science Fiction*, he opened an essay ostensibly about cosmic rays with a withering attack on Reagan, whose strategic-defense concept was, Asimov declared, "the wish-fulfillment dream of a shallow mind." The same applied by extension to Reagan's supporters, notably an author of "far-right persuasion" who was a "well-known apostle of the righteousness of violence."[46] Inescapably, Asimov viewed SDI proponents as idiotic warmongers.

Pournelle responded to counter Asimov's direct appeal to science-fiction fans. Working with publisher Jim Baen, he established a new magazine, *Far Frontiers*, to combat what they saw as a leftward shift in the genre and encourage a return to "traditional" military-themed science fiction. Its frequent op-eds about SDI asked readers to support the program. The venture lasted only seven issues;[47] Heinlein, who had supported it, continued to advocate for SDI in his works. He dedicated his penultimate novel, *The Cat Who Walked through Walls*, to his fellow council members, nine of whom, including Pournelle and Niven, were "men to have at your back."[48] The martial image is unsurprising, given that the book was about a weapons program. Heinlein also found ways to bring the military directly into the intra-genre debate. He began to work with Lt. Gen. Daniel Graham, a retired Army officer who had been deputy director of the CIA and Reagan's campaign advisor on military affairs in 1976 and 1980.

Graham was a leading advocate of missile defense and spoke about it frequently with Reagan. He founded a group, High Frontier, to lobby for investment in SDI and send issue papers to policy makers. Heinlein donated over $40,000 to the group and wrote the introduction to Graham's 1983 nonfiction book *High Frontier*, the subtitle of which assured readers, "There Is a Defense against Nuclear War."[49] In his introduction, Heinlein called SDI "the best news I have heard since V-J day" and argued that relying only on nonnuclear systems, as Graham urged, was "as non-aggressive as a bullet-proof vest." (It apparently did not concern him that many would see wearing a bulletproof vest as evidence of readiness to act aggressively.) Heinlein also dismissed lamentations of its high cost; he "was not in a position to judge this" but in any case did not "give a damn," as a "man with a burst appendix can't afford to dicker over the cost of surgery."[50] Heinlein confidently promised, on the basis of his experience as an engineer four decades previously, that the technical issues were surmountable. Pournelle too contributed to the book, writing a preface that similarly claimed his past scientific work as authority for his conviction that SDI was feasible.[51]

Though the novelists cast their support for SDI in scientific terms, it was not their expertise that pleased Graham. He was aware that both were decades removed from research in their fields and understood only vaguely how the program would work. However, they were well known in the science-fiction community and could reach a large audience with ease. He chose Tor Books to approach for *High Frontier*, a publisher then as now best known for science fiction and fantasy. Tor's decision to publish Graham's nonfictional work, ultimately issuing a mass-market version, suggests its editors believed science-fiction fans would embrace a fairly technical look at the Strategic Defense Initiative. Graham, for his part, felt sci-fi readers might be predisposed favorably.

Meanwhile, journalists sought out science-fiction authors for pieces on Star Wars. They happily quoted Nobel Prize–winning scientists, politicians, military leaders, and the like. A profile of Graham listed as supporters of the *High Frontier* group a former chairman of the Joint Chiefs of Staff, Teller, Aldrin, and Heinlein, whose opinions, by implication, were equally relevant and valuable as those of "nationally prominent figures in the military and scientific community."[52] Politicians too wanted to tap into the writers' audience. Gingrich developed a long-term friendship with Pournelle, who provided the introduction to Gingrich's first book, *Window of Opportunity*, cowritten with his second wife, Marianne Gingrich, and noted military-science-fiction author David Drake (the Hammer's Slammers series, etc.). The book offered policy prescriptions for the United States and focused on space exploration as a way to create an "opportunity society." The cover art was more akin to that of a lower-tier sci-fi novel than a typical political campaign book: a small planet earth dwarfed by a giant bald eagle soaring in outer space and a space shuttle hurtling toward the reader. Tor Books published this work as well.[53] Gingrich had met Pournelle and Drake, with both of whom he would maintain close relationships, at the 1983 World Science Fiction Convention in Atlanta, as well as Pournelle's SDI ally Baen.[54] Gingrich embarked with Drake and Pournelle (who later dropped out) on a fiction project that would become Gingrich's first novel, an alternative history of World War II in which the United States and Germany never fight each other.

The prominence of sci-fi's Big Three in the SDI reflected the significant strides the genre made from its pulp-magazine origins. Readers of John Campbell's *Astounding Science Fiction* and of Burroughs' John Carter novels in the 1920s and 1930s carried their love of such writing with them into adulthood and its golden age of the 1940s and 1950s. The continued growth of science fiction and its expansion into television and movies made it a particularly valuable channel for messages about technology. Science-fiction writers became translators of policy, speaking to the imaginations of Americans hungry to think about the future usefully. They sold a vision that could make or break a policy.

The relationship between fiction and policy is not that of a one-way street; the case of SDI shows how much influence politicians and "policy wonks" could have on writers of fiction. Reagan's enthusiastic embrace of what sci-fi writers saw as "their lane" led them to feel obliged to reckon with his strategic-defense concept. In Pournelle's words, it "damn near split science fiction in America in half" and exposed in the genre political divides that remain stark into the present day.[55] While these intramural controversies would likely have come to light without SDI, Reagan's speech marked the beginning of a public literary civil war.

SOVIET STAR WARS

Reagan greatly appreciated the efforts of science-fiction writers on his behalf. He praised "the important work that [Graham] and [his] colleagues have done to prepare the way for a more secure America." In particular, he was appreciative of High Frontier's "efforts to help us build a national consensus" in favor of SDI.[56] Reagan also thanked the Citizens' Advisory Council for its "verve and vision."[57] Science-fiction writers who inserted SDI into narratives, fictional and otherwise, pleased Reagan tremendously. Their presentation of Star Wars in a way that was approachable for a large audience made them important assets for the administration.

Science-fiction authors were not the only writers to draw inspiration from SDI and seek to promote it with their work. Tom Clancy embraced missile defense and made it the central theme of his fourth book, *The Cardinal of the Kremlin*. Published in 1988 as the last of the Jack Ryan novels to appear during Reagan's presidency, it was clearly intended to build popular support for SDI. A *New York Times Magazine* profile called Clancy a "champion . . . of Ronald Reagan's Strategic Defense Initiative program" and quoted the author as saying that if the United States did not "go forward with it, we're stupid." Clancy believed "it can work" and argued that the Russians "think it can work" too— the best possible argument in favor of the program.[58]

The Cardinal of the Kremlin portrays a race between the United States and Soviet Union to develop a working missile-defense system. It opens with the scuttling by the Americans of the *Red October*, giving Clancy an opportunity to have Ryan, now working on arms-control issues, pontificate about nuclear weapons. Clancy's protagonist recalls seeing the submarine's missiles and recoils at the memory of these "ghastly things."[59] He rejects the utility of arms reduction, on the ground that even destroying half of all weapons leaves the framework of MAD intact. Ryan concludes the United States needs to "eliminate the damned things or figure out something to keep them from working" and "had to do the latter before [it] can attempt the former."[60] Within the first forty pages of the book, then, Clancy demonstrated his support for both SDI and the Reykjavík framework, specifically Reagan's stance that SDI was not a roadblock to peace but its guarantor. The book drives this point home in its concluding chapter, in which Ryan delivers a message to the Soviet general secretary, clearly an avatar of Gorbachev. The Soviet wryly notes that Ryan sounds like the American president, which pleases the analyst, who adds, "He's right."[61] Here was the central theme of the book: Reagan was right.

Structurally, *The Cardinal of the Kremlin* is like Clancy's other books. American characters are unambiguously virtuous and capable. The lead American researcher on SDI, Maj. Alan Gregory, has been valedictorian at West Point, holds several PhDs, and is "already being talked about in the same breath as Cambridge's Stephen Hawking or Princeton's Freeman Dyson."[62] Soviet characters are foils by which to expose the flaws of their country's system. The eponymous cardinal is a longtime U.S. mole at the highest level of the Soviet government. Despite three citations as a Hero of the Soviet Union, "Col. Mikhail Semyonovich Filitov" has chosen to work for his nation's sworn enemy. He feels the nation has betrayed the sacrifices of the Great Patriotic War (i.e., the Eastern Front of World War II) and, as with Ramius in *The Hunt for Red October*, the regime is responsible for the death of his wife. It has also killed both of his sons, who followed their father into the military; one has died in the suppression of the 1956 Hungarian Revolt.[63] With *The Cardinal of the Kremlin* Clancy continued to advance the Reagan themes of gallant American servicemembers, Russians who would choose freedom, and a Soviet system that betrays them in the name of the power of the few.

Though depicting both nations as having advanced missile-defense programs, this time Clancy broke from reality and made the Soviets the more advanced. A U.S. spy plane's detection of a Soviet test leads the officer in charge of the American program to declare the Russians are "at least three years ahead of us."[64] As in *The Hunt for Red October*, the revelation that the Soviets are ahead of the United States technologically sets off a flurry of activity. In this case, the Soviets' brutal past comes back to haunt them. Under the protection of the CIA is a member of the Afghan mujahedeen, a former math teacher, who has lost his wife and child in a jet attack during the Soviet occupation of Afghanistan. He leads a raid that destroys the Soviet's main research facility, a loss that, combined with the theft of secrets by Filitov, sets up the Soviet Union to be overtaken by the United States.

Notwithstanding Clancy's exaggeration of how far along the Soviet missile-defense program was, he captured the significant concern about it in the Reagan administration. Kenneth deGraffenreid, the NSC director for intelligence programs, believed previous administrations "had not given enough attention to what the Soviets were doing in strategic defense."[65] He meant not just missile defense but also the ability to disrupt U.S. command and control of strategic weapons. Studies in the wake of Able Archer revealed a number of vulnerabilities, and the NSC worried that Soviets might have gained access to the American ICBM launch and control networks.[66] A 1983 White House screening of the movie *Wargames* led Reagan to second that concern. In the movie a young hacker breaks into U.S. strategic systems and nearly launches the nation's arsenal. Reagan asked the Joint Chiefs shortly afterward whether what the movie showed could happen. Taken aback by the unexpected question and its unlikely source, the chiefs could not answer but promised to investigate. They returned to tell Reagan the problem was "worse than you can possibly imagine" and pledged to work on a solution.[67]

Reagan was also convinced the Soviets were subverting the restrictions of the ABM Treaty and were well along in developing their own missile-defense system. This belief also led him to doubt that the Soviet Union was actually deterred by the logic of MAD but rather intended to upend the strategic balance they claimed to uphold.[68] Failure to match or exceed their progress could allow a Soviet first strike. Intelligence reports did provide evidence of Soviet research activity. Shultz's and Weinberger's October 1985 joint report "Soviet Strategic Defense Programs," a declassified glimpse at the subject for the American public, identified a four-part "Soviet Approach" to missile defense. The report alleged the Soviets sought first the "destruction and disruption of the West's nuclear associated command, control and communications."

Then the Soviets would destroy American weapons before launch and, third, attempt the "interception and destruction of surviving weapons" while in flight.[69] Finally, they would improve the protection of their own key personnel and infrastructure.

The bulk of the report focused on the third objective, the interception and destruction of in-flight missiles. Research was ongoing at Pechora in northern Russia, Krasnoyarsk in Siberia, and Sary Shagan in Kazakhstan on radars for tracking and on directed-energy weapons.[70] However, even as late as 1989 the most advanced site, at Sary Shagan, was still able to track only satellites, not missiles. American scientists who visited the location doubted the systems there would ever be viable as ABM weapons.[71] The secretaries' report painted a darker picture. It claimed an alternate site in Kazakhstan already successfully tested interceptor missiles that could destroy a satellite and that these would soon be repurposed to destroy missiles.[72] Shultz and Weinberger used this dubious claim to justify both U.S. research to balance Soviet capabilities and accusations of hypocrisy to Moscow.

Reagan echoed these arguments in a radio address a week after the report's release. He stated the Soviets employed over ten thousand scientists and engineers in their strategic-defense program, a scale that obliged Americans to "realize that our SDI research program is crucial to maintain the military balance and protect the liberty and freedom of the West." He predicted the United States would "welcome the day when the Soviet Union can shoot down any incoming missile"—if, in a key caveat, the United States could do the same. Reagan's vision was of replacing MAD with a "balance of safety" that was "not only morally preferable [but] may result in getting rid of nuclear weapons altogether."[73]

That all of this happened a month before Reagan's first meeting with Gorbachev suggests that it was part of an attempt to shape the agenda of the upcoming summit in Geneva. There SDI was a frequent topic; Gorbachev flatly denied the accusations of the report but hedged that "both of us do research in space of course." He declared that Soviet research was solely for peaceful purposes, in an ironic echo of Reagan's own claims about SDI. Throughout the summit Gorbachev acknowledged Reagan's vision for missile defense "on a human level" but as the leader of the competing great power "could not possibly agree" to allow the American research—and echo of what he had told Vice

President Bush during their first meeting following the funeral of Konstantin Chernenko, Gorbachev's predecessor. The new general secretary had railed against SDI, fearing a "scientific and technological revolution" that the Soviets could not duplicate but that "could set in motion irreversible and uncontrollable processes."[74] The official opinion of the USSR would remain that SDI would start an extraterrestrial arms race.

Soviet military leadership framed their own research differently. During the Reykjavík summit the chief of the Soviet General Staff, Marshal of the Soviet Union Sergei Akhromeyev, admitted to Poindexter that the sites in Kazakhstan were conducting research into missile defense. He and others at the highest levels of the Soviet military "had such high regard for US technology and research and development" that they were certain if the United States pursued SDI it would succeed. The exchange convinced Poindexter that their objections were not tied to the ABM Treaty but rather fear of a technological breakthrough that the Soviets lacked the resources and expertise to match.[75] Accordingly, at Reykjavík, Reagan pledged "to share the benefits of SDI" with them, hoping the offer would "ensure that the Soviets understood [the United States was] not interested in a first strike capability." The United States "would share the fruits of [its] research" freely as a matter of its own self-interest—if "everyone had access to the relevant technology it would be a threat to no one," and there would be no incentive to launch a first strike certain to fail.[76]

However, as Poindexter later reflected, "the Soviets didn't believe us" and had found it far too risky to concede the point when they "couldn't really be assured that [the United States] would share the technology."[77] Certainly, there was little reason for the Soviet leadership to see the offer as genuine. SDI would be massively expensive and advanced, and the Reagan administration had been aggressively preventing any military technology from Soviet hands. However, Reagan was in fact sincere. In internal meetings he stated his desire "simply [to] make all the information available about each other's systems." SDI was for him an essential step to abolishing nuclear weapons, and if giving away advanced technology was the price, he was willing to pay it, once the United States had achieved conventional superiority. During a 1987 National Security Planning Group meeting, Reagan predicted that "someday people are going to ask why we didn't do something now about getting rid of nuclear weapons." He associated them with Armageddon, prophesied by the biblical Book of Revelations as the last battle, between good and evil; his recent Bible study on the topic had told him that the "end times" would begin with the destruction "of many cities."[78]

Apocalyptic fears explain why Reagan did not call on the Soviets to end their own research in Iceland. He mentioned to Gorbachev that he believed the Soviets were aggressively violating the ABM Treaty but "did not talk about it much." Instead, Reagan just asked the Soviets to allow the Americans to do the same research without politicking. Gorbachev declared this "not an acceptable request," as a new system would run counter to the narrative that the two sides were about to "start reductions."[79] Since it could not bear a program on the scale of the American one, Gorbachev recognized, the better strategic move for the Soviet Union was to prevent an expensive competition that might not produce usable results for either side.

Weinberger remained concerned about a Russian SDI program long after there was any credible possibility of its bearing fruit. Frustrated by the cuts in military spending during the Clinton administration, he turned to fiction to warn of the danger. Weinberger told Margaret Thatcher of the project, explained that it had come about because the United States let its "defense stagnate," and asked the former prime minister to write the foreword, which she agreed to do.[80] *The Next War*, cowritten with Hoover Institution scholar Peter Schweizer, presented a series of fictional vignettes the authors felt would assist readers to grasp "tough strategic choices."[81] Weinberger hoped that as wargames did for Pentagon analysts and as *Red Storm Rising* had for Reagan, they would provide readers memorable ways to view his preferred policies.

As we have seen, of course, in chapter 4, Weinberger was a longtime believer in the importance of popular fiction. He often reviewed books with a conservative outlook seeking to raise their profile and popularity.[82] One not already noted was William F. Buckley Jr.'s *Mongoose R.I.P.* The author, a conservative icon, was a natural ally of Weinberger, who unsurprisingly gave the book a favorable review. If the book did not depict the CIA of the 1960s in "the best light," it did treat the agency's work as often "critically important and frequently highly dangerous." Weinberger rejoiced that Buckley was "no John LeCarre" [*sic*] who always seemed "to delight in the blunders and weaknesses of the United States and its allies."[83] The review thrilled Buckley, who sent Weinberger flowers in thanks.[84]

With his own *The Next War*, Weinberger sought to become like the authors he admired and tell powerful and relevant stories. In one of the vignettes the Russians continue to research missile defense after the United States abandons it. They unveil the "Magic Chain" in 2006 and, safe from retaliation, launch an invasion of Eastern Europe to reclaim their empire. America is left "naked, unable to retaliate" and must stand by as Russia completes its conquest of all Europe and demands $100 billion each year from the United States, the United Kingdom, and Japan.[85] A crash U.S. program produces two years later a Brilliant Pebbles–style system that, as the story ominously ends, Russian leaders resolve to test with a massive nuclear launch. The vignette was a naked attempt to scare Americans into greater defense spending: the Russian Federation of the mid-1990s could not support such expenditures any more than the Soviet Union had been able to in the eighties. The vignette, and the book in general, was an artless effort to emulate the success of Clancy in building support for an aggressive defense policy.

In fact, the book project consciously sought to evoke Clancy. Weinberger and Schweizer provided him an advance reader's copy and asked for an endorsement they could use. They assured Clancy he could be as effusive as he wanted, since they reserved "the entire back of the dust jacket" for his comments.[86] He did not fill the space, however, sending only a short blurb calling *The Next War* "a well presented and thought-provoking look into an undetermined future."[87] Weinberger also solicited and received prepublication praise from Kissinger ("*The Next War*, through fiction, lays out some chilling but plausible scenarios") and General Vessey, now retired ("An exciting and eminently readable tale to give readers an important civics lesson").[88] However, the praise of neither a former secretary of state and national security advisor nor a well-regarded four-star general, with between them nearly a century of expertise in national security matters, compared to a freelance author with none. Only Clancy's blurb appeared on the dust jacket.[89] He was now, within a decade of his debut, the nation's leading writer of war stories.

The Cardinal of the Kremlin continued Clancy's string of success. It sold more than 1.2 million copies in 1988, the most of any hardcover that year.[90] It also garnered more critical praise than his previous outings. Robert Lekachman, who had also reviewed his previous books for the *New York Times*, upgraded his description of Clancy's writing from "undistinguished prose" only to "workman-like" but also declared the "unmasking of the title's secret agent" to be "as sophisticated an exercise in the craft of espionage" as any he had encountered. The review praised the book for keeping "readers well abreast of current politics" but criticized its open embrace of SDI.[91]

The review, despite its favorable elements, drew the ire of Daniel Graham, who wrote the editors to complain about its "deplorable bit of snide ax-grinding." High Frontier's founder claimed Clancy had made a "very clear and very persuasive case for SDI" and that insinuation that it amounted to "a leaky defense [being] worse than no defense" was tantamount to "censorship of [that is, by] the literati against all books that offend their politics." Graham insisted that Reagan's notion that it would "be better to save lives" was echoed by the central message of *The Cardinal of the Kremlin*, that "defense, not vengeance, [was] the proper function of the military."[92] Lekachman responded that he was "in excellent company of many eminent scientists who oppose the enterprise as a dangerous and expensive scientific fantasy." He also complained of the special access that must have allowed him to explain "esoteric details of lasers, mirrors, satellites, software, and heaven knows what else." The Pentagon had "acted astutely" in granting it but, the reviewer declared, by doing so had acknowledged that "the best defense of Star Wars [was] indeed fictional."[93]

The reviewer's accusation was accurate, as Clancy had received significant access for his research. A *Newsweek* article accompanying the book release trumpeted Clancy's time spent at the National Training Center in Fort Irwin, California, at the Navy bases and activities in Norfolk, Virginia, and in the headquarters of both the FBI and CIA. A Pentagon spokesperson went on record to declare enthusiastically that "everybody's willing to talk to Clancy," since "he's one of the good guys." The article also revealed that Clancy had been given information— the precise coordinates of a Soviet research facility and the number and types of its buildings—that would not only be top secret but require "compartmentalized" access. The author had then contracted a commercial company to take satellite imagery of the location so he could claim his data were in the public domain and fair to use.[94] A more honest defense would have been to cite the Pentagon Papers case, but this would likely have damaged his reputation as one of the good guys.

Pournelle, who traveled with Clancy on one of the research trips, acknowledged that both authors learned things that were classified, to which they should not have had access. They had accordingly rarely discussed technology directly.[95]

Clancy viewed these research excursions as part of "The Great Chain," his information conduit: he could spend time in officers' clubs and elsewhere around
bases to gain material about how the military operated and details of how key
systems worked. Peter Zimmerman, a former arms-control official, argued in
Newsweek that Clancy was "the authorized winked-at way [cleared personnel
have long been trained to resist precisely such approaches] to leak information
that would help the military-procurement budget."[96]

The openness extended to unclassified and nonmilitary systems. As Clancy
researched for *The Cardinal of the Kremlin* the director of the U.S. Information Agency (USIA), Charles Wick, invited him to tour his agency's WorldNet
facility, the hub of a satellite television network that spread American view-
points globally. Clancy later wrote Wick that WorldNet had "the potential to
remake the world" and could represent the "most useful, most cost-effective tool
of American diplomacy."[97] Wick happily forwarded the letter to Reagan, hoping a favorable word from one of the president's favorite authors would lead to
more support for the program.[98] For his part, Clancy included WorldNet in the
book: late in the novel Jack Ryan asks if USIA still has that "global tv operation
going," prompting a response referring to WorldNet as "one hell of a program."[99]
The scene was completely unnecessary to the plot but allowed Clancy to repay a
favor and keep the door open for future access.

Clancy's special access demonstrated the eagerness of government officials
to attempt to shape popular culture in their favor and reinforce positive narratives about their work. Clancy received from this benefits beyond fodder for his
techno-thrillers. That Pentagon officials actively praised him and sought him
out burnished his personal reputation as an expert, which in turn reinforced the
perception of "realism" in his narratives. During publicity tours for *The Cardinal
of the Kremlin*, Clancy enjoyed hinting he would soon work for the Pentagon.
After all, there were "people on the inside who say [he belonged] there." Clancy
would not take just any job, though, it "would have to be something useful."[100]
He let listeners imagine what "useful" would mean, though he certainly hoped
they pictured something high ranking. Actually, the author never seriously considered entering government service once he "hit it big," and there is no evidence
he received an offer that was anything other than polite talk and ego puffery.
However, the public notion that he might do so benefited both himself and the
Reagan and G. H. W. Bush administrations.

Publicly evoking Jack Ryan was a good bet for policy makers, and just as they had with *Red Storm Rising*, members of Congress immediately made use of Clancy's newest book. In a speech deriding opponents of SDI, Robert Dornan entered a recent Clancy *Wall Street Journal* op-ed into the *Congressional Record* and demanded his colleagues take time to "contemplate his analysis."[101] The piece equated opponents of the program with Luddites (referring to early-nineteenth-century English machinery wreckers) and inaccurately claimed that opposition to SDI boiled down to a belief that "it can't be done, because it hasn't been done, and therefore we ought not even try doing it."[102] It pointed to advances in personal computers as proof that issues of processing speed could be overcome.

The speed with which Dornan brought Clancy's article to the House floor is telling—the very day of its publication. Dornan believed it worthwhile to point to the article in debate immediately as a means of showing "expert" support and claiming the implicit popular mandate. That Clancy had no scientific background, official access to the SDI program, or any specific counter to the issues the OTA was likely to raise did not matter. What was important to Dornan was that the novelist shaped the public narrative in a way favorable to his own policy goals. In acting on that belief Dornan played his part in a symbiotic relationship.

Though he never publicly commented on it, probably because it appeared so late in his time in office, Reagan both read and appreciated *The Cardinal of the Kremlin*. However, on the shelves in his postpresidential office Reagan kept forty-four books. The majority were biographies of Reagan and nonfiction books with clear ties to his life such as *The Cubs at Catalina*. Still, when the Reagan Library took possession of the collection its staff found only a single work of fiction, *The Cardinal of the Kremlin*.[103] The book's naked advocacy for SDI and open praise for Reagan tied it to the autobiographical portion of the book collection; its presence on the shelf was testimony to the vast importance of Clancy's work for the former president.

The United States has not brought to life the program of Reagan's imagination. Although there were successful missile-intercept tests in the 2010s and early 2020s, the United States still has not deployed a system of the scale and scope promised in 1983. In its early years the pursuit of SDI both helped and hindered the causes of arms control, nuclear abolition, and peace with the

Soviet Union. Archives in Moscow document the deep concern of Soviet leaders about it.[104] Gorbachev feared the United States might succeed, in which case his nation would lack the economic and technical capacity to respond.[105] His strident efforts to get Reagan to drop SDI reflect this point. Gorbachev also took his case to the American public directly. Following a 1985 interview he conducted with *Time*, American officials recognized that Gorbachev's "primary summit objective [at Geneva] was to kill SDI."[106] At an NSC meeting just before Geneva, Casey assessed that while the CIA could not list everything the Soviets sought to achieve, its analysts were "fairly certain" that Gorbachev's "principal concern at the present time is our SDI program."[107] Gorbachev's concern was how it threatened his domestic agenda. Any new arms race, even for defensive weapons, would interfere with Gorbachev's sweeping economic reforms. It was this economic problem that led him to seek a "sharp improvement of relations with the United States."[108]

In the eyes of the Soviet military SDI reinforced the need to quicken the reaction time of its own strategic systems. Reagan's deployment of Pershing II missiles already reduced to approximately eight minutes the time a Soviet leader had to contemplate options when faced with nuclear war—a vanishingly small time to consider the fate of millions.[109] The lack of time to respond and lack of resources to produce an SDI-like defense led the Soviets to invest in the "Dead Hand," an opportunity for revenge. In the event a U.S. first strike decapitated the USSR—annihilated or isolated its leaders—duty officers in a secret location could launch a missile that, from altitude, would radio orders to the rest of the Soviet arsenal to fire on preselected targets. Unlike SDI, the Dead Hand became operational during the Cold War, with a successful test in 1984 just a year after Reagan announced his vision of a defensive shield.[110]

SDI's strategic success was in forcing Moscow to recognize that it could not compete with the United States without substantial economic reform. It laid bare the financial and technological gaps between the two nations. One of Matlock's pretended memos from Chernyaev to Gorbachev captured this point: the Soviet advisor states that the Soviet investment in space defense was "not enough to buy a year's supply of toilet paper for the Pentagon." Furthermore, it suggested, the U.S. military could see savings by cutting their purchases of "such non-essentials" and giving "everyone a subscription to *Pravda* and [let] them use it the way we do."[111]

Whether the program was feasible did not matter as long as the Soviets believed it was. While this dynamic was not Reagan's intent, it was effective. The vast expense to which the United States went for strategic defense became a feature of the program rather than a flaw, reinforcing Soviet desires to move away from unwinnable arms races and focus on domestic economic conditions. Similar calculations about proxies in Eastern Europe and the war in Afghanistan led to Soviet drawbacks from both zones in the late 1980s. In effect, both actual and projected costs put the United States in a position to win massive concessions in negotiations and shape Europe in its interest. Gorbachev could choose either to compete, and likely fail, or remake the economic basis of his nation. He wisely selected the latter option, though ultimately it too would fail.

In *The Impossible Presidency*, historian Jeremi Suri argues that SDI demonstrated Reagan's leadership through vision and promise rather than detail, his choice of "mission over management."[112] Gil Troy similarly holds that Reagan's "vision represented his keystone contribution to the 1980s";[113] the Reagan administration became a "cultural and political phenomenon" thanks to Reagan's "preference for story-telling over policymaking."[114] Reagan's 1983 SDI speech set off flurries in both political circles and popular culture. His inability to define his vision explicitly to those around him led to disagreement about how seriously he took it. That Reagan could, however, articulate it by means of stories, without specifics, was in many ways a double-edged sword. Relatable parables open to individual interpretation attracted many supporters but diluted the effectiveness of the message itself and opened the door to misdeeds. Not only "policy wonks" could in this environment command arcane detail well enough to influence national strategy. Both supporters and opponents of Reagan's views took advantage of this and increasingly used popular culture in shaping public opinion about strategic issues. The democratization of the debate allowed for greater creativity and imagination but also risked oversimplification of critical issues.

CONCLUSION

INTO THE
SUNSET

Illusions of Clean Endings

lancy's *Clear and Present Danger* contained a surprising acknowledgment: Gen. Colin Powell had supplied the idea for the book.[1] They had met at a Nashville, Tennessee, award ceremony in 1988 and struck up a friendship. Powell later recalled that the two "hit it off right away," as Clancy was "deeply involved in military affairs."[2] Serving at the time as Reagan's national security advisor, Powell appreciated what Clancy's work did for the military, in particular the Navy.[3] He also felt the Army might benefit from the author's work in a similar fashion.

Shortly after the awards ceremony, the two discussed "the work the military was doing in South America to cut the flow of drugs."[4] Powell discussed the challenges of operating in Colombia and the unconventional forces and techniques the United States used to combat the cartels.[5] The conversation led Clancy to expand on his 1983 idea for a novel about a U.S. Coast Guard cutter, the USCG *Panache*, and link it into the Jack Ryan universe.[6] While the *Panache* is important to the novel that resulted, most of the action involves land-based special operations forces—clear evidence of the influence of Powell's advice and insight.

The departure from heavily nautical themes is not the only divergence in *Clear and Present Danger* from Clancy's established "brand." It is a more reflective work than its predecessors and does not advance a uniformly positive narrative about the United States. With *Clear and Present Danger* Clancy clearly struggles to reconcile the revelations of Iran-Contra with his pro-Reagan worldview. As the *New York Times* review noted, "echoes of Iran-Contra are clear and present" throughout the work, as are concerning issues about the military and the drug war.[7] In the novel's acknowledgments Clancy closes by thanking Powell and active-duty personnel who helped his research with a morose wish "that America serve [them] as faithfully as they serve her."[8]

One of the novel's villains is the national security advisor, "Vice Adm. James Cutter," who uses the NSC to run a secret, illegal war against a cartel and takes a vague presidential statement as his license to do so. Threatened with exposure, Cutter betrays the Special Forces teams operating in Colombia, trading their locations to the cartels for promises of "success" in future drug busts. Ryan is able to save a small group of soldiers with the help of a CIA operative, "Mr. Clark." Back in Washington a CIA operative shows Cutter a recording of his deal with the cartels, warns that his arrest is imminent, and suggests the national security advisor "handle things himself—for the good of the service."[9] Cutter commits suicide.

Ryan gets to grandstand in the Oval Office. In stark contrast to the ending of *The Cardinal of the Kremlin*, where Ryan proclaimed how right the president had been, in *Clear and Present Danger* he lambasts the president for the poor management that allowed the illegal operation to occur. He fears it is impossible for him to "be connected with something like this . . . and not be corrupted by it."[10] The president eventually accepts responsibility and intentionally "tanks" his reelection bid to avoid scandal and protect people who believed they had been acting lawfully. Ryan finds some solace in that and concludes the president was "still a man of honor, whatever mistakes he'd made."[11]

Ryan's Oval Office conversation was a thinly veiled representation of Clancy's own struggle. His admiration for Reagan had been evident in both *The Hunt for Red October* and *The Cardinal of the Kremlin*; now he and the nation were stunned by the scale of Iran-Contra's duplicity, immorality, and illegality. In the wake of Reagan's televised apology after the release of the Tower Commission, national approval of his handling of foreign policy plummeted to 33 percent.[12] The scandal nearly doomed his presidency; there was open discussion of impeachment. Reagan's personal standing recovered over time; Americans largely chose to blame others in his administration instead. In his diary, Reagan recorded that the response to his apology was overwhelmingly positive: calls to the White House surged and polls suggested 93 percent of Americans viewed it favorably.[13] He would leave office in January 1989 with a 63 percent approval rating.[14]

Clancy, like many of his fellow citizens, blamed national security advisors Bud McFarlane and John Poindexter. At a 1990 luncheon at the U.S. Naval Academy, Clancy and Poindexter found themselves seated together. Clancy, accurately sensing the former naval officer did not like him, disingenuously assured Poindexter that "Cutter" was not based on him.[15] However, the closeness of Cutter's biography to Poindexter's was inescapable, as was public knowledge of Clancy's penchant for drawing on real-world figures for characters. In fact, Cutter's suicide in the book was likely a reference to McFarlane's recent attempt to overdose on Valium, tormented by "a sense of having failed the country."[16] Poindexter dismissed the writer's protestations of coincidence and believed Clancy both arrogant and insecure.[17] Though Poindexter had indeed engaged in illegal activity, he likely found the implication of Clancy's novel that he would openly trade the lives of American servicemembers for political benefit beyond the pale.

Otherwise, few in 1990 viewed Clancy so negatively. *Clear and Present Danger* continued the author's string of best sellers. Even the departure of Reagan did not dint the popularity of Clancy in the White House, as its next occupant too was a major fan. George H. W. Bush counted *Red Storm Rising* among his favorite books and like Reagan developed a personal relationship with Clancy. Speaking in Baltimore to commemorate the 175th anniversary of "The Star-Spangled Banner," Bush was pleased to have the chance to talk with Clancy. In his speech the president thanked his friend for "the marvelous contribution he's made to our literary world and . . . the national security interests of the United States."[18] A few months later, Bush hosted Clancy in the White House.

In February 1990, Bush personally called the head of the Motion Picture Association of America to request an advance print of the forthcoming film adaptation of *The Hunt for Red October*. At the time the movie's producer was unsure it was ready, but soon a copy went to the White House for a screening.[19] Bush hosted a party to view it, two weeks prior to its theatrical release. Clancy and James Earl Jones attended, along with such high-ranking defense officials as Scowcroft, Powell, Gates, and Inman.[20] The attendance of so many important national security voices showed the continued influence of Clancy's work and its importance to the Bush administration's goals. Although Bush often struggled with the "whole vision thing," Clancy's books aided him in forming one of war as clean and surgical.[21] The stunning, rapid success of the United States in the first Iraq War, broadcast to millions of living rooms as if for entertainment on CNN, promised a future of uncontested U.S. military might and a new world order.

Technical marvels and desert explosions masked the outsourcing of diplomatic and strategic planning of the conflict to the military, a trend that began in the Reagan years and would persist and escalate over the next four decades. Administration officials allowed military leaders to dictate the terms ending the war, with the result that Gen. Norman Schwarzkopf, who led the coalition forces, and his staff at Central Command concluded a peace that left the Iraqi dictator, Saddam Hussein, in place and with significant military power—power that he quickly turned against his own people, slaughtering Kurds and Shia, groups he feared would overthrow him. The peace terms also created an environment that necessitated long-term U.S. military presence in Saudi Arabia and Kuwait, generated a large-scale humanitarian crisis in Iraq, and preconditioned another invasion of Iraq in 2003 and its subsequent occupation. Though the fact was not apparent in 1991, the end of Desert Storm was a spectacular failure of vision and an example of haphazard decision making.

Bush avoided, however, a similarly tempting, easy peace in Europe. His administration greatly disappointed Gorbachev by not aggressively following up on the openings created by Reagan. Instead, it undertook a deliberate, months-long review of U.S.-Soviet policy.[22] Caution was still evident as late as 1991, when Bush warned the Ukrainian parliament against seeking total escape from the Soviet Union, warning, "Freedom is not the same as independence." He further cautioned the legislators that "Americans will not support those who seek independence in order to replace far-off tyranny with local despotism."[23] The speech stunned many in the United States, and the media quickly labeled it the "Chicken Kiev speech."[24] In his memoirs Bush defended it: pushing the Soviet republics to break away, he had feared, would lead to violence on a massive scale.[25] His caution was prudent, and his administration's handling of the events leading to the demise of the Soviet Union on Christmas of 1991 reflected impressive statesmanship. It demonstrated deep cultural understanding, empathy, and deliberate assessment of risk.

These qualities were absent at the end of Desert Storm. The final chapter of Edward Said's *Culture and Imperialism* stridently charges that the apparent fiasco was part of a "cultural war against Arabs." That accusation is inaccurate and overlooks the agency of Hussein and other regional actors, but Said also puts forward another, more persuasive, explanation for this failure of vision and long-term strategy: a crucial change in America's cultural perception of its power. Throughout the conflict, he argues, American officials and the media portrayed it "as a painless Nintendo exercise" and further developed the "image of Americans as virtuous clean warriors" that Reagan and Clancy advanced in the 1980s.[26] Desert Storm was a Clancy novel brought to life, and a Clancy novel never ends poorly for America. The good guys win.

Popular culture eagerly embraced this conceptualization of the war. Companies raced to advertise and sell the war to Americans. T-shirts, patriotic commercials, and even two different sets of collectible trading cards flooded screens and markets.[27] Desert Storm's brevity, the small number of American casualties, and the outpouring of international support it elicited made it tantalizing entertainment for most Americans and promised them an easy future. American technical superiority had turned the conflict from a serious campaign into "a turkey-shoot."[28] Dramatic images of miles upon miles of flaming Iraqi tanks and trucks screamed that Americans should no longer fear the ghost of Vietnam and its aftermath. Interventions from now on would be clean, quick, decisive, and popular with all but villainous, mustache-twirling dictators.

Though he was not president at the time, Reagan was essential to the creation of the spectacle of Desert Storm. It was his beau ideal of war. Throughout his time in office Reagan had portrayed servicemembers as gallant, virtuous, brave, and, if equipped with advanced weapons, unstoppable. They would end the Cold War and release freedom from its beleaguered Western sanctuary at last. Media coverage of Desert Storm seemed to copy Reagan's rhetoric almost verbatim. Melani McAlister argues in *Epic Encounters* that it praised the military as "a microcosm of the US population . . . drawn from small towns and communities around the nation" and embodying the "diversity of the United States."[29] Reagan had spoken in the same way, referring to Michener's "Admiral Tarrant." Reagan's military found superlative people "where we've always found them, in our villages and towns, on our city streets, in our shops, and on our farms."[30] The rhetoric was and is not entirely unfounded. The fact that the American armed forces draw on the breadth of identities and experiences present in the United States constitutes one of its greatest strengths.

Reagan's faith in technology too seemed well founded in the wake of Desert Storm. The war was full of good news for the Pentagon, just as Clancy's *Red Storm Rising* had been. Each of the major conventional weapons programs that had been fielded or expanded during the Reagan years worked nearly flawlessly, giving a decisive edge to U.S. forces. In particular, the Abrams tank proved itself far and away the best in the world at the time. Equivalent Soviet systems (such as the Iraqis operated) could not match it for range or firing rate and could not penetrate its armor. Against the backdrop of the nearly unlimited resources the United States brought into the region before the war and its unchallenged control of the skies, engagements between U.S. systems and those made in the Warsaw Pact played out even more one-sidedly than in a Clancy novel.

Throughout his life, and certainly in his years as president, Reagan saw war and the U.S. military in this manner, through the lens of fiction. One of the lasting legacies of his administration is that long after he left office many Americans still not only saw the military in the same way but drew on the same sorts of stories. He rightly recognized the importance of national will in strategic calculation and succeeded in changing popular narratives about the use of military power. However, these successes were to incentivize future policy makers and the broader population to oversimplify matters of national security. Americans responded with a surge in popular support because Reagan told them they could do their patriotic duty without sacrifice. This assumption further subverted the civil-military dynamic and empowered the military-industrial complex of which Eisenhower, one of Reagan's political mentors, had warned. Increasingly, politicians running for office in later years sought to demonstrate support for the troops without substantive conversation about what that meant. National support for the military thus became a vast but shallow ocean.

In *The New American Militarism*, Andrew Bacevich argues that "no one did more to affirm [Reagan's] military mythology and perpetuate the use of soldiers as political props than did Bill Clinton."[31] Needing to distance himself from his own past declarations of hatred for the military and avoidance of service in Vietnam, Clinton embraced Reagan's rhetoric. In an address unveiling "A New

Covenant for American Security," Clinton shared with pride an episode from his time as governor of Arkansas. He had invited veterans of all wars to take part in a parade and believed it resulted in "Vietnam veterans finally being given the honor they deserved all along."[32] Clinton did not quite agree with Reagan's notion of the nobility of war, but that he now felt compelled to praise publicly the veterans of a war he despised and the service he had disdained in his youth is telling. Anything short would likely have left Clinton unelectable. The politically safe and beneficial course was feel-good, easy rhetoric about "the troops," not discourse about their global employment.

Had wars after Desert Storm continued to unfold like the ones of Reagan's imagination, the drawbacks of his legacy would be less important than they have proved to be. As it is, the three decades after success in the gulf demonstrated that technology in the hands of a free people is not enough to win. American intervention in Somalia failed. Policy makers were unwilling to intervene in Rwanda, fearing a potential quagmire. Actions in concert with NATO in the former Yugoslavia failed to stop ethnic cleansing. A major attack by a foreign actor took place on continental American soil for the first time since 1812. Insurgencies in Iraq and Afghanistan bedeviled troops on the ground, and the wars that festered there, the nation's longest, demonstrated massive failures in strategic thought. Too frequently the United States relied solely on the power of its technology and the training of its soldiers, sparing little or no thought for cultural context. Successive generations of political and military leaders affirmed their belief in Reagan's vision and in the face of failure barely reassessed it at all. Hubristic optimism reigned.

Clinton shared Reagan's love of the Clancy books and his way of employing stories. During the 1992 campaign a *New York Times* profile spoke highly of Clinton's having read Marcus Aurelius and Gabriel Garcia Márquez but dismissed the candidate's love of Clancy and Ludlum as escapism in "grocery store trash." The article also noted that Clinton had recently viewed one of Reagan's favorite movies, *High Noon*, nineteen times. On the trail he demonstrated a "memory for characters, actors, directors, situations, and punchlines" that rivaled Reagan's and was an important part of his charisma and ability to connect with voters.[33] Although there is little evidence that Clinton used narratives in policy making in the same way Reagan did, he did recognize the importance of pop culture in getting messages to broad audiences.

Clinton's admiration of Clancy was not reciprocated. Though the author acknowledged Clinton's personal charm as "like a physical force," he detested the new direction of national security policy and accused Clinton of taking a "shit on the military pretty comprehensively."[34] These feelings likely contributed to Clancy's decision to end his 1994 novel *Debt of Honor* with an attack that kills the president and most of Congress. Being at odds with the president's policies did not negatively affect Clancy's bottom line, however. The media environment Reagan had shaped remained largely intact, and if movies in the 1990s were less bombastic and jingoistic than 1980s films like *Top Gun* and *First Blood Part II*, they largely continued to portray the U.S. military positively. Clancy's own presence expanded greatly. Numerous film adaptations of his works appeared, and his video-game brand became ubiquitous. The label "Tom Clancy's" became shorthand for "realistic," high-tech military adventure.

Clancy's relevance persisted after his death. A March 2018 report from the House Intelligence Committee seeking to clear the Trump campaign of accusations of collusion with Moscow declared that "only Tom Clancy . . . could take this series of inadvertent contacts with each other . . . and weave that into some sort of fictional page turner spy thriller."[35] The Russian embassy in the United States tweeted its agreement, attaching images of the covers of two Clancy novels, *Rainbow Six* and *Debt of Honor*.[36] Prominent use of Clancy as a metaphor showed the author's legacy as a common reference point and underlined the importance of pop culture in political discussion.

Fiction is a powerful tool. It sparks imagination and creates lasting, even permanent impressions. Well-told stories offer vicarious experiences with and of unfamiliar people, places, and systems. Ideally, a good narrative can build empathy and understanding in readers and help them frame complex issues. An immersive story can make an issue seem real just as a dramatic photo or video can. For policy makers it can yield a benefit similar to that of a well-run wargame or tabletop exercise. Both varieties of synthetic experience attempt to arm leaders with foreknowledge of decisions they may need one day to make and of their consequences. They can reduce strategic surprise and allow for creative planning of "branches and sequels" (in the military term of art) to exploit success or respond to failure.

Reagan's use of *Red Storm Rising*, though controversial, fit this mold. It served to reinforce more traditional materials and what he heard from his advisors. The book afforded a creative space in which Reagan could imagine what the next ten years would bring. In the end, Reagan's reading revealed to him an opportunity few others saw. He pursued this vision with aggressive negotiations. While his attempt fell short at Reykjavík, a dam soon burst, with the elimination by the Intermediate-Range Nuclear Forces Treaty of an entire class of nuclear weapons for the first time. Fiction in conjunction with other materials here spurred decision and ultimately successful action. However, the use of fiction in this manner carries significant risk. It is essential that decision makers communicate explicitly and consciously about the lessons they are drawing from narrative. Without clarity and common understanding among subordinate executives, the benefits of stories became dangerous liabilities.

Vision is essential to strategy. Defining what success looks like is a fundamental leadership task, as is sharing and using the vision to broaden support and build consensus. The boldness of Reagan's strategic vision was the greatest strength of his administration. He compellingly argued for a return to the Manichean conceptualization of the Cold War and presented a path for doing so and winning. It oversimplified greatly but resonated with most Americans. While it was not because of Reagan's actions that the Cold War ended, his choices as president were essential to its ending when it did and as peacefully as it did. In that light, Bush's admission of discomfort with the "vision thing" is damning. Despite its capable, prudent statecraft in Europe and the broad coherence of its global objectives, the administration did not offer anything for Americans to understand and get behind. Envisioning, and selling, a national future requires imagination and creativity. It also requires fiction. A good strategy imagines an environment that does not yet exist and identifies ways to make it a reality.

Reagan's uses of fiction provide plenty of examples of the risk. He too often assumed everyone interpreted stories exactly as he did and simply referred to, say, *High Noon* and westerns as shorthand. While the white-hat/black-hat model arguably worked in the 1980s European context, in which Soviet oppression of Eastern Europe contrasted with the broad freedoms of the West, it was appallingly reductionist in Central and South America. Reagan's desire to be "Marshal Kane" against the Sandinistas demonstrated a lack of understanding of the region and rested on racist stereotypes propagated by his source material. It, combined with Reagan's ambiguity, also enabled widespread illegality in his administration. Reagan gave the NSC what amounted to a blank check by using *High Noon* to express what he wanted to happen. Predictably, some took this as license to subvert Congress and support a morally bankrupt group committing horrific violations of human rights.

His primary failure in this regard was indifference to detail. There is no defense for his abdication of oversight over the NSC. It was also a failure of imagination that came from Reagan's intellectual incuriosity about the region. His interest in Russia and Europe led him to read widely about them to understand their peoples and structures; Koestler, Massie, Solzhenitsyn, and others humanized the people beyond the Iron Curtain for Reagan. The empathy that marked his comments about them reflect this reading. He made no such effort with regard to the global South. He viewed that part of the world through the imperialist lens of Kipling and Burroughs and attributed to its peoples the same lack of agency as such people suffered in L'Amour's westerns.

Reagan is hardly the only politician guilty of seeking comforting sources. The period from 1980 to 2020 saw an explosion of sources in both news and popular culture that individuals with a wide variety of outlooks found comforting; the result was the fracturing of common understandings and shared media experiences. The highest-rated television shows of 2020 would have faced cancelation for poor "audience draw" in 1980, and contemporary best sellers would not have cracked the top ten in that era. In many ways this development is positive, in that, for instance, it opens creative spaces to groups previously excluded and creates for all an opportunity to engage with a broader array of experiences. However, only an audience willing to seek out such experiences can reap their benefit. Too frequently, prominent policy makers fall back on the comforting bromides of sources friendly to their respective opinions and rail against countervailing ones. Bad-faith actors refuse to see uncomfortable realities as anything other than "fake," preferring to create (often conspiratorial) narratives reinforcing their own egos and objectives. The result is an often-toxic public discourse and a very real threat of political violence.

The seeds were present in the Reagan administration. While president he enabled many with hateful views, and his own rhetoric often left large parts of the population feeling explicitly excluded by his vision. Though it is difficult to argue it was intentional, Reagan's tone deafness on racial issues and his failure to act in the face of the AIDS crisis represent shortcomings of leadership that made the country poorer. They came from his inability to view the world from the perspective of groups with identities different from his own. The empathy extended to populations behind the Iron Curtain was absent with regard to the LGBTQ community, African Americans, and many others. Also, a desire to avoid conflict meant that egregious slights toward those communities by members of his administration went uncorrected, which suggested tacit approval from the Oval Office. They collectively represent a stain on Reagan's legacy, and the resentment with which many view the former president is understandable.

That he did not intend the divisiveness to which his administration contributed does not absolve Reagan, but it does set him apart from many of his successors. Reagan's rhetoric tended toward building metaphorical bridges and highlighting the importance of others' achievements. Reagan rarely praised himself, frequently preferring to tell jokes at his own expense to engender goodwill from audiences. The modern tendency toward self-aggrandizement, open attacks on unfavorable media, and creation of "alternative facts" reflects conscious attempts to divide and demean the American people. Counterintuitively, fiction and narrative offer together a potential fix. Policy makers who engage broadly and seek diversity in the popular culture they consume themselves will be better able to empathize and build bridges.

Reagan's rhetoric and actions, then, helped create the modern political environment and keep him prominent in contemporary discussions. Somewhat ironically, his legacy receives the same simplification and compression Reagan himself employed when telling stories. He is often cast as either saint or demon, with little middle ground, and presented as a caricature to advance or oppose policy. The continued ubiquity of Reagan's name in political life reflects both his transformative skill as a politician and the importance of his service as president. He entered office intent on improving the position of the United States in the Cold War and on charting a path to win it. While the Cold War did not end during his administration, the United States had effectively won it by the time Reagan left office. This was the case not solely because of Reagan. The miraculously peaceful end of the Cold War came because of the remarkable confluence of farsighted leadership in both countries, the fact that the Soviet Union was on the verge of economic ruin, and courageous resistance by peoples of Eastern Europe. Reagan's administration set conditions in each regard and hastened the end but cannot claim the lion's share of credit.

The administration failed the global South. While much of modern Central and South America now embraces democratic norms, it does so despite, not because of, Reagan. The United States was certainly not the only malign actor in the region, but the disregard for human rights displayed by Cuba, the Sandinistas, and others does not excuse or explain such disregard being shown by the United States. Failure to recognize either local agency or the reasons the local populaces did not see the United States as acting in good faith perpetuated belief in American imperialism and empowered autocrats. These adverse results clearly detract from the overall geopolitical success of the Reagan administration. However, they do not erase the more important successes in Europe— more important because the Cold War represented an existential threat to the United States as Reagan entered office. That threat effectively did not exist when he left it.

A testament to this success came at Reagan's funeral. Gorbachev chose to fly to the District of Columbia to pay final respects to his former counterpart and adversary. While he rejected the notion that the United States won the Cold War, Gorbachev did perceive that Reagan had restored the self-confidence of America. Without this, the end of the conflict would likely have played out far differently. In a poignant moment, the final Soviet leader stood alone next to Reagan's casket and rested his hand on it. When asked why, Gorbachev responded he just "gave him a pat."[37] The fraternal gesture from the leader of the "Evil Empire" attests to the power and reach of Reagan's vision.

Fiction was essential to this vision. Narrative sparked creativity and provided the synthetic experience necessary to the success of Reagan's presidency. It helped define Reagan's conception of the powerful pairing of technology and a free people that worked in the moment. The results of the failure of subsequent leaders to adapt to new circumstances of their times and imagining how they were changing the vision points to a need for their successors to add creativity to their standard and more traditional sources of thought. Fiction cannot be used in a vacuum, and it is not a panacea. However, its purposeful and sustained use can add nuance and empathy to policy and make timely recognition of opportunity more likely. Stories and narrative are necessary to grand strategy and leadership.

NOTES

Introduction

1. Caspar Weinberger, "President Reagan: Mastermind," *Saturday Night Live*, NBC, December 6, 1986.
2. David Stockman, *The Triumph of Politics: Why the Reagan Revolution Failed* (New York: Harper & Row, 1986), 5.
3. Bob Greene, "Triumph of Politics Is a Triumph of Hype," *Chicago Tribune*, May 14, 1986.
4. Michael Kinsley, "In the Land of the Magic Asterisk," *New York Times*, May 11, 1986.
5. Stockman, *Triumph of Politics*, 10.
6. Stockman.
7. George Shultz, *Turmoil and Triumph: My Years as Secretary of State* (New York: Scribner's, 1995).
8. Caspar Weinberger, *Fighting for Peace: Seven Critical Years in the Pentagon* (New York: Warner Books, 1990), 33.
9. Lou Cannon, *President Reagan: The Role of a Lifetime* (New York: Simon & Schuster, 1991), 132.
10. Edmund Morris, *Dutch: A Memoir of Ronald Reagan* (New York: Random House, 1999), xxiii, xxv.
11. Edmund Morris, "Five Myths about Ronald Reagan," *Washington Post*, 4 February 2011.
12. John Patrick Diggins, *Ronald Reagan: Fate, Freedom, and the Making of History* (New York: W. W. Norton, 2007), xvii.
13. Rick Perlstein, *The Invisible Bridge: The Fall of Nixon and the Rise of Reagan* (New York: Simon and Shuster, 2014), xv–xvi.
14. John Lewis Gaddis, *The Cold War: A New History* (New York: Penguin, 2005), 197.
15. Gaddis, 196.
16. Duncan White, *Cold Warriors: Writers Who Waged the Literary Cold War* (New York: HarperCollins, 2014), 14.
17. Christina Klein, *Cold War Orientalism: Asia in the Middlebrow Imagination, 1945–1961* (Berkeley: University of California Press, 2003), 6.

18. Klein, 8.

19. Edward Said, *Culture and Imperialism* (New York: Vintage Books, 1993), 71.

20. Melani McAlister, *Epic Encounters: Culture, Media, & U.S. Interests in the Middle East since 1945* (Berkeley: University of California Press, 2001), 6.

21. Charles Hill, *Grand Strategies: Literature, Statecraft, and World Order* (New Haven, CT: Yale University Press, 2010), 8.

22. Hill, 5.

23. Paul Musgrave and J. Furman Daniel, "Synthetic Experiences: How Popular Culture Matters for Images of International Relations," *International Studies Quarterly* 61, no. 3 (September 2017).

24. Musgrave and Daniel.

25. Draft of Reagan's commencement address at West Point, Folder: West Point Speech and Back Up File (1), Box 8: Speechwriting, White House, Office Of: Research Office, 1981–1989, Ronald Reagan Library.

Chapter 1. Raised on Mars

1. Ronald Reagan, "Farewell Address to the Nation," Washington, DC, January 11, 1989.

2. Draft of Reagan's commencement address at West Point.

3. Draft of Reagan's commencement address at West Point.

4. Vice Adm. John Poindexter, interview with the author, telephone, West Point, NY, August 19, 2017.

5. Stockman, *Triumph of Politics*, 5.

6. Stockman, 308.

7. Anatoly Dobrynin, *In Confidence: Moscow's Ambassador to America's Six Cold War Presidents* (New York: Times Books, 1995), 519.

8. Charles Powell to Colin Budd, October 14, 1986, PREM-19-1759, The National Archives of the United Kingdom, Kew, United Kingdom [hereafter TNA].

9. Charles Powell, Baron Powell of Bayswater to author, email, August 19, 2016.

10. Weinberger, *Fighting for Peace*, 33.

11. Weinberger; Shultz, *Turmoil and Triumph*.

12. Reagan, "Farewell Address to the Nation."

13. Cannon, *Role of a Lifetime*, 293.

14. Ronald Reagan and Richard Hubler, *Where's the Rest of Me?* (New York: Van Rees, 1965), 12.

15. Reagan, *Where's the Rest of Me?* 8.

16. Reagan, *Where's the Rest of Me?* 15.

17. Michael Deaver and Mickey Herskowitz, *Behind the Scenes: In Which the Author Talks about Ronald and Nancy Reagan . . . and Himself* (New York: William Morrow, 1987), 43.

18. Tom Reed, interview with author, Austin, TX, October 16, 2014.

19. Reagan to the Children of Troy, in Rebecca Greenfield, "Ronald Reagan's Letter to the Library and Other Finds from 1971," Theatlantic.com, May 12, 2011.

20. Ronald Reagan to Helen P. Miller, September 3, 1981, in *Reagan: A Life in Letters*, ed. Kiron Skinner, Annelise Anderson, and Martine Anderson (New York: Free Press, 2003), 7.

21. Jerry Griswold, "I'm a Sucker for Hero Worship," *New York Times*, August 30, 1981.

22. Reagan, *Where's the Rest of Me?* 7.

23. Reagan, *Where's the Rest of Me?*

24. Griswold, "I'm a Sucker for Hero Worship."

25. "Dinner Hosted by the Gorbachevs in Geneva, 19 November 1985," Memorandum of Conversation, Reagan-Gorbachev Meetings in Geneva November 1985, National Security Archive, Washington, DC.

26. "Dinner Hosted by the Gorbachevs."

27. Cannon, *Role of a Lifetime*, 42.

28. Griswold, "I'm a Sucker for Hero Worship."

29. Reagan to Miller.

30. Sam Weller, "Ray Bradbury, the Art of Fiction No. 203," *Paris Review*, no. 192 (Spring 2010).

31. Irwin Porges, *Edgar Rice Burroughs* (Provo, UT: Brigham Young University Press, 1975), 49, 65.

32. Porges, 70.

33. Edgar Rice Burroughs, *Princess of Mars* (Chicago: A. C. McClung, 1917).

34. Edgar Rice Burroughs, *The Gods of Mars* (Chicago: A. C. McClung, 1918).

35. Edgar Rice Burroughs, *Warlord of Mars* (Chicago: A. C. McClung, 1919).

36. Burroughs, *Princess of Mars*.

37. Griswold, "I'm a Sucker for Hero Worship."

38. Burroughs, *Princess of Mars*

39. Reagan, *Where's the Rest of Me?* 8.

40. "Address at Commencement Exercises at the United States Air Force Academy," Colorado Springs, CO, May 30, 1984.

41. Cannon, *Role of a Lifetime*, 214.

42. Reagan to Cyndi Davis, undated circa early 1970s, in Skinner, Anderson, and Anderson, *Reagan: A Life in Letters*, 679.

43. Ronald Reagan, "Address to the Nation on the Explosion of the Space Shuttle *Challenger*," Washington, DC, January 28, 1986, *Ronald Reagan Presidential Foundation & Institute*, reaganfoundation.org.

44. Jeremi Suri, *The Impossible Presidency: The Rise and Fall of America's Highest Office* (New York: Basic Books, 2017), 240.

45. Morris, *Dutch*, xii.

46. "Remarks at the National Conference of the Building and Construction Trades Department, AFL-CIO," Washington, DC, March 30, 1981.

47. "Lyn Nofziger Oral History," Miller Center, University of Virginia, March 6, 2003.

48. Ronald Reagan, "11 April 1981," in *The Reagan Diaries*, ed. Douglas Brinkley (New York: HarperCollins, 2007).

49. Ronald Reagan, *An American Life: The Autobiography* (New York: Simon & Schuster, 1990), 269.

50. Ronald Reagan to Jean B. Wright, March 13, 1984, in Skinner, Anderson, and Anderson, *Reagan: A Life in Letters*, 6.

51. Lawrence Tagg, *Harold Bell Wright: Storyteller to America* (Tucson, AZ: Westernlore, 1986).

52. Harold Bell Wright, *That Printer of Udell's* (Chicago: Book Supply, 1903), 11, 14.

53. Wright, 19.

54. Reagan, *Where's the Rest of Me*, 13.

55. Wright, *That Printer of Udell's*, 315.

56. Wright, 319.

57. Morris, *Dutch*, 40.

58. Reagan to Wright, 6.

59. Griswold, "I'm a Sucker for Hero Worship."

60. Ronald Reagan, "A Time for Choosing," televised speech, October 27, 1964.

61. Ronald Reagan, "Address to the National Association of Evangelicals," Orlando, FL, March 8, 1983.

62. Diggins, *Fate, Freedom, and the Making of History*, 14.

63. Diggins.

64. Reagan tells two slightly different versions of the story, in one the score being 0–0, in the other 3–3. On the basis of a combing of the pitch-by-pitch tracker on baseballreference .com, the game he describes was played on April 24, 1935, the only instance during Reagan's time at WHO in which the Cubs and Cardinals entered the ninth tied with Dean pitching.

65. Reagan, *Where's the Rest of Me?* 64.

66. "Cubs–Pirates," *Chicago Cubs Baseball*, WGN, September 30, 1988.

67. "Cubs–Pirates"; Reagan to Buzzy Sisco, December 24, 1985, in Skinner, Anderson, and Anderson, *Reagan: A Life in Letters*, 33.

68. James Clarity and Warren Weaver, "Briefing: Reagan at the Bat," *New York Times*, October 2, 1984.

69. In 2016 the Cubs won the World Series, ending a 108-year streak without a championship. Go Cubs Go!

70. Reagan, *Where's the Rest of Me?* 49.

71. Reagan, *Where's the Rest of Me?* 50. Reagan actually failed to make the block, thereby nearly costing his team the game.

72. Reagan, *Where's the Rest of Me?*

73. Morris, *Dutch*, 112.

74. Reagan to Paul Loyet, circa September 1968, in Skinner, Anderson, and Anderson, *Reagan: A Life in Letters*.

75. Reagan, *Where's the Rest of Me?* 72.

76. Reagan, *Where's the Rest of Me?* 117.

77. Kate Smith's rendition is played during the "seventh-inning stretch" at all home Yankees games.

78. Skinner, Anderson, and Anderson, *Reagan: A Life in Letters*, 132.

79. Timothy Snyder, *Bloodlands: Europe between Hitler and Stalin* (New York: Basic Books, 2010), 411.

80. Skinner, Anderson, and Anderson, *Reagan: A Life in Letters*, 132.

81. The purges of the Great Terror killed over 750,000 and decimated the senior leaders of the Red Army. By purging them Stalin removed any serious contender to his power but also left the Soviets at a significant military disadvantage at the start of the war.
82. Stephen Whitfield, *The Culture of the Cold War* (Baltimore, MD: Johns Hopkins University Press, 1991), 127–28.
83. Morris, *Dutch*, 542–43.
84. Jack Matlock, *Reagan and Gorbachev: How the Cold War Ended* (New York: Random House, 2005), 6.

Chapter 2. Friendly Witness

1. "Daily Diary of President Ronald Reagan," entry for December 12, 1983, Reagan Library [hereafter Daily Diary, [date]).
2. Ronald Reagan, "Remarks at the Annual Convention of the Congressional Medal of Honor Society in New York City," New York City, NY, December 12, 1983.
3. "Remarks at the Annual Convention of the Congressional Medal of Honor Society."
4. "Remarks at the Annual Convention of the Congressional Medal of Honor Society."
5. A number of pilots and crew members did receive Medals of Honor for refusing to bail out of planes when others were too wounded to do so with them: Maj. Horace Carswell, Maj. Donald Pucket, 1st Lt. Donald Gott, and Sgt. Archibald Mathies. However, in each case the citation is for an attempt to make an emergency landing, implying an intent to save the wounded crew member rather than to share his death. Similarly, there are citations for pilots who gave their parachutes to wounded comrades: 2nd Lt. David Kingsley and 2nd Lt. William Metzger. In the case of Kingsley, the plane was in extremis when he gave up his parachute. Metzger attempted, unsuccessfully, to crash-land.
6. Cannon, *Role of a Lifetime*, 59.
7. Ronald Reagan, "Commencement Address at William Woods College," in *Echoes from the Woods*, June 1952, Ronald Reagan Subject Collection, Box 1, Hoover Institution Archives.
8. Reagan, "Time for Choosing."
9. Diggins, *Fate, Freedom, and the Making of History*, 15.
10. Abraham Lincoln, "Annual Address to Congress," Washington DC, 1 December 1862, available at https://www.presidency.ucsb.edu/documents/second-annual-message-9.
11. Thomas Paine, *Common Sense; Addressed to the Inhabitants of America*, [...] (London: H. D. Symonds, 1792).
12. Ronald Reagan to Otis Carney, November 1979, in Skinner, Anderson, and Anderson, *Reagan: A Life in Letters*, 259
13. Ronald Reagan, "Address Accepting the Nomination at the Republican National Convention in Detroit," Detroit, MI, 17 July 1980.
14. Steven Hayward, *The Age of Reagan: The Conservative Counterrevolution, 1980–1989* (New York: Three Rivers, 2009), 13.
15. Diggins, *Fate, Freedom, and the Making of History*, xviii–xix.
16. Diggins, 2.

17. Reagan, *Where's the Rest of Me?* 311.
18. T.M.P., "An Old Picture from Warners," *New York Times*, June 11, 1949.
19. Reagan, *Where's the Rest of Me?* 175.
20. Ronald Reagan to Fred F. Fielding, March 4, 1985, in Skinner, Anderson, and Anderson, *Reagan: A Life in Letters*, 133.
21. "Hold Your Hats, Boys," *Time*, October 7, 1946.
22. *Jurisdictional Disputes in the Motion-Picture Industry: Hearings before a Special Subcommittee of the Committee on Education and Labor*, House of Representatives, 80th Cong., 1st Sess., 1990 (1948).
23. *Jurisdictional Disputes in the Motion-Picture Industry*, 1973.
24. *Jurisdictional Disputes in the Motion-Picture Industry*, 1977.
25. Peter Schweizer, *Reagan's War: The Epic Story of His Forty-Year Struggle and Final Triumph over Communism* (New York: Doubleday, 2002), 9.
26. *Communist Activities among Professional Groups in the Los Angeles Area*, Part 1, *Hearings before the House Un-American Activities Committee*, House of Representatives, 82nd Cong., 2nd Sess., 2450 (1952).
27. "Hold Your Hats, Boys."
28. Reagan, *Where's the Rest of Me?* 155.
29. Reagan.
30. *Communist Infiltration of the Motion Picture Industry, Hearings before the House Un-American Activities Committee*, House of Representatives, 80th Cong., 1st Sess. (1947).
31. Reagan, *Where's the Rest of Me?* 165.
32. Reagan.
33. Dalton Trumbo, "The Oscar Syndrome," *Playboy*, April 1960.
34. Ronald Reagan to Hugh Hefner, July 4, 1960, in Skinner, Anderson, and Anderson, *Reagan: A Life in Letters*, 148.
35. Schweizer, *Reagan's War*, 18.
36. Arthur Koestler, *The God That Failed* (New York: Harper & Row, 1949), 44.
37. Koestler, *God That Failed*, 57.
38. Koestler, *God That Failed*, 68.
39. Arthur Koestler, *Darkness at Noon* (London: Macmillan, 1940) 3.
40. Koestler, *Darkness at Noon*, 43.
41. Koestler, *Darkness at Noon*.
42. Koestler, *Darkness at Noon*, 244.
43. J. Arch Getty and Oleg Naumov, *The Road to Terror: Stalin and the Self-Destruction of the Bolsheviks, 1932–1939* (New Haven, CT: Yale University Press, 2010), 227.
44. Getty and Naumov, *Road to Terror*, 227.
45. Nikoli Bukharin to Josef [Joseph] Stalin, December 10, 1947, in Getty and Naumov, *Road to Terror*, 220.
46. Morris, *Dutch*, 291.
47. Richard English, "What Makes a Hollywood Communist?" *Saturday Evening Post*, May 19, 1951, 30–31.
48. English.

49. Reagan, *Where's the Rest of Me?* 163.

50. Lee Zhito, "Picture Business," *Billboard*, June 16, 1951, 2.

51. Koestler, *Darkness at Noon*, 5.

52. Kenneth deGraffenreid, interview with author, telephone, West Point, NY, September 5, 2017; David Anderson, "Chambers' MD Farm Rejected as Landmark," *Washington Post*, April 27, 1988.

53. Bruce Craig, "Whittaker Chambers' Pumpkin Patch," *Washington Post*, May 22, 1988.

54. Craig.

55. Ronald Reagan, "Remarks at the Conservative Political Action Conference Dinner," Washington DC, March 20, 1981.

56. Reagan, "Address to the National Association of Evangelicals."

57. Thomas Reed, *The Reagan Enigma, 1964–1980* (Los Angeles: Figueroa, 2014), 13.

58. Whittaker Chambers, *Witness* (New York: Regnery History, 1952), 101.

59. Chambers, 49; Sam Tanenhaus, *Whittaker Chambers: A Biography* (New York: Modern Library, 1998), 44.

60. House Committee on Un-American Activities, *Investigation of Communist Espionage Activities* (Washington, DC: U.S. Government Printing Office, August 25, 1948), 571.

61. Christopher Andrew and Vasili Mitrokhin, *The Sword and the Shield: The Mitrokhin Archive and the Secret History of the KGB* (New York: Basic Books, 1999), 134.

62. Tanenhaus, *Whittaker Chambers*, 461.

63. Tanenhaus, 463.

64. Reagan, *Where's the Rest of Me?* 152.

65. Reagan, 185.

66. Chambers, *Witness*, 358.

67. Chambers, 358, 701.

68. Chambers, 358.

69. Reagan to Heffner.

70. Reagan, *Where's the Rest of Me?* 268.

71. Reagan, 271.

72. Reagan, 270.

73. Ronald Reagan, "Are Liberals Really Liberal?" draft speech circa 1962, Ronald Reagan Subject Collection, Box 1, Hoover Institution Archives.

74. Reagan, *Where's the Rest of Me?* 270.

75. "Transcript of a 1948 Radio Broadcast," Ronald Reagan Subject Collection, Box 1, Hoover Institution Archives.

76. Chambers, *Witness*, introduction.

77. Reagan, "Commencement Address at William Woods College."

78. Paul Kengor, *God and Ronald Reagan: A Spiritual Life* (New York: Harper Collins, 2004), 80.

79. Reed, interview.

80. Ronald Reagan, *U.S. National Security Strategy*, National Security Decision Directive [hereafter NSDD] 32 (Washington, DC: White House, May 20, 1982).

81. Chambers, *Witness*, foreword.

82. Chambers.

83. Chambers.

84. Kengor, *God and Ronald Reagan*, 85.

85. Dobrynin, *In Confidence*, 527.

86. Dobrynin, 477, 480.

87. Reagan, "Address to the National Association of Evangelicals."

88. Reagan, "Address to the National Association of Evangelicals."

89. William Inboden, *Religion and Foreign Policy, 1945–1960: The Soul of Containment* (Cambridge, UK: Cambridge University Press, 2008), 4.

90. Tanenhaus, *Whittaker Chambers*, 470, 509.

91. Ronald Reagan, "Remarks at the Presentation Ceremony for the Presidential Medal of Freedom," March 26, 1984.

92. "Remarks at the Presentation Ceremony for the Presidential Medal of Freedom."

Chapter 3. Cowboy Values

1. "Richard Nixon and Ronald W. Reagan on 26 October 1971," Conversation 013-008, *Presidential Recordings Digital Edition* [*Nixon Telephone Tapes: 1971*, ed. Ken Hughes] (Charlottesville: University of Virginia Press, 2014–), available at http://prde.upress.virginia.edu/conversations/4002192.

2. Andrew Bacevich, *The New American Militarism: How Americans Are Seduced by War* (Oxford, UK: Oxford University Press, 2013), 106.

3. Reed, interview.

4. Thomas Reed, *The Reagan Enigma, 1964–1980* (Los Angeles: Figueroa Press, 2014), 248.

5. "Remarks at the Presentation Ceremony for the Presidential Medal of Freedom."

6. Ronald Reagan, "Remarks at a White House Barbecue for the Professional Rodeo Cowboy Association," September 24, 1983.

7. James Barron, "Louis L'Amour, Writer, Is Dead; Famed Chronicler of West Was 80," *New York Times*, June 13, 1988.

8. Louis L'Amour, *Education of a Wandering Man* (New York: Bantam Books, 1990), chap. 1.

9. Barron, "Louis L'Amour, Writer, Is Dead."

10. L'Amour, *Education of a Wandering Man*; Meyer Berger, "Painter Relives Tragic Parting Each Year at Station Door: L'Amour from West," *New York Times*, February 14, 1955.

11. Louis L'Amour, "The Gift of Cochise," *Colliers*, July 5, 1952.

12. Michael Marsden, "Louis L'Amour's *Hondo*: From Literature to Film to Literature," *Literature Film Quarterly* (January 1999).

13. Louis L'Amour, *Hondo* (1953; repr. New York: Bantam Books, 2016).

14. L'Amour, *Hondo*, 26.

15. L'Amour, *Hondo*, 179.

16. Reagan, *Where's The Rest of Me?* 204.

17. Reagan, *Where's the Rest of Me?* 279.

18. Ronald Reagan to Dr. and Mrs. Norman Sprague Jr., August 13, 1984, in Skinner, Anderson, and Anderson, *Reagan: A Life in Letters*.

19. "Remarks at a White House Barbecue for the Professional Rodeo Cowboy Association."

20. John Miller, "Western Civ," *National Review*, May 4, 2009.

21. Hayward, *Age of Reagan*, 561.

22. Ronald Regan to Earl Smith, June 29, 1979, in Skinner, Anderson, and Anderson, *Reagan: A Life in Letters*, 488.

23. Diggins, *Fate Freedom, and the Making of History*, 257.

24. "Issue Paper Prepared in the Bureau of Intelligence and Research," January 30, 1981, in U.S. State Dept., *Foreign Relations of the United States* [hereafter *FRUS*] *1981–1989*, vol. 3, *Soviet Union, January 1981–January 1983*, ed. James Graham Wilson (Washington, DC: Office of the Historian, 2016).

25. "Minutes of a National Security Council Meeting," February 6, 1981, in *FRUS 1981–1989*, vol. 3.

26. Charles Hill, interview with author, telephone, West Point, NY, April 3, 2016.

27. Ronald Reagan to LtGen Victor Krulak, USMC (Ret.), March 11, 1985, in Skinner, Anderson, and Anderson, *Reagan: A Life in Letters*, 503.

28. Prescott Bush Jr. to William Casey, April 5, 1984, in Personal Papers of William J. Casey, Box 321, Hoover Institution Archives, Stanford, CA.

29. William Casey to Prescott Bush Jr., July 9, 1984, in The Personal Papers of William J. Casey, Box 321, Hoover Institution Archives, Stanford, CA.

30. "October 16, 1981," in Brinkley, *Reagan Diaries*, 44.

31. "National Security Council Meeting: Strategy toward Cuba and Central America," *The Reagan Files*, November 10, 1981, thereaganfiles.com.

32. John Poindexter, interview with the author, Skype, West Point, NY, August 19, 2017.

33. Poindexter, interview.

34. Weinberger, *Fighting for Peace*, 353.

35. Ronald Reagan, "Address to the Nation on Iran-Contra," Washington, DC, March 4, 1987.

36. David Rosenbaum, "Iran-Contra Hearings: Poindexter Says He Withheld Iran-Contra Link from Reagan; Testimony Gratifies President; Admiral on Stand," *New York Times*, July 16, 1987.

37. Ronald Reagan, "Address to the Nation on the Iran Arms and Contra Aid Controversy and Administration Goals," Washington, DC, August 12, 1987.

38. Colin Powell, with Joseph E. Persico, *My American Journey* (New York: Random House, 1995), 334.

39. Ronald Reagan to Laurence Beilenson, in Skinner, Anderson, and Anderson, *Reagan: A Life in Letters*, 471.

40. Ronald Reagan, "Address before a Joint Session of the Congress on the State of the Union," Washington, DC, February 6, 1985.

41. Whitfield, *Culture of the Cold War*, 149.

42. James Michener, *The Bridges at Toko-Ri* (New York: Fawcett Books, 1952), 126.

43. Hedda Hopper, "Looking at Hollywood: An Empty Camera Slices Ham Off an Egotistical Film Actor," *Chicago Tribune*, April 8, 1953; "Lash of Fear," *General Electric Theater*, NBC, October 16, 1955.

44. Ronald Reagan, "Address at the Commencement Exercises at the United States Military Academy," May 27, 1981.

45. "Reagan Country: The Ronald Reagan Presidential Foundation Member Newsletter," July 2012, *Ronald Reagan Presidential Foundation & Institute*, reaganfoundation.org, accessed July 7, 2017.

46. Rudyard Kipling, "If," 1910.

47. Rudyard Kipling, "The White Man's Burden: Or the United States in the Philippines."

48. Ronald Reagan, "Remarks to Administration Officials on Domestic Policy," Washington, DC, December 13, 1988.

49. "Airisms from the Four Winds," *Flight*, January 20, 1921.

50. Hannah Arendt, *The Origins of Totalitarianism* (New York: Harcourt, Brace, 1951), 208–9.

51. Arendt, 208, 211.

52. Ronald Reagan, "Rhodesia and Majority Rule," March 4, 1977, Ronald Reagan Subject Collection, Box 9, Hoover Institution Archives, Stanford, CA.

53. Ronald Reagan, "Reprint of a Radio Program Entitled Rhodesia," Ronald Reagan Subject Collection, Box 9, Hoover Institution Archives, Stanford, CA.

54. "December 7, 1984," in Brinkley, *Reagan Diaries*, 285.

55. Ronald Reagan to Pieter Botha, January 4, 1986, *Margaret Thatcher Foundation*, margaretthatcher.org.

56. Ronald Reagan, "South Africa and Apartheid," Washington, DC, July 23, 1986.

57. Peggy Noonan, *When Character Was King: A Story of Ronald Reagan* (New York: Viking, 2001), 34.

58. Noonan.

59. Michener, *Bridges at Toko-Ri*, 36.

60. Michener, 35, 38.

61. Michener, 123.

62. Ronald Reagan, "Remarks on Presenting the Medal of Honor to Master Sergeant Roy P. Benavidez," Arlington, VA, February 24, 1981.

63. Weinberger, *Fighting for Peace*, 52.

64. Robert Pear, "Veteran Pleads Case to Congressmen," *New York Times*, June 21, 1983.

65. Ronald Reagan, "Statement on Armed Forces Day," Washington, DC, May 16, 1981; Ronald Reagan, "Radio Address to the Nation on Armed Forces Day," Washington, DC, May 15, 1982.

66. Ronald Reagan, "Remarks at a White House Ceremony Honoring Hispanic Americans in the United States Armed Forces," September 16, 1983, Washington, DC.

67. Klein, *Cold War Orientalism*, 125–26.

68. Daniel Inouye, "James A. Michener," *Congressional Record–House*, September 17, 1962.

69. Klein, *Cold War Orientalism*, 125.

70. Michener, *Bridges at Toko-Ri*, 75.

71. Michener, *Bridges at Toko-Ri*, 79.

72. James Michener, "Bald Eagle of the *Essex* has Wings Clipped: Four Narrow Escapes Are Called Enough," *Chicago Tribune*, February 6, 1952.

73. Michener, "Bald Eagle of the Essex has Wings Clipped," 8.

74. Michener, *Bridges at Toko-Ri*, 68.

75. Reagan, "Commencement Address at William Woods College."
76. Michener, *Bridges at Toko-Ri*, 58.
77. Kipling, "If."
78. H. W. Brands, *Reagan: The Life* (New York: Doubleday, 2015), 154.
79. Ronald Reagan to Mark Hatfield, May 5, 1980, Ronald Reagan Subject Collection, Box 3, Hoover Institution Archives.
80. Bacevich, *New American Militarism*, 108.
81. Reagan, "Commencement Address at William Woods College."
82. Ronald Reagan, "Do Your Kids Belong to Uncle Sam?" February 13, 1979, Ronald Reagan Subject Collection, Box 9, Hoover Institution Archives.
83. Bacevich, *New American Militarism*, 108.

Chapter 4. Up from the Depths

1. Reagan "Address at the Commencement Exercises of the United States Military Academy."
2. Reagan, "United States Military Academy."
3. Reagan, "United States Military Academy."
4. "May 27, 1981," in Brinkley, *Reagan Diaries*, 21.
5. Memorandum, Caspar Weinberger, memorandum to Ronald Reagan, April 17, 1981, Folder: "West Point Speech and Back Up File (1)," Box 8: Speechwriting, White House Office Of: Research Office, 1981–1989, Ronald Reagan Library.
6. Draft of Reagan's Commencement address at West Point.
7. Representative Dana Rohrabacher, interview with author, telephone, West Point, NY, July 18, 2017.
8. Hill, interview.
9. Rohrabacher, interview.
10. Reagan to Frank McCarthy, March 10, 1970, in Skinner, Anderson, and Anderson, *Reagan: A Life in Letters*, 151.
11. Gil Troy, *Morning in America: How Ronald Reagan Invented the 1980s* (Princeton, NJ: Princeton University Press, 2005), 11.
12. Ernest Marshall, letter to Michael Deaver, September 3, 1982, Folder: NCAA Football Halftime Address, Box 66: Speechwriting, White House Office of: Research Office, 1981–1989, Ronald Reagan Library.
13. Marshall to William Sadler, October 6, 1982, Folder: NCAA Football Halftime Address, Box 66: Speechwriting, White House Office of: Research Office, 1981–1989, Ronald Reagan Library.
14. "Presidential Taping: Salute to Veterans for NCAA Football Halftime November 8, 1982," Folder: NCAA Football Halftime Address, Box 66: Speechwriting, White House Office of: Research Office, 1981–1989, Ronald Reagan Library.
15. McAlister, *Epic Encounters*, 252.
16. William Hogan, "A Bookman's Notebook: Clark Kerr Speaks on the University," *San Francisco Chronicle*, October 30, 1963.

17. Ronald Reagan to Allen Drury, July 15, 1981, in Skinner, Anderson, and Anderson, *Reagan:* in *Ronald Reagan: A Life in Letters*, 284.

18. Phil Gailey and Warren Weaver, "Briefing: Weinberger's Faith," *New York Times*, August 23, 1982.

19. Allen Drury to Caspar Weinberger, January 5, 1984, Box 600, Papers of Caspar Weinberger, Library of Congress.

20. Allen Drury, *Pentagon* (New York: Doubleday, 1986), afterword.

21. Weinberger to Drury, February 9, 1984; Drury to Weinberger, April 12, 1984; Weinberger to Drury, April 24, 1984.

22. Drury, *Pentagon*, 583.

23. Larry Bond and Chris Carlson, interviews with the author, Springfield, VA, October 20–21, 2014.

24. Tom Clancy to Larry Bond, February 19, 1982, personal papers of Larry Bond.

25. Representative William Broomfield to Max Friedersdorf, March 17, 1981, White House Office of Records Management [hereafter WHORM] Subject File: Public Relations, PR 005-01 008386-018157, Box 37, Ronald Reagan Library.

26. Tom Clancy to Susan Richards, March 8, 1985, personal papers of Larry Bond.

27. Bond, interview.

28. Gregory Young, "Mutiny on the *Storozhevoy*: A Case Study on Dissent in the Soviet Navy," master's thesis, Naval Postgraduate School, March 1982, 29. The author later expanded the thesis into a book with coauthor Nate Braden: *The Last Sentry: The True Story that Inspired the Hunt for Red October*, published by the Naval Institute Press in 2013.

29. Clancy to Richards, February 5, 1983.

30. Robert Andrews, "'Tugboat' Surprises the Battleships of New York Publishing Industry," Associated Press, March 11, 1985.

31. Deborah Grosvenor, interview with author, Austin, TX, November 11, 2014.

32. Andrews, "'Tugboat.'"

33. Grosvenor, interview.

34. Clancy to Richards, February 5, 1983.

35. Clancy to Richards, November 1, 1984.

36. John Alden, "Bookshelf: The Cold War at 50 Fathoms," *Wall Street Journal*, October 22, 1984.

37. Richard Setlowe, "Adrift with Subplots," *Los Angeles Times*, December 28, 1984.

38. Scott Dance and Justin George, "Tom Clancy 82M Estate Focus of Tussle between Widow, Lawyer," *Baltimore Sun*, September 18, 2014.

39. Clancy to Richards, February 5, 1985.

40. Reed, interview.

41. Kenneth Adelman, interview with the author, Austin, TX, January 19, 2017.

42. Grosvenor, interview; Patricia Blake, "One of Their Subs Is Missing: An Insurance Broker's Novel Has the White House Reading," *Time*, March 4, 1985, http://content.time.com/.

43. Adelman, interview.

44. DeGraffenreid, interview.

45. Blake, "One of Their Subs Is Missing"; Edwin McDowell, "Publishing: Doing Right by a Book," *New York Times*, March 22, 1985.

46. Clancy to Richards, March 8–19, 1985.

47. "March 13, 1985," in Brinkley, *Reagan Diaries*, 308.

48. Clancy to Richards, March 8–19, 1985.

49. Tom Clancy, letter to Ronald Reagan, March 14, 1985, WHORM Subject File: Public Relations, PR 005-01 008386-018157, Box 37, Ronald Reagan Library.

50. Rohrabacher, interview.

51. Tom Clancy, *The Hunt for Red October* (Annapolis, MD: Naval Institute Press, 1984).

52. Clancy, 102.

53. Clancy, 197.

54. Clancy, 45.

55. Alden, "Cold War at 50 Fathoms."

56. Bond, interview.

57. Reagan to George, undated draft, in Skinner, Anderson, and Anderson, *Reagan: A Life in Letters*, 150.

58. Bacevich, *New American Militarism*, 111.

59. "August 13, 1982," in Brinkley, *Reagan Diaries*, 150.

60. "June 29, 1985," in Brinkley, *Reagan Diaries*, 477.

61. "Reagan Gets Idea from Rambo for Next Time," *Los Angeles Times*, June 1, 1985.

62. President Reagan talking to actor Sylvester Stallone with his wife Sasha Czack and Joan Clark during a White House party and showing of the film *Victory* in the Red Room, photograph, July 24, 1981, Ronald Reagan Library, C3215-6, Ronald Reagan Library; President and Nancy Reagan posing with actor Sylvester Stallone and Brigette Nielsen during a state dinner for Prime Minister Lee Kuan Yew of Singapore, photograph, October 8, 1985, C31323-10.

63. Bond, interview.

64. Clancy, *Hunt for Red October*, 96.

65. Clancy, 140–41, 184.

66. Shultz, *Turmoil and Triumph*.

67. Clancy to Richards, March 8–19 1985.

68. *The Hunt for Red October*, film, directed by John McTiernan, Paramount.

69. Cannon, *Role of a Lifetime*, 293.

70. Rohrabacher, interview.

71. Ronald Reagan, "First Inaugural Address," January 20,1981, Washington, DC.

72. Rohrabacher interview.

73. Reagan, "First Inaugural Address."

74. Reagan, "Remarks on Presenting the Medal of Honor."

75. Mark Lawrence, "Policymaking and the Uses of the Vietnam War," in *The Power of the Past: History and Statecraft*, ed. Hal Brands and Jeremi Suri (Washington, DC: Brookings Institution, 2015).

76. Ronald Reagan, "Peace: Restoring the Margins of Safety," Chicago, IL, August 18, 1980.

77. Ronald Reagan to Mr. and Mrs. Elwood Wagner, April 23, 1971, in Skinner, Anderson, and Anderson, *Reagan: A Life in Letters*, 771.

78. Reagan to the Wagners.

79. Clancy, *Hunt for Red October*, 44.
80. Clancy, 58.
81. Clancy, 37.
82. Adm. Bobby Inman, interview with author, Austin, TX, November 2015.
83. Clancy, *Hunt for Red October*, 102.
84. Clancy, 309.
85. Clancy, 309.
86. Ronald Reagan, "Address at the Commencement Exercises of the United States Naval Academy," Annapolis, MD, May 22, 1985.
87. "May 22, 1985," in Brinkley, *Reagan Diaries*, LOC 10781.
88. Hill, interview.
89. Ronald Reagan, "Remarks on the Signing of the Intelligence Identity Protection Act," Langley, VA, June 23, 1982.
90. DeGraffenreid, interview.
91. Clancy, *Hunt for Red October*, 272.
92. Hill, interview.
93. Dobrynin, *In Confidence*, 477.
94. "Memorandum from Secretary of Defense Weinberger to the Counselor to the President (Meese)," March 17, 1981, in *FRUS 1981–1988*, vol. 3, Document 30, 83.
95. Reagan, "First Inaugural Address."
96. Carnes Lord, memorandum to Richard Allen, April 27, 1981, Folder: "West Point Speech and Back Up File (1)," Box 8: Speechwriting, White House Office of: Research Office: Records, 1981–1989, Ronald Reagan Library.
97. Ronald Reagan, "Address at Commencement Exercises at the University of Notre Dame," South Bend, IN, May 17, 1981.
98. John Paul II, *Dives in Misericordia*, November 30, 1980.
99. John Paul II, *Dives in Misericordia*; Reagan, "Address at Commencement Exercises of the University of Notre Dame."
100. Ronald Reagan, "Address to British Parliament," London, UK, June 8, 1982.
101. Gail Yoshitani, *Reagan on War: A Reappraisal of the Weinberger Doctrine, 1980–1984* (College Station: Texas A&M University Press, 2012), 11.
102. Clancy, *Hunt for Red October*, 26.
103. Clancy, 33.
104. Chambers, *Witness*.
105. Lee Zhito, "Picture Business," *Billboard* June 16, 1951, 2.
106. Clancy, *Hunt for Red October*, 18.
107. Bacevich, *New American Militarism*, 117.
108. Grosvenor, interview.
109. Reagan, "Address at Commencement Exercises at the United States Air Force Academy."
110. NSDD-32.
111. "Draft Study Prepared by the Policy Planning Staff," in *FRUS 1981–1988*, vol. 3, Document 13.

112. "Action Memorandum from the Assistant Secretary of State–Designate for European Affairs (Eagleburger) and the Director of the Bureau of Political and Military Affairs (Burt) to Secretary of State Haig," March 16, 1981, in *FRUS 1981–1988*, vol. 3, Document 28, 96.

113. Ronald Reagan, *U.S. Relations with the USSR*, NSDD 75 (Washington, DC: White House, January 17, 1983).

114. Reagan, "Address at Commencement Exercises at the United States Air Force Academy."

115. Memorandum, "U.S. Foreign Policy: A Look Ahead," May 18, 1984, Folder: Foreign Policy Background for President's Trip to Europe, Notebook (1 of 2), RAC Box 8, NSC Executive Secretariat: Trip File, Ronald Reagan Library.

116. Clancy to Richards, March 1985.

117. Grosvenor, interview.

118. Clancy to Richards, March 1985.

119. Clancy, *Hunt for Red October*, 176.

120. Clancy, 211, 213.

121. Rohrabacher, interview.

122. Jeremy Treglown to Caspar Weinberger, August 9, 1985, Box 596, Papers of Caspar Weinberger, Library of Congress.

123. Kay Liesz to Caspar Weinberger, August 14, 1985, Box 596, Papers of Caspar Weinberger, Library of Congress.

124. Caspar Weinberger, review of *The Hunt for Red October*, by Tom Clancy, *Times Literary Supplement*, October 18, 1985.

125. Caspar Weinberger, review of *Patriot Games*, by Tom Clancy, *Wall Street Journal*, August 5, 1987.

126. Robert Ludlum, *The Bourne Supremacy* (New York: Random House, 1986).

127. Caspar Weinberger, review of *The Bourne Supremacy*, by Robert Ludlum, *Wall Street Journal*, Caspar Weinberger Papers, Library of Congress.

128. Clancy to Richards, March 1985

129. Bacevich, *New American Militarism*, 116.

130. Robert Merry, "Tom Clancy and Ronald Reagan," *National Interest*, October 3, 2013.

131. Clancy to Richards, March 1985.

132. *Rambo: First Blood Part II*, film, directed by George Cosmatos, TriStar Pictures, 1985.

133. Perlstein, *Invisible Bridge*, 117.

134. *Rocky IV*, film, directed by Sylvester Stallone, United Artists, 1985. In the movie, Creed embraces Cold War rhetoric before his death, arguing that his bout means something because "it's us against them" and promising that Rocky will understand its importance when it is over.

135. *Back to the Future*, film, directed by Robert Zemeckis, Universal Pictures, 1985.

136. John Lehman, *Oceans Ventured: Winning the Cold War at Sea* (New York: W. W. Norton, 2018), 90.

137. *Top Gun*, film, directed by Tony Scott, Paramount, 1986.

Chapter 5. Techno-Thriller Rising

1. Margaret Thatcher to Ronald Reagan, October 13, 1986, PREM-19-1759, TNA.
2. "Prime Minister's Talk with President Reagan," October 13, 1986, PREM-19-1759, TNA.
3. Powell to Budd.
4. Powell to author.
5. Powell to Budd.
6. Ken Adelman, *Reagan at Reykjavik: Forty-Eight Hours That Ended the Cold War* (New York: Broadside Books, 2014), 12.
7. Poindexter, interview.
8. Cannon, *Role of a Lifetime*, 294.
9. Adelman, interview.
10. "Remarks to American Military Personnel and Their Families in Keflavik, Iceland" Keflavik, Iceland, October 12, 1986.
11. Rohrabacher, interview.
12. "Memorandum of Conversation," 12 October 1986 in *FRUS*, vol. 5, *Soviet Union, March 1985–1986*, ed. Elizabeth Charles (Washington, DC: U.S. Government Printing Office, 2020), Document 308.
13. Briefing Book, "Selected National Security Issues," December 1985, Folder: Selected National Security Issues December 1985 [Copy 1], RAC Box 9, NSC Executive Secretariat: Trip File, Ronald Reagan Library.
14. Judith Miller, "Reagan Endorses Rise in Atomic Warheads by 380 over Carter Goal," *Washington Post*, March 22, 1982.
15. Matlock, *Reagan and Gorbachev*, 78
16. Weinberger, *Fighting for Peace*, 334.
17. Hill, interview.
18. Special Meeting of Foreign and Defense Ministers, Brussels Belgium, December 12, 1979.
19. "Address to the National Press Club on Arms Reduction and Nuclear Weapons," Washington, DC, November 18, 1981.
20. Reagan to Rumsfeld, October 26, 1979,
21. "Reprint of a Radio Program Entitled 'SALT,' Commentary by Ronald Reagan," Ronald Reagan Subject Collection, Box 8, Hoover Institution on War Revolution and Peace, Hoover Institution Archives.
22. "Reprint of Radio Program Entitled 'Neutron Bomb II,' Commentary by Ronald Reagan," Ronald Reagan Subject Collection, Box 8, Hoover Institution on War Revolution and Peace, Hoover Institution Archives.
23. Mary Thornton, "45% in Poll Say Chance of Nuclear War on the Rise," *Washington Post*, March 24, 1982.
24. Ronald Reagan, "Radio Address to the Nation on Congressional Inaction on Proposed Legislation," August 11, 1984.
25. Alan Moore and Dave Gibbons, *Watchmen* (New York: DC Comics, 1986).
26. Frank Miller, *The Dark Knight Returns* (New York: DC Comics, 1986).

27. Theodore Seuss, *The Better Butter Battle* (New York: Random House, 1984).

28. Gloria Goodall, "From Dr Seuss, an Arms Race Allegory about Yooks and Zooks," *Christian Science Monitor*, March 2, 1984.

29. Betty Jean Lifton, "Children's Books," *New York Times*, February 26, 1984.

30. John Corry, "The Day After: TV as a Rallying Cry," *New York Times*, November 20, 1983.

31. David Hoffman and Lou Cannon, "ABC's 'The Day After,'" *Washington Post*, November 18, 1983.

32. Jack Matlock, interview by author, tape recording, Austin, TX, September 23, 2014.

33. "October 10, 1983" and "November 16, 1983," in Brinkley, *Reagan Diaries*, 186, 199.

34. Margot Henriksen, *Dr. Strangelove's America: Society and Culture in the Atomic Age* (Berkeley: University of California Press, 1997), 51.

35. *The Day the Earth Stood Still*, film, directed by Robert Wise, 20th Century Fox, 1951.

36. Ronald Reagan, "Radio Address to the Nation on the Tricentennial Anniversary Year of German Settlement in America," June 25, 1983.

37. Cannon, *Role of a Lifetime*, 42, 251.

38. Paul Lettow, *Ronald Reagan and His Quest to Abolish Nuclear Weapons* (New York: Random House, 2005), xi.

39. Lettow, 3–5.

40. Lettow, 23.

41. Adelman, interview.

42. James Graham Wilson, *The Triumph of Improvisation: Gorbachev's Adaptability, Reagan's Engagement, and the End of the Cold War* (Ithaca, NY: Cornell University Press, 2014).

43. Reagan, "Time for Choosing."

44. Carl von Clausewitz, *On War*, ed. and trans. Michael Howard and Peter Paret (Princeton, NJ: Princeton University Press, 1976), chap. 1, sec. 4.

45. Dwight Eisenhower, "Crusade for Freedom Speech," Denver, CO, September 4, 1950, available at http://latimesblogs.latimes.com/washington/2010/09/labor-day-speech-ike-eisenhower-1950.html.

46. Reagan Ronald. "Crusade for Freedom," Radio Free Europe Advertisement, circa 1950s, available at https://www.youtube.com/watch?v=SVy1K_xX5pg.

47. Reagan, "Address to British Parliament."

48. R. W. Apple, "President Urges Global Crusade for Democracy" *New York Times*, June 9, 1982.

49. William Inboden, "Grand Strategy and Petty Squabbles," in *The Power of the Past: History and Statecraft*, ed. Hal Brands and Jeremi Suri (Washington, DC: Brookings Institution Press, 2016), 168.

50. U.S. Army Dept., *Operations*, Field Manual [FM] 100-5 (Washington, DC: U.S. Government Printing Office, 1976), 1–5. The title of this field manual is often given as *Active Defense*.

51. John Romjue, *From Active Defense to AirLand Battle: The Development of Army Doctrine 1973–1982* (Washington, DC: U.S. Government Printing Office, 1984), 19.

52. Romjue, 36.

53. Poindexter, interview.

54. Harold Brown to Zbigniew Brzezinski, memorandum, April 30, 1979, in *Harold Brown: Offsetting the Soviet Military Challenge, Documentary Supplement*, Office of the Secretary of Defense, ed. Edward Keefer (Washington, DC: Historical Office, 2017), 802, 803.

55. "Memorandum from the Counselor-Designate of the Department of State (McFarlane) to the Director-Designate of Policy Planning (Wolfowitz)," in *FRUS 1981–1988*, vol. 3, Document 13; Eagleburger and Burt to Secretary of State Haig.

56. NSDD-32.

57. Ronald Reagan, "Address at Commencement Exercises at Eureka College," Eureka, IL, May 9, 1982.

58. David Fouquet, "NATO's Own Comparison with Warsaw Pact Strength Puts East Ahead," *Christian Science Monitor*, May 5, 1982.

59. Joseph Luns, *NATO and Warsaw Pact Force Comparison: 1982* (Brussels, BE: NATO Information Service, 1982), foreword. The start date of 1962 for the period of neglect likely was chosen to embrace many reasons for the decline. The Vietnam War, U.S. disengagement with Europe, domestic European discontent with the Cold War, and Soviet buildup and aggressiveness all played roles.

60. "National Security Council Meeting on Theater Nuclear Forces Negotiation Timing," April 30, 1981, Washington, DC, Ronald Reagan Library.

61. Jack Nelson, "Reagan Urges Nuclear Freeze: But Only after U.S. Catches Up with Russia," *Los Angeles Times*, April 1, 1982.

62. Ronald Reagan, "The President's News Conference," Washington, DC, March 31, 1982.

63. "Memorandum of Conversation," October 12, 1986, WHORM Subject File: FO006-11, Ronald Reagan Library.

64. John Poindexter, memorandum to Ronald Reagan, "Why We Can't Commit to Eliminating All Nuclear Weapons within 10 Years," October 16, 1986, RAC Box 3, Alton Keel Files, Ronald Reagan Library.

65. Poindexter, interview.

66. Transcript, "JCS Meeting with the President," December 19, 1986, Folder: JCS Response–NSDD 250, December 19, 1986 (1 of 4), RAC Box 12, Robert Linhard Files, Ronald Reagan Library.

67. Ronald Reagan, *Post-Reykjavik Follow-Up*, NSDD 250 (Washington, DC: White House, November 3, 1986).

68. Caspar Weinberger to Ronald Reagan, memorandum "Post-Reykjavik Activities: NSDD 250," December 5, 1986, Folder: JCS Response–NSDD 250, December 19, 1986 (1 of 4), RAC Box 12, Robert Linhard Files, Ronald Reagan Library.

69. Richard Nixon and Henry Kissinger, "A Real Peace," *National Review*, May 22, 1987, 34.

70. James Mann, *The Rebellion of Ronald Reagan: A History of the End of the Cold War* (New York: Penguin Books, 2009), 47; Bartholomew Sparrow, *The Strategist: Brent Scowcroft and the Call of National Security* (New York: PublicAffairs, 2015), 550.

71. George Will, ". . . Another Ten Divisions . . . ," *National Review*, May 22, 1987.

72. Charles Wick to John Poindexter, memorandum, "SDI and INF Dominate Revitalized Strategic Debate in Post-Reykjavik Europe," October 17, 1986, Folder: Post-Iceland (3 of 4), RAC Box 2, Alton Keel Files, Ronald Reagan Library.

73. "Reykjavik Summit, French Reaction," October 3, 1986, PREM-19-1759, TNA.

74. "Reykjavik: Initial German Reactions," October 14, 1986, PREM-19-1759, TNA.

75. Sir Anthony Acland, cable to Foreign Ministry, October 18, 1986, PREM-19-1759, TNA.

76. Washington to London, diplomatic cable, October 30, 1986, PREM-19-1759, TNA.

77. Tom Clancy, *Red Storm Rising* (New York: Putnam's Sons, 1986), 32, 34.

78. John Hackett, *The Third World War: August 1985* (New York: Macmillan, 1978), 138

79. Stephen Webbe, "World War III: A Novel Warning," *Christian Science Monitor*, August 7, 1980.

80. Adam R. Seipp, "Visionary Battle Scenes: Reading Sir John Hackett's *The Third World War, 1977–85*," *Journal of Military History* 83, no. 4 (October 2019).

81. "Paperback Best Sellers: Trade," *New York Times*, June 1, 1980.

82. Hackett, *Third World War*.

83. Ronald Reagan to the *Baltimore Sun*, June 26, 1984, in Skinner, Anderson, and Anderson, *Reagan: A Life in Letters*, 285.

84. Reagan, "Address at the Commencement of Eureka College."

85. Briefing Book, "Selected National Security Issues."

86. Adelman, interview.

87. Odd Arne Westad, *The Cold War: A World History* (New York: Hachette Books, 2017), 6.

88. Jeffrey Engel, *When the World Seemed New: George H. W. Bush and the End of the Cold War* (Boston: Houghton Mifflin Harcourt, 2017), 53.

89. Westad, *Cold War*, 523.

90. Central Intelligence Agency, "A Comparison of Warsaw Pact and NATO Defense Activities, 1976–86," *Freedom of Intelligence Act Electronic Reading Room*, 1987, 4, v.

91. Briefing Book, "Selected National Security Issues."

92. "Comparison of Warsaw Pact and NATO Defense Activities, 1976–86," vi.

93. Briefing Book, "Selected National Security Issues."

94. "National Security Council Meeting: Soviet Defense and Arms Control Objectives," November 30, 1984, Washington, DC, Ronald Reagan Library.

95. Robert Lekachman, "Virtuous Men and Perfect Weapons," *New York Times*, July 27, 1986.

96. Clancy, *Red Storm Rising*, 329, 332.

97. Romjue, *From Active Defense to AirLand Battle*, 45.

98. Bond and Carlson, interviews.

99. Reagan, "Address at Commencement Exercises at the United States Air Force Academy."

100. Acland to Foreign Ministry, 20.

101. "Wednesday, April 8, 1987," in Brinkley, *Reagan Diaries*.

102. Poindexter, interview.

103. Acland to Foreign Ministry, 20.

104. "Memorandum of Conversation between General Secretary Yuri Andropov and Averell Harriman," June 2, 1983, Moscow, USSR, *National Security Archive*, https://nsarchive.gwu.edu/document/17311-document-11-memorandum-conversation-between.

105. Dobrynin, *In Confidence*, 523.

106. Jeane Kirkpatrick, "Comments to the UN General Assembly, New York City, September 5, 1983," *New York Times*, September 7, 1983, available at https://www.nytimes.com/1983/09/07/world/transcript-of-kirkpatrick-address-on-korean-airliner-to-security-council.html.

107. Ronald Reagan, "Address to the Nation on the Soviet Attack on a Korean Civilian Airliner," September 5, 1983.

108. Nate Jones, "Able Archer Electronic Briefing Book," *National Security Archive*, n.d., https://nsarchive2.gwu.edu/NSAEBB/NSAEBB427/#_ftn1.

109. U.S. Military Airlift Command, "Reforger 83\Crested Cap 83\Display Determination 83\Autumn Forge 83 After Act Report," *National Security Archive*, December 8, 1983, https://nsarchive.gwu.edu/project/able-archer-83-sourcebook.

110. "Unpublished Interview with former Soviet Head of General Staff Marshal Sergei Akhromeyev," *National Security Archive*, January 10, 1990, https://nsarchive.gwu.edu/project/able-archer-83-sourcebook.

111. Simon Miles, *Engaging the Evil Empire: Washington Moscow and the Beginning of the End of the Cold War* (Ithaca, NY: Cornell University Press, 2020), 81.

112. Wilson, *Triumph of Improvisation*, 78.

113. Greg Myre, "Stanislav Petrov, 'The Man Who Saved the World,' Dies at 77," *National Public Radio*, September 18, 2017

114. Miles, *Engaging the Evil Empire*, 81

115. The President's Foreign Advisory Board, "The Soviet War Scare," *National Security Archive Electronic Briefing Book*, February 15, 1990, https://nsarchive.gwu.edu/project/able-archer-83-sourcebook.

116. Ronald Reagan, *American Life*, 588–89.

117. Ronald Reagan diary entry for June 14, 1984, available at https://nsarchive.gwu.edu/project/able-archer-83-sourcebook.

118. Ronald Reagan, "Address to the Nation and Other Countries on United States–Soviet Relations," January 16, 1984.

119. Reagan, "Address to the Nation and Other Countries on United States–Soviet Relations."

120. Matlock, interview.

121. Reagan, "Address to the Nation and Other Countries on United States–Soviet Relations."

122. Reagan, "Address to the Nation and Other Countries on United States–Soviet Relations."

123. Matlock, interview. Matlock was preceded in this position by Richard Pipes, an academic who took a much harder line with regard to the Soviet Union.

124. Matlock, interview.

125. Matlock, *Reagan and Gorbachev*, 195.

126. Mock memorandum from Soviet Foreign Policy Assistant Chernyayev [*sic*] to Soviet Secretary General Gorbachev, June 9, 1986, in *FRUS 1981–1988*, vol. 5, 983.

127. Suzanne Massie, *Trust but Verify: Reagan, Russia, and Me* (Rockland: Maine Authors, 2013), 99.

128. Massie, 165–66.

129. Mann, *Rebellion of Ronald Reagan*, 64.

130. Bond, interview.

131. Clancy, *Red Storm Rising*.

132. Clancy, *Red Storm Rising*, 88.

133. Anton Chekhov, "The Cherry Orchard," in *Plays*, trans. Elisaveta Fen (London: Penguin, 1954). The American strategist George Kennan was a reader of Chekhov and often spoke of a more genuine "Chekhovian self" in his own personality.

134. Ezra Vogel, *Deng Xiaoping and the Transformation of China* (Cambridge, MA: Belknap of Harvard University Press, 2013).

135. Ronald Reagan, "Address at Moscow State University," Moscow, USSR, May 31, 1988.

136. Reagan had read Aleksandr Solzhenitsyn's *Gulag Archipelago* and *A Day in the Life of Ivan Denisovich* but would likely have argued that these works, and Pasternak's *Doctor Zhivago* as well, were exceptions that proved the rule, given the postpublication treatment of the authors.

137. Ronald Reagan, "Address from the Brandenburg Gate," West Berlin, Federal Republic of Germany, June 12, 1987.

138. Mann, *Rebellion of Ronald Reagan*, 185.

139. Mann, 181.

140. Jack Matlock, *Superpower Illusions: How Myths and False Ideologies Led America Astray—and How to Return to Reality* (New Haven, CT: Yale University Press, 2010).

141. Memorandum, "U.S. Foreign Policy: A Look Ahead," May 18, 1984, Folder: Foreign Policy Background for President's Trip to Europe–Notebook (1 of 2), RAC Box 8, NSC Executive Secretariat: Trip File, Ronald Reagan Library.

142. John Cole, interview with Margaret Thatcher, BBC, December 17, 1984.

143. Poindexter, interview.

144. Ronald Reagan to Jesse Zeeman in Skinner, Anderson, and Anderson, *Reagan: A Life in Letters*, 538.

145. Bernard Weinraub, "Wiesel Confronts Reagan on Trip; President to Visit Bergen-Belsen; Survivor of Holocaust Urges Him Not to Stop at German Cemetery," *New York Times*, April 20, 1985.

146. Ronald Reagan to Colonel Barney Oldfield, in Skinner, Anderson, and Anderson, *Reagan: A Life in Letters*.

147. "Friday, November 30, 1984," in Brinkley, *Reagan Diaries*.

148. Mann, *Rebellion of Ronald Reagan*, 185.

149. Reagan, "Commencement Address at Eureka College,"

150. Clancy, *Red Storm Rising*, 284.

151. Clancy, *Red Storm Rising*, 330.

152. Clancy, *Red Storm Rising*, 82.

153. Bond, interview.

154. Matlock, interview.

155. Bond, interview.

156. Robert Pear, "For the Patient Reader, Military Secrets are Self-Revealing," *New York Times*, August 30, 1987.

157. Central Intelligence Agency, "Employee Bulletin, No. 1341," February 12, 1986, and "Memorandum for Mr. Casey," February 24, 1986, *Freedom of Information Act Electronic Reading Room,* https://www.cia.gov/readingroom/.

158. Clancy to Richards, February 5, 1985.

159. Clancy to Richards, March 8, 1985.

160. Bond, interview.

161. *Hearings on National Defense Authorization Act for Fiscal Year 1990: H.R. 2461 and Oversight of Previously Authorized Programs* (Washington, DC: U.S. Government Printing Office, 1990), 333–35.

162. Bond, interview.

163. Bond, interview.

164. Bond, interview.

165. Peter Perla, interview with author, notes, October 23, 2014, Arlington, VA. Perla still works with the CNA, where he is referred to as the "Peyton Manning of war gaming."

166. Perla, interview. For further reading on wargaming and its value see Matthew B. Caffrey Jr., *On Wargaming,* Newport Paper No. 43 (Newport, RI: Naval War College Press, 2019), available at https://digital-commons.usnwc.edu/usnwc-newport-papers/44/ [sic].

167. Newt Gingrich, "National Defense Authorization Act for Fiscal Year 1987," *Congressional Record,* August 13, 1986, 21173.

168. Clancy, *Red Storm Rising,* 484.

169. Gingrich, "National Defense Authorization Act for Fiscal Year 1987."

170. Thomas Downey, "National Defense Authorization Act for Fiscal Year 1987," *Congressional Record* August 13, 1986, 21174.

171. Walter Hixson, "*Red Storm Rising*: Tom Clancy Novels and the Cult of National Security," *Diplomatic History* 17, no. 4 (October 1993).

172. Peter Osterlund and Donald Rheem, "Quayle: Wide Appeal but Untried on National Stage," *Christian Science Monitor,* August 18, 1988.

173. Lisa Belkin, "Quayle Discards His Script on Military Issues and Raises Eyebrows," *New York Times,* September 9, 1988.

174. Bond, interview.

175. Paul Musgrave and J. Furman Daniel, "Synthetic Experiences: How Popular Culture Matters for Images of International Relations," *International Studies Quarterly* 61, no. 3 (September 2017).

176. Clancy to Richards, February 5, 1985.

177. "OPS Session 2—*Red Storm Rising*: A Case Study," U.S. Naval War College, Personal Papers of Larry Bond.

178. "OPS Session 2."

179. "Best Sellers," *New York Times,* August 3, 1986, and August 24, 1986; Edwin McDowell, "Author of 'Hunt for Red October' Stirs Up a 'Red Storm,'" *New York Times,* August 12, 1986.

180. *The Books of the Century: 1980–1989,* http://www.ocf.berkeley.edu/~immer/books1980s.

181. Bond, interview.

182. Wilson, *Triumph of Improvisation,* 11.

183. Poindexter, interview.

184. Acland to Foreign Ministry.

185. Wilson, *Triumph of Improvisation*, 111.

186. Matlock, *Reagan and Gorbachev*, 209.

Chapter 6. Pebbles from Space

1. Ronald Reagan, "Address to the Nation on Defense and National Security," Washington, DC, March 23, 1983.

2. Reagan, "Address to the Nation on Defense and National Security."

3. Robert McFarlane, draft memorandum to Bud Clark, March 22, 1983, Folder 15, Box 73, William P. Clark Papers, Hoover Institution Archives.

4. Shultz, *Turmoil and Triumph*.

5. DeGraffenreid, interview.

6. Poindexter, interview.

7. Poindexter, interview.

8. Strobe Talbott, "The Risks of Taking of Shields," *Time*, April 4, 1983.

9. David Alpern, David Martin, Mary Lord, and William Cook, "A New Nuclear Heresy," *Newsweek*, April 4, 1983.

10. Sparrow, *Strategist*, 228.

11. Alpern, Martin, Lord, and Cook, "Nuclear Facts, Science Fictions."

12. David Alpern, "Nuclear Facts, Science Fictions," *New York Times*, March 27, 1983.

13. Hayward, *Age of Reagan*, 297.

14. Alpern, "Nuclear Facts, Science Fictions."

15. Lou Cannon, "President Seeks Futuristic Defense against Missiles," *Washington Post*, March 24, 1983.

16. Reagan to LtGen V. H. Krulak, February 4, 1985, in Skinner, Anderson, and Anderson, *Reagan: A Life in Letters*, 122.

17. Morris, *Dutch*, xii.

18. Reagan, "Address at Commencement Exercises at the United States Air Force Academy."

19. Larry Niven, email, West Point, NY, August 15, 2017.

20. Jerry Pournelle, interview with author, Skype, West Point, NY, August 19, 2017.

21. Pournelle, interview.

22. Niven, email.

23. Pournelle, interview.

24. Pournelle, interview; Niven, email.

25. Pournelle, interview.

26. Rohrabacher, interview.

27. Pournelle, interview; Reagan, "Address to the Nation on Defense and National Security."

28. Pournelle, interview.

29. Pournelle, interview.

30. Thomas Disch, *On SF* (Ann Arbor: University of Michigan Press, 2005), 211.

31. Jerry Pournelle and Dean Ing, *Mutual Assured Survival* (New York: Baen Books, 1985).

32. Disch, *On SF*, 211.

33. "Paperback Best Sellers: May 18, 1986," *New York Times*, May 18, 1986.

34. Pournelle, interview.

35. Pournelle, interview; Niven, email.

36. Gerald Jones, "Science Fiction," *New York Times*, September 8, 1985.

37. Niven, email.

38. Arthur C. Clarke, "On Golden Seas," in *The Collected Stories of Arthur C. Clarke* (New York: Macmillan, 2002), 935–37.

39. William Patterson, *Robert Heinlein: In Dialogue with His Century*, vol. 2, *The Man Who Learned Better* (New York: Macmillan, 2014), 446.

40. Neil McAleer, *Arthur C. Clarke: The Authorized Biography* (New York: McGraw-Hill, 1992), 325.

41. Arthur C. Clarke, "1992: What Is to Be Done?," *Bulletin of Atomic Scientists*, May 1992, available at https://thebulletin.org/.

42. McAleer, *Arthur C. Clarke*, 325.

43. Isaac Asimov, *I, Asimov: A Memoir* (New York: Random House, 1995)

44. Marjorie Hunter and Warren Weaver Jr., "Briefing: Science Fiction," *New York Times*, August 2, 1985.

45. William Broad, "Sci-Fi Writers Speak Up over Real-Life 'Star Wars,'" *Chicago Tribune*, March 21, 1985.

46. Isaac Asimov, "Out of the Everywhere," in *Out of the Everywhere: Thoughts on Science From the Master* (New York: Doubleday, 1990), 29.

47. Michael Ashley, *Science Fiction Rebels: The Story of the Science-Fiction Magazines from 1981–1990* (Liverpool, UK: Liverpool University Press, 2016), 213.

48. Robert Heinlein, *The Cat Who Walks through Walls* (New York: Putnam's Sons, 1985)

49. Daniel Graham, *High Frontier: There Is a Defense against Nuclear War* (New York: Tor Books, 1984); Martin Morse Wooster, "Questioning Authority," *National Review*, September 8, 2014.

50. Robert Heinlein, quoted in Graham, 7–8.

51. Jerry Pournelle, quoted in Graham, 13.

52. Tom Nugent, "Daniel Graham: Sheriff of the 'High Frontier,'" *Washington Times*, November 1, 1983.

53. Newt Gingrich, David Drake, and Marianne Gingrich, *Window of Opportunity: A Blueprint for the Future* (New York: Tor Books, 1984)

54. David Streitfield, "The Speaker Also Writes," *Washington Post*, June 12, 1995.

55. Pournelle, interview. There remains considerable controversy in the sci-fi community about what constitutes "real" science fiction and about the role of military science fiction. A vocal minority known alternatively as the "Sad (or Rabid) Puppies" sought repeatedly to hijack the Hugo Awards in the mid-2010s to protest themes of inclusion and perceived political correctness. Many authors associated with Baen Books and Pournelle were involved. At Pournelle's death in September 2017 the reaction of the community was mixed, owing in large part to his outspoken political views.

56. Reagan to Graham, *High Frontier*, quoting Reagan to Graham, June 3, 1983.

57. Disch, *On SF,* 211.

58. Patrick Anderson, "King of the Techno-Thriller," *New York Times Magazine,* May 1, 1988.

59. Tom Clancy, *The Cardinal of the Kremlin* (New York: Putnam's Sons, 1988), 21.

60. Clancy, *Cardinal of the Kremlin,* 37.

61. Clancy, *Cardinal of the Kremlin,* 536.

62. Clancy, *Cardinal of the Kremlin,* 51.

63. Clancy, *Cardinal of the Kremlin,* 211.

64. Clancy, *Cardinal of the Kremlin,* 119.

65. DeGraffenreid, interview.

66. Nate Jones, *Able Archer 83: The Secret History of the NATO Exercise That Almost Triggered Nuclear War* (New York: New Press, 2016), 308n58.

67. Christopher Fuller, "The Reagan Administration and the Roots of US Cyber (In) Security," in *Ronald Reagan and the Transformation of International Politics in the 1980s Conference,* Clements Center for National Security, Austin, TX, January 19, 2017.

68. DeGraffenreid, interview.

69. Caspar Weinberger and George Shultz, "Soviet Strategic Programs," [CIA] *Freedom of Information Act Electronic Reading Room,* October 1985, 7.

70. Weinberger and Shultz, 12.

71. Bill Keller, "American Team Gets Close Look at Soviet Laser," *New York Times,* July 9, 1989.

72. Weinberger and Shultz, "Soviet Strategic Programs," 14.

73. Ronald Reagan, "Radio Address to the Nation on Soviet Strategic Defense Programs," Camp David, MD, October 12, 1985.

74. "Telegram from the Embassy in the Soviet Union to the Department of State" in *FRUS 1981–1988,* vol. 5, 12.

75. Poindexter, interview.

76. "Geneva Summit Memorandum of Conversation Second Private Meeting," November 19, 1985, Ronald Reagan Library.

77. "Geneva Summit Memorandum of Conversation Second Private Meeting."

78. "Review of United States Arms Control Positions: National Security Planning Group Meeting," *The Reagan Files,* September 8, 1987, thereaganfiles.com.

79. "Memorandum of Conversation," October 11, 1986. in *FRUS,* vol. 5, Document 302.

80. Caspar Weinberger to Margaret Thatcher, June 25, 1996, Part III, Box 41, Caspar Weinberger Papers, Library of Congress.

81. Caspar Weinberger and Peter Schweizer, *The Next War* (New York: Regnery, 1996), xxiv.

82. Claudia Rosett to Caspar Weinberger, February 18, 1986, Part III, Box 43, Caspar Weinberger Papers, Library of Congress.

83. Caspar Weinberger, "Mongoose R.I.P." *Wall Street Journal,* January 13, 1988.

84. Caspar Weinberger to William Buckley, January 21, 1988, Part III, Box 43, Caspar Weinberger Papers, Library of Congress.

85. Weinberger and Schweizer, *Next War,* 226.

86. Peter Schweizer to Tom Clancy, August 20, 1996, Part III, Box 41, Caspar Weinberger Papers, Library of Congress.

87. Tom Clancy to Caspar Weinberger, August 26, 1996, Part III, Box 42, Caspar Weinberger Papers, Library of Congress.
88. Suzanne McFarlane to Ileana Gonzalez, October 18, 1996, Part III, Box 41, Caspar Weinberger Papers, Library of Congress; Jack Vessey to Ileana Gonzalez, October 14, 1996, Part III, Box 41, Caspar Weinberger Papers, Library of Congress.
89. Weinberger and Schweizer, *Next War*.
90. Edwin McDowell, "Top-Selling Books of 1988: Spy Novel and Physics," *New York Times*, February 2, 1989.
91. Lekachman, "Virtuous Men and Perfect Weapons."
92. Daniel Graham, "Clancy's Star Wars," *New York Times*, August 28, 1988.
93. Robert Lekachman "Clancy's Star Wars," *New York Times*, August 28, 1988.
94. Evan Thomas, "The Art of the Techno-Thriller," *Newsweek*, August 9, 1998.
95. Pournelle, interview.
96. Thomas, "Art of the Techno-Thriller."
97. Tom Clancy to Charles Wick, October 17, 1987, ID#525617, FG298, WHORM Subject File, Ronald Reagan Library.
98. Charles Wick to Ronald Reagan, November 5, 1987, ID#525617, FG298, WHORM Subject File, Ronald Reagan Library.
99. Clancy, *Cardinal of the Kremlin*, 608.
100. Thomas, "Art of the Techno-Thriller."
101. Robert Dornan, "OTA: The Home of Modern-Day Luddites," *Congressional Record*, April 28, 1988, 9484.
102. Tom Clancy, "Luddites Are Wrong about SDI Too," *Wall Street Journal*, April 28, 1988.
103. "Books from Personal Bookshelves from Behind Ronald Reagan's Desk at Office of Ronald Reagan," Ronald Reagan Library.
104. Hayward, *Age of Reagan*, 631.
105. William Taubman, *Gorbachev: His Life and Times* (New York: W. W. Norton, 2017), 263.
106. "Memorandum from William Stearman of the National Security Council Staff to the President's Assistant for National Security Affairs," in *FRUS 1981–1988*, vol. 5, 317.
107. "Minutes of a National Security Council Meeting, Washington, September 20, 1985, 11 am–12:07 pm," in *FRUS 1981–1988*, vol. 5, 370.
108. "Minutes of a National Security Council Meeting, Washington, September 20, 1985, 11 am–12:07 pm."
109. The President's Foreign Intelligence Advisory Board, "The Soviet War Scare," February 15, 1990, reprinted in Jones, *Able Archer 83*, 121.
110. David Hoffman, *The Dead Hand: The Untold Story of the Cold War Arms Race and Its Dangerous Legacy* (New York: Random House, 2009), 147–52.
111. "Mock Memorandum from Soviet Foreign Policy Assistant Chernyaev to Soviet General Secretary Gorbachev (9 June 86)," in *FRUS 1981–1988*, vol. 5, 1018.
112. Suri, *Impossible Presidency*, 239–40.
113. Troy, *Morning in America*, 2.
114. Troy, 11.

Conclusion

1. Tom Clancy, *Clear and Present Danger* (New York: Putnam's Sons, 1989).
2. Eliza Gray, "Colin Powell Remembers Tom Clancy," *Time*, October 2, 2013.
3. Colin Powell, email to author, West Point, NY, August 25, 2016. Secretary Powell communicated with the author through his longtime personal assistant Peggy Cifrino, who relayed questions to him and sent the answers to the author.
4. Gray, "Colin Powell Remembers Tom Clancy."
5. Powell to author.
6. Tom Clancy, letter to Susan Richards, 5 February 1983, available at piedtype.com.
7. David Wise, "Clear and Present Danger," *New York Times*, August 13, 1989.
8. Clancy, *Clear and Present Danger*.
9. Clancy, *Clear and Present Danger*, 649.
10. Clancy, *Clear and Present Danger*, 650.
11. Clancy, *Clear and Present Danger*, 655.
12. Brands, *Reagan: The Life*, 653.
13. Brands.
14. Gerhard Peters, "Final Presidential Job Approval Ratings," *The American Presidency Project*, http://www.presidency.ucsb.edu/data/final_approval.php. This web-based resource has been edited since 1999 by John T. Woolley and Gerhard Peters of the University of California, Santa Barbara.
15. Poindexter, interview.
16. Maureen Dowd, "The White House Crisis: McFarlane Suicide Attempt—'What Drove Me to Despair,'" *New York Times*, March 2, 1987.
17. Poindexter, interview.
18. George H. W. Bush, "Remarks at the Ceremony Commemorating the 175th Anniversary of 'The Star-Spangled Banner,'" Baltimore, MD, September 7, 1989.
19. Tevi Troy, "What's Playing at the White House Movie Theater?" *Washingtonian Magazine*, February 2011.
20. Matt Novak, "The White House Screening of *The Hunt for Red October* Had Celebrities, Spies and (Maybe) a Sex Scandal," Gizmodo.com, April 26, 2016, https://paleofuture.gizmodo.com/. Though not a typical academic source, this article contains photo rolls and a guest list obtained via Freedom of Information Act request from the George H. W. Bush Presidential Library.
21. Engel, *When the World Seemed New*, 8.
22. Engel.
23. George H. W. Bush, "Remarks to the Supreme Soviet of the Republic of Ukraine," Kiev, Ukraine, August 1, 1991.
24. John-Thor Dahlburg, "News Analysis: Bush's 'Chicken Kiev' Talk—an Ill-Fated US Policy," *Los Angeles Times*, December 19, 1991.
25. George H. W. Bush and Brent Scowcroft, *A World Transformed* (New York: Knopf, 1998), 592.
26. Said, *Culture and Imperialism*, 301.

27. McAlister, *Epic Encounters*, 241. As a seven-year-old, the present author was proud of his complete collection of Pro Set Desert Storm Trading Cards.

28. Rick Atkinson and William Claiborne, "Allies Surround Republican Guard, Say Crippled Iraqis Are Near Defeat," *Washington Post*, February 27, 1991.

29. McAlister, *Epic Encounters*, 250.

30. Reagan, "Remarks on Presenting the Medal of Honor to Master Sergeant Roy P. Benavidez."

31. Bacevich, *New American Militarism*, 117.

32. Bacevich, 121.

33. William Honan, "Books, Books, and More Books: Clinton an Omnivorous Reader," *New York Times*, December 10, 1992.

34. Blake Hounshell, "Tom Clancy Sounds Off on Colin Powell, Politicians," ForeignPolicy .com, October 20, 2008.

35. Nicholas Fandos, "Despite Mueller's Push, House Republicans Declare No Evidence of Collusion," *New York Times*, March 12, 2018.

36. @RusEMBUSA, Twitter.com, March 12, 2018.

37. Robert Kaiser, "Gorbachev: We All Lost the Cold War," *Washington Post*, June 11, 2004.

BIBLIOGRAPHY

Archival Sources

American Presidency Project, University of California Santa Barbara, Santa Barbara, CA

Center for Military History, Washington, DC

Central Intelligence Agency Freedom of Information Act Electronic Reading Room

U.S. State Department, *Foreign Relations of the United States*. Office of the Historian. Washington, DC
——. *1981–1989*. Vol. 3, *Soviet Union, January 1981–January 1983*. Edited by James Graham Wilson, 2016.
——. *1981–1989*. Vol. 5, *Soviet Union, March 1985–October 1986*. Edited by Elizabeth Charles, 2020.

Hoover Institution Archives, Stanford University, Palo Alto, CA
Ronald Reagan Subject Collection.
William J. Casey Papers.
William P. Clark Papers.

Library of Congress
Caspar Weinberger Papers.
Congressional Record.
Hearings before the House Un-American Activities Committee.
Hearings on National Defense Authorization Act.
Hearings before a Special Subcommittee of the Committee on Education and Labor.

The National Archives of the United Kingdom
PREM-19-1759.

National Security Archive (online), George Washington University, Washington, DC
Able Archer '83 Sourcebook.
Electronic Briefing Book 172.

Personal Papers of Larry Bond

Ronald Reagan Library, Simi Valley, CA
Alton Keel Files.
Daily Diary of President Ronald Reagan.
Michael Deaver Files.
National Security Decision Directives.
NSC Executive Secretariat: Trip File.
Robert Linhard Files.
Ronald Reagan Files.
Transcripts of National Security Council Meetings.
White House, Office Of: Research Office, 1981–1989.
White House Office of Records Management [WHORM] Subject File.
White House Photo Collection.

Interviews Conducted by the Author

Adelman, Kenneth. Notes. Austin, TX, January 19, 2017.
Bond, Larry. Tape Recording. Springfield, VA, October 20, 2104.
Carlson, Chris. Tape Recording. Springfield, VA, October 20, 2014.
DeGraffenreid, Kenneth. Telephone. West Point, NY, September 5, 2017.
Grosvenor, Deborah. Telephone. Austin, TX, November 11, 2014.
Hill, Charles. Telephone. West Point, NY, April 3, 2017.
Inman, Bobby, Adm. Notes. Austin, TX, November 2015.
Matlock, Jack. Tape Recording. Austin, TX, September 23, 2014.
Niven, Larry. Email. West Point, NY, August 15, 2017.
Perla, Peter. Notes. Arlington, VA, October 23, 2014.
Poindexter, John. Skype. West Point, NY, August 19, 2017.
Pournelle, Jerry. Skype. West Point, NY, August 19, 2017.
Powell, Charles. Email. West Point, NY, August 19, 2017.
Powell, Colin. Email. West Point, NY, August 25, 2016.
Reed, Tom. Tape Recording. Austin, TX, October 16, 2014.
Rohrabacher, Dana. Telephone. West Point, NY, July 18, 2018.

Ronald Reagan Public Statements, American Presidency Project

"A Time for Choosing." televised speech, October 27, 1964.
"Address Accepting the Nomination at the Republican National Convention in Detroit."
        Detroit, MI, July 17, 1980.
"Address before a Joint Session of the Congress on the State of the Union." Washington, DC,
        6 February 1985.
"Address to British Parliament." London, UK, June 8, 1982.
"Address at Commencement Exercises at Eureka College." Eureka, IL, May 9, 1982.

"Address at Commencement Exercises at the United States Air Force Academy." Colorado
     Springs, CO, May 30, 1984.
"Address at the Commencement Exercises at the United States Military Academy." West Point,
     NY, May 27, 1981.
"Address at the Commencement Exercises of the United States Naval Academy." Annapolis,
     MD, May 22, 1985.
"Address from the Brandenburg Gate." West Berlin, Federal Republic of Germany, June 12, 1987.
"Address to the Nation on Defense and National Security." Washington, DC, March 23, 1983.
"Address to the Nation on the Iran Arms and Contra Aid Controversy and Administration
     Goals." Washington, DC, August 12, 1987.
"Address to the Nation on Iran-Contra." Washington, DC, March 4, 1987.
"Address to the Nation and Other Countries on United States–Soviet Relations." Washington,
     DC, January 16, 1984.
"Address to the Nation on the Soviet Attack on a Korean Civilian Airliner." Washington, DC,
     September 5, 1983.
"Address to the National Association of Evangelicals." Orlando, FL, March 8, 1983.
"Address to the National Press Club on Arms Reduction and Nuclear Weapons." Washington,
     DC, 18 November 1981.
"Farewell Address to the Nation." Washington, DC, January 11, 1989.
"First Inaugural Address." Washington, DC, January 20, 1981.
"Peace: Restoring the Margins of Safety." Chicago, IL, August 18, 1980.
"The President's News Conference." Washington, DC, March 31, 1982.
"Presidential Taping: Salute to Veterans for NCAA Football Halftime." November 8, 1982.
"Radio Address to the Nation on Armed Forces Day." May 15, 1982.
"Radio Address to the Nation on Congressional Inaction on Proposed Legislation." August 11,
     1984.
"Radio Address to the Nation on Soviet Strategic Defense Programs." Camp David, MD,
     October 12, 1985.
"Radio Address to the Nation on the Tricentennial Anniversary Year of German Settlement in
     America." June 25, 1983.
"Remarks to Administration Officials on Domestic Policy." Washington, DC, December 13,
     1988.
"Remarks to American Military Personnel and Their Families in Keflavik, Iceland." Keflavik,
     Iceland, October 12, 1986.
"Remarks to American Troops at Camp Liberty Bell." Seoul, South Korea, November 13, 1983.
"Remarks at the Annual Convention of the Congressional Medal of Honor Society in New
     York City." New York City, NY, December 12, 1983.
"Remarks at the Conservative Political Action Conference Dinner." Washington, DC, February 26,
     1982.
"Remarks at the Conservative Political Action Conference Dinner." Washington, DC, March 20,
     1981.
"Remarks at a Luncheon for Recipients of the National Medal of Arts." Washington, DC,
     May 18, 1983.

"Remarks at the National Conference of the Building and Construction Trades Department, AFL-CIO." Washington, DC, March 30, 1981.

"Remarks at the Presentation Ceremony for the Presidential Medal of Freedom." Washington, DC, March 26, 1984.

"Remarks on Presenting the Medal of Honor to Master Sergeant Roy P. Benavidez." Arlington, VA, February 24, 1981.

"Remarks on the Signing of the Intelligence Identity Protection Act." Langley, VA, June 23, 1982.

"Remarks at a White House Barbecue for the Professional Rodeo Cowboy Association." Washington, DC, September 24, 1983.

"Remarks at a White House Ceremony Honoring Hispanic Americans in the United States Armed Forces." Washington, DC, September 16, 1983.

"Reprint of Radio Program Entitled 'Neutron Bomb II,' Commentary by Ronald Reagan." Ronald Reagan Subject Collection, Box 8, Hoover Institution on War Revolution and Peace.

"Reprint of a Radio Program Entitled 'SALT,' Commentary by Ronald Reagan." Ronald Reagan Subject Collection, Box 8, Hoover Institution on War Revolution and Peace.

"Second Inaugural Address." Washington, DC, January 21, 1985.

"South Africa and Apartheid." Washington, DC, 23 July 1986.

"Statement on Armed Forces Day." Washington, DC, May 16, 1981.

Journals, Periodicals, Broadcasters, and News Services

Associated Press
Atlantic
Baltimore Sun
Baseball Reference
Billboard
Box Office Mojo
British Broadcasting Company
Chicago Tribune
Christian Science Monitor
Flight
Foreign Policy
Kirkus Reviews
Los Angeles Times
National Interest
National Public Radio
National Review
New York Times
New York Times Magazine
Newsweek
Paris Review
Playboy
San Francisco Chronicle

Saturday Evening Post
Time
Times Literary Supplement
Wall Street Journal
Washington Post
Washingtonian Magazine

Printed Works of Fiction

Burroughs, Edgar Rice. *The Gods of Mars*. Chicago: A. C. McClung, 1918.
———. *Princess of Mars*. Chicago: A. C. McClung, 1917.
Chekov, Anton. "The Cherry Orchard." In *Plays*, translated by Elisaveta Fen. London: Penguin, 1954.
Clancy, Tom. *The Cardinal of the Kremlin*. New York: Putnam's Sons, 1988.
———. *Clear and Present Danger*. New York: Putnam's Sons, 1989.
———. *Debt of Honor*. New York: Putnam's Sons, 1994.
———. *The Hunt for Red October*. Annapolis, MD: Naval Institute Press, 1984.
———. *Red Storm Rising*. New York: Putnam's Sons, 1986.
Clark, Arthur C. "On Golden Seas." In *The Collected Stories of Arthur C. Clarke*. New York: Macmillan, 2002.
Drury, Allen. *Pentagon*. New York: Doubleday, 1986.
Hackett, John. *The Third World War: August 1985*. New York: Macmillan, 1978.
Heinlein, Robert. *The Cat Who Walks through Walls*. New York: Putnam's Sons, 1985.
Kipling, Rudyard. "If," 1910.
———. "The White Man's Burden: The United States in the Philippine Islands," 1899.
Koestler, Arthur. *Darkness at Noon*. London: Macmillan, 1940.
L'Amour, Louis. "The Gift of Cochise." *Colliers*, July 5, 1982.
———. *Hondo*. New York: Bantam Books, 2016.
Ludlum, Robert. *The Bourne Supremacy*. New York: Random House, 1986.
Michener, James. *The Bridges at Toko-Ri*. New York: Fawcett Books, 1952.
Miller, Frank. *The Dark Knight Returns*. New York: DC Comics, 1986.
Moore, Alan, and Dave Gibbons. *Watchmen*. New York: DC Comics, 1986.
Seuss, Theodore. *The Better Butter Battle*. New York: Random House, 1984.
Weinberger, Caspar, and Peter Schweizer. *The Next War*. New York: Regnery, 1996.
Wright, Harold Bell. *That Printer of Udell's*. Chicago: Book Supply, 1903.

Television Shows and Films

Back to the Future. Film directed by Robert Zemeckis. Universal Pictures, 1985.
The Bridges at Toko-Ri. Film directed by Mark Robson. Paramount, 1954.
Chicago Cubs Baseball. WGN, 1948–2019.
General Electric Theater. National Broadcasting Company, 1953–1962.
Hondo. Film directed by John Farrow. Warner Bros., 1953.

The Hunt for Red October. Film directed by John McTiernan. Paramount, 1990.
Rambo: First Blood Part II. Film directed by George Cosmatos. TriStar Pictures, 1985.
Rocky IV. Film directed by Sylvester Stallone. United Artists, 1985.
Saturday Night Live. National Broadcasting Company, 1975–.
Top Gun. Film directed by Tony Scott. Paramount, 1986.

Published Primary Sources

Asimov, Isaac. *I, Asimov: A Memoir*. New York: Random House, 1995.
"Out of the Everywhere." In *Out of the Everywhere: Thoughts on Science from the Master*. New York: Doubleday, 1990.
Bush, George H. W. "Remarks at the Ceremony Commemorating the 175th Anniversary of 'The Star-Spangled Banner,'" Baltimore, MD, 7 September 1989, American Presidency Project.
———. "Remarks to the Supreme Soviet of the Republic of Ukraine." Kiev, Ukraine, 1 August 1991, American Presidency Project.
Bush, George H. W., and Brent Scowcroft. *A World Transformed*. New York: Knopf, 1998.
Chambers, Whittaker. *Witness*. New York: Regnery History, 1952.
Clancy, Tom, to Larry Bond, February 19, 1982. Personal papers of Larry Bond.
——— to Susan Richards, February 5, 1983. Accessed on Piedtype.com.
——— to Susan Richards, November 1, 1984. Accessed on Piedtype.com.
——— to Susan Richards, February 5, 1985. Accessed on Piedtype.com.
——— to Susan Richards, March 1985. Accessed on Piedtype.com.
Deaver, Michael, and Mickey Herskowitz. *Behind the Scenes: In Which the Author Talks about Ronald and Nancy Reagan . . . and Himself*. New York: William Morrow, 1987.
Dobrynin, Anatoly. *In Confidence: Moscow's Ambassador to America's Six Cold War Presidents*. New York: Times Books, 1995.
Gingrich, Newt, David Drake, and Marianne Gingrich. *Window of Opportunity: A Blue Print for the Future*. New York: Tor Books, 1984.
Graham, Daniel O. *High Frontier: There Is a Defense against Nuclear War*. New York: Tor Books, 1984.
John Paul II. *Dives in Misericordia*, November 30, 1980.
Kennan, George. *The Kennan Diaries*. Edited by Frank Costigliola. New York: W. W. Norton and Co, 2014.
Koestler, Arthur. *The God That Failed*. New York: Harper & Row, 1949.
L'Amour, Louis. *Education of a Wandering Man*. New York: Bantam Books, 1990.
Lehman, John. *Oceans Ventured: Winning the Cold War at Sea*. New York: W. W. Norton, 2018.
Luns, Joseph. *NATO and Warsaw Pact Force Comparison: 1982*. Brussels: NATO Information Service, 1982.
"Lyn Nofziger Oral History." Miller Center, University of Virginia, 6 March 2003.
Massie, Suzzane. *Trust but Verify: Reagan, Russia, and Me*. Rockland: Maine Authors, 2013.
Office of the Secretary of Defense. *Harold Brown: Offsetting the Soviet Military Challenge, Documentary Supplement*. Edited by Edward Keefer. Washington, DC: Historical Office, 2017.

Orwell, George. *George Orwell: A Life in Letters*. Edited by Peter Davison. New York: Liveright, 2010.

———. *Homage to Catalonia*. Orlando, FL: Harvest, 1952.

Powell, Colin. *My American Journey*. With Joseph E. Persico. New York: Random House, 1995.

Pournelle, Jerry, and Dean Ing. *Mutual Assured Survival*. New York: Baen Books, 1985.

"Reagan Country: The Ronald Reagan Presidential Foundation Member Newsletter." July 2012. ReaganFoundation.org, accessed July 7, 2017.

Reagan, Ronald. *An American Life: The Autobiography*. New York: Simon & Schuster, 1990.

———. *The Reagan Diaries* edited by Douglas Brinkley. New York: HarperCollins, 2007.

———. *Ronald Reagan: A Life in Letters*. Edited by Kiron Skinner, Annelise Anderson, and Martine Anderson. New York: Free Press, 2003.

Reagan, Ronald, and Richard Hubler. *Where's the Rest of Me?* New York: Van Rees, 1965.

Reagan, Ronald, to Pieter Botha, 4 January 1986, *Margaret Thatcher Foundation*, margaretthatcher.org.

Reed, Thomas. *The Reagan Enigma, 1964–1980*. Los Angeles: Figueroa, 2014.

"Richard Nixon and Ronald W. Reagan on 26 October 1971." Conversation 013-008, *Presidential Recording Digital Edition* [*Nixon Telephone Tapes: 1971*, edited by Ken Hughes]. Charlottesville: University of Virginia Press, 2014–.

Romjue, John. *From Active Defense to AirLand Battle: The Development of Army Doctrine, 1973–1982*. Washington, DC: U.S. Government Printing Office, 1984.

Russian Embassy to the United States, @RusEMBUSA, twitter.com, March 12, 2018.

Shultz, George. *Turmoil and Triumph: My Years as Secretary of State*. New York: Scribner's, 1995.

Special Meeting of Foreign and Defense Ministers, Brussels, Belgium, NATO, December 12, 1979.

Stockman, David. *The Triumph of Politics: Why the Reagan Revolution Failed*. New York: Harper & Row, 1986.

U.S. Army Dept., *Operations*, Field Manual [FM] 100-5. Washington, DC: U.S. Government Printing Office, 1976.

Weinberger, Caspar. *Fighting for Peace: Seven Critical Years in the Pentagon*. New York: Warner Books, 1990.

Published Secondary Sources

Adelman, Ken. *Reagan at Reykjavik: Forty-Eight Hours That Ended the Cold War*. New York: Broadside Books, 2014.

Andrew, Christopher, and Vasili Mitrohkin. *The Sword and the Shield: The Mitrokhin Archive and the Secret History of the KGB*. New York: Basic Books, 1999.

Arendt, Hannah. *The Origins of Totalitarianism*. New York: Harcourt, Brace, 1951.

Ashley, Michael. *Science Fiction Rebels: The Story of Science-Fiction Magazines from 1981–1990*. Liverpool, UK: Liverpool University Press, 2016.

Bacevich, Andrew. *The New American Militarism: How Americans Are Seduced by War*. Oxford, UK: Oxford University Press, 2013.

The Books of the Century: 1980–1989. Http://www.ocf.berkeley.edu/~immer/books1980s.

Brands, H. W. *Reagan: The Life*. New York: Doubleday, 2015.

————. *What Good Is Grand Strategy? Power and Purpose in American Statecraft from Harry S. Truman to George W. Bush*. Ithaca, NY: Cornell University Press, 2014.

Cannon, Lou. *President Reagan: The Role of a Lifetime*. New York: Simon & Schuster, 1991.

————. *Reagan*. New York: Perigee Books, 1982.

Clausewitz, Carl Von. *On War*. Edited and translated by Michael Howard and Peter Paret. Princeton, NJ: Princeton University Press, 1976.

Diggins, John Patrick. *Ronald Reagan: Fate, Freedom, and the Making of History*. New York: W. W. Norton, 2007.

Disch, Thomas. *On SF*. Ann Arbor: University of Michigan Press, 2005.

Engel, Jeffrey. *When the World Seemed New: George H. W. Bush and the End of the Cold War*. Boston: Houghton Mifflin Harcourt, 2017.

Fuller, Christopher. "The Reagan Administration and the Roots of US Cyber (In)Security." In *Ronald Reagan and the Transformation of International Politics in the 1980s Conference*. Clements Center for National Security, Austin, TX, January 19, 2017.

Gaddis, John Lewis. *The Cold War: A New History*. New York: Penguin Books, 2005.

Getty, J. Arch, and Oleg Naumov. *The Road to Terror: Stalin and the Self-Destruction of the Bolsheviks, 1932–1939*. New Haven, CT: Yale University Press, 2010.

Hayward, Steven. *The Age of Reagan: The Conservative Counterrevolution, 1980–1989*. New York: Three Rivers, 2009.

————. *The Age of Reagan: The Fall of the Old Liberal Order, 1964–1980*. New York: Forum, 2001.

Henriksen, Margot. *Dr. Strangelove's America: Society and Culture in the Atomic Age*. Berkeley: University of California Press, 1997.

Hill, Charles. *Grand Strategies: Literature, Statecraft, and World Order*. New Haven, CT: Yale University Press, 2010.

Hixson, Walter. "Red Storm Rising: Tom Clancy Novels and the Cult of National Security." *Diplomatic History* 17, no. 4 (October 1993).

Hoffman, David. *The Dead Hand: The Untold Story of the Cold War Arms Race and Its Dangerous Legacy*. New York: Random House, 2009.

Inboden, William. "Grand Strategy and Petty Squabbles." In *The Power of the Past: History and Statecraft*. Edited by Hal Brands and Jeremi Suri. Washington, DC: Brookings Institution, 2016.

Jones, Nate. *Able Archer 83: The Secret History of the NATO Exercise That Almost Triggered Nuclear War*. New York: New Press, 2016.

Kengor, Paul. *God and Ronald Reagan: A Spiritual Life*. New York: HarperCollins, 2004.

Klein, Christina. *Cold War Orientalism: Asia in the Middlebrow Imagination, 1945–1961*. Berkeley: University of California Press, 2003.

Lawrence, Mark. "Policymaking and the Uses of the Vietnam War." In *The Power of the Past: History and Statecraft*. Edited by Hal Brands and Jeremi Suri. Washington, DC: Brookings Institution, 2016.

Leffler, Melvyn. *For the Soul of Mankind: The United States, the Soviet Union, and the Cold War*. New York: Hill & Wang, 2007.

Lettow, Paul. *Ronald Reagan and His Quest to Abolish Nuclear Weapons*. New York: Random House, 2005.

Mann, James. *The Rebellion of Ronald Reagan: A History of the End of the Cold War*. New York: Penguin Books, 2009.

Matlock, Jack. *Reagan and Gorbachev: How the Cold War Ended*. New York: Random House, 2005.

———. *Superpower Illusions: How Myths and False Ideologies Led America Astray and How to Return to Reality*. New Haven, CT: Yale University Press, 2010.

Marsden, Michael. "Louis L'Amour's *Hondo*: From Literature to Film to Literature." *Literature Film Quarterly*, January 1, 1999.

McAleer, Neil. *Arthur C. Clarke: The Authorized Biography*. New York: McGraw-Hill, 1992.

McAlister, Melani. *Epic Encounters: Culture, Media, & U.S. Interests in the Middle East since 1945*. Berkeley: University of California Press, 2001.

Miles, Simon. *Engaging the Evil Empire: Washington, Moscow, and the Beginning of the End of the Cold War*. Ithaca, NY: Cornell University Press, 2020.

Morris, Edmund. *Dutch: A Memoir of Ronald Reagan*. New York: Random House, 1999.

Musgrave, Paul, and J. Furman Daniel. "Synthetic Experiences: How Popular Culture Matters for Images of International Relations." *International Studies Quarterly* 61, no. 3 (September 2017).

Nau, Henry. *Conservative Internationalism: Armed Diplomacy under Jefferson, Polk, Truman and Reagan*. Princeton, NJ: Princeton University Press, 2013.

Noonan, Peggy. *When Character Was King: A Story of Ronald Reagan*. New York: Viking, 2001.

Patterson, William. *Robert Heinlein: In Dialogue with His Century*. Vol. 2, *The Man Who Learned Better*. New York: Macmillan, 2014.

Perlstein, Rick. *The Invisible Bridge: The Fall of Nixon and the Rise of Reagan*. New York: Simon & Schuster, 2014.

Porges, Irwin. *Edgar Rice Burroughs*. Provo, UT: Brigham Young University Press, 1975.

Said, Edward. *Culture and Imperialism*. New York: Vintage Books, 1993.

Saposs, David. *Communism in American Labor Unions*. New York: McGraw-Hill, 1956.

Schweizer, Peter. *Reagan's War: The Epic Story of His Forty-Year Struggle and Final Triumph over Communism*. New York: Doubleday, 2002.

Snyder, Timothy. *Bloodlands: Europe between Hitler and Stalin*. New York: Basic Books, 2010.

Sparrow, Bartholomew. *The Strategist: Brent Scowcroft and the Call of National Security*. New York: PublicAffairs, 2015.

Steill, Benn. *The Battle of Bretton Wood: John Maynard Keynes, Harry Dexter White and the Making of a New World Order*. Princeton, NJ: Princeton University Press, 2013.

Suri, Jeremi. *The Impossible Presidency: The Rise and Fall of America's Highest Office*. New York: Basic Books, 2017.

Tanenhaus, Sam. *Whittaker Chambers: A Biography*. New York: Modern Library, 1999.

Tagg, Lawrence. *Harold Bell Wright: Storyteller to America*. Tucson, AZ: Westernlore, 1986.

Taubman, William. *Gorbachev: His Life and Times*. New York: W. W. Norton, 2017.

Taylor IV, F. Flagg. "Arthur Koestler's Trail of Darkness." *Modern Age* (October 2016).

Troy, Gil. *Morning in America: How Ronald Reagan Invented the 1980s*. Princeton, NJ: Princeton University Press, 2005.

Vogel, Ezra. *Deng Xiaoping and the Transformation of China*. Cambridge, MA: Belknap of Harvard University Press, 2013.

Westad, Odd Arne. *The Cold War: A World History*. New York: Hachette Books, 2017.

White, Duncan. *Cold Warriors: Writers Who Waged the Literary Cold War*. New York: HarperCollins, 2014.

Whitfield, Stephen. *The Culture of the Cold War*. Baltimore, MD: Johns Hopkins University Press, 1991.

Wilentz, Sean. *The Age of Reagan: A History, 1974–2008*. New York: Harper Books, 2008.

Wilson, James Graham. *The Triumph of Improvisation: Gorbachev's Adaptability, Reagan's Engagement and the End of the Cold War*. Ithaca, NY: Cornell University Press, 2014.

Yoshitani, Gail. *Reagan on War: A Reappraisal of the Weinberger Doctrine, 1980–1984*. College Station: Texas A&M University Press, 2012.

Young, Gregory. "Mutiny on the *Storozhevoy*: A Case Study on Dissent in the Soviet Navy." Master's thesis, Naval Postgraduate School, March 1982.

INDEX

The Third World War (Hackett), 118–19
This Is the Army (1943 film) (Curtiz), 34
Thunman, Nils R. "Ron," 104–5, 135
"A Time for Choosing" (1964 campaign
     speech), 30, 39, 113
Top Gun (1986 film) (Scott), 8, 106, 173
Tower Commission, 67, 167
Treptow, Martin, 92–93
"triumph of good over evil" belief, 18, 23,
     29, 31
The Triumph of Politics (Stockman), 2, 3, 68
Trotsky, Leon, 37
Troy, Gil, 83, 165
Truman, Harry S., 78
Trumbo, Dalton, 44, 47, 52, 68
Tukhachevsky, Mikhail, 46
Tutu, Desmond, 72
Twain, Mark, 19
2001: A Space Odyssey (Clarke), 150

Udell, George (fictional character), 29, 30
Udell Falkner, Amy (fictional character),
     29, 30
United Nations (UN): Outer Space treaties,
     148; Reagan's criticisms of, 57–58, 94;
     UN Resolution 2758, 57, 71, 94
United States: as "last best hope," 39–40;
     Reagan's reading of fiction relating to, 9;
     tensions with Soviet Union, 124–26
U.S. military: as all-voluntary force, 77,
     78–79, 80, 81; American engagement
     with, 12; communist aggression and,
     144; Michener and, 76; militarization
     of foreign policy, 12; military draft,
     78–79; National Security Decision
     Directive 32, 54, 101; National Security
     Decision Directive 75, 102; negative
     representations of, 27; Operation Desert
     Storm, 84, 105, 169, 170, 171; popu-
     lar culture and, 16, 82, 105, 169, 173;
     post–World War II expansion of, 78;
     public perceptions of, 11, 75, 81–82,
     170; Reagan's reading of fiction relating
     to, 9, 69; Reagan's romanticized vision of,
     58, 69, 74, 75, 92, 170–71; restoration
     of honor of, 81–82, 92, 95–96; in Saudi

Arabia and Kuwait, 169; sporting events
     and, 83–84; technology and, 79, 101–6,
     120–21, 171
U.S. Naval Academy speech (1985), 96
U.S. Navy: Clancy and, 95, 104–5, 136,
     140, 166; support for *Top Gun* (1986
     film) (Scott), 106; wargaming and, 137

Vassilii (fictional character), 48
Vatican, 99, 141
Vessey, John W., Jr., 121, 144, 160
Vietnam Syndrome, 14, 92
Vietnam War, 93; film representations of,
     8, 82, 91, 105; My Lai Massacre, 94;
     POWs, 75; Reagan on draft during,
     78; Reagan's new narrative of, 92–95;
     whitewashing of, 83
Vietnamese refugee boat story, 13–14
violence, in popular culture, 90–91
vision(s): creation of, 4; farewell address and,
     4, 13; of free society, 24, 144; as Reagan's
     contribution, 165; religion and Cold
     War, 30, 37, 54; specifics of less concern
     than, 66; strategic vision, 174, 177; use of
     narrative to communicate, 2, 25
Vonnegut, Kurt, 130

wargames, 137–38, 142, 159
Wargames (1983 film) (Badham), 110, 141
Warload of Mars (Burroughs), 22
Warsaw Pact, 11, 111–12, 115, 117, 118,
     120, 121, 132, 134–35
Watchmen (Moore and Gibbons), 111
Wayne, John, 61, 62, 68, 70
Weinberger, Caspar: budget proposals,
     15; Dobrynin and, 98; Drury and,
     84; fictional works, 12, 159, 160; on
     ICBMs, 116; on Iran-Contra issue, 66;
     on popular support for U.S. military,
     82; on Reagan's use of stories/jokes, 3,
     15–16; *Red Storm Rising* (Clancy) and,
     121; review of Clancy's books, 104, 106;
     review of Ludlum's books, 104; reviews
     of, 159; on Russian SDI program, 159;
     "Soviet Strategic Defense Programs"
     report, 156–57; on Soviet Union, 109

West Point commencement address (1981), 69–70, 73, 80, 81–82, 92

Westad, Odd Arne, 120

westerns: Central American policy and, 63, 65, 67; moral code in, 10–11, 59, 70; protagonists in, 62; Reagan's reading of, 9, 74. *See also* cowboy stories; L'Amour, Louis

Where's the Rest of Me? (Reagan), 18

White, Duncan, 5–6

White, Harry Dexter, 50–51

white hat/black hat analogy: Carter, John (fictional character), 22; Cold War and, 10, 56, 93, 98, 174; Nicaragua and, 67–68, 174

"The White Man's Burden" (1899 poem) (Kipling), 70–71

"White Man's Burden" ideology, 18, 22–23, 59, 70–71

Wick, Charles, 162

Wiesel, Elie, 133

William Woods commencement address (1952), 39, 54, 73, 77, 78, 79

Wilson, James Graham, 113

Witness (Chambers), 10, 49–50, 51, 54, 55, 56, 88

World War II: 40th anniversary commemoration, 133–34; Chambers during, 50; First Motion Picture Unit, 34; Gingrich's alternative history novel on, 153; Heinlein and Asimov during, 151; L'Amour during, 61; mass rape by Soviets during, 34, 129; OSS operatives in, 97; Reagan's service in, 34, 35; stories referencing, 14, 38; technological advances after, 120; U.S. military expansion after, 78; Vietnam War comparison to, 93

World War III: Clancy to Reagan on, 88; in *The Day After* (1983 TV film) (Meyer), 111; provocations for, 124; in *Red Storm Rising* (Clancy), 118, 121–22, 138; in *The Third World War* (Hackett), 118–19; Warsaw Pact and, 132

WorldNet, 162

Wright, Harold Bell, 10, 16, 28–29, 71. See also *That Printer of Udell's* (Wright)

writings of Reagan: after assassination attempt, 27; *An American Life* (Reagan), 27; on *The Day After* (1983 TV film), 111–12; "Do Your Kids Belong to Uncle Sam?" 79; empathy in, 126; on future vision, 123; insights from, 3; "Killed in Action" (short story), 73–74; on response to his apology, 168; on Sandinistas, 65; on speech at Annapolis, 96; on West Point graduations, 81–82; *Where's the Rest of Me?* (Reagan), 18

Zimmerman, Peter, 162

ABOUT THE AUTHOR

Benjamin Griffin is an Army officer who earned his PhD in history from the University of Texas at Austin. He teaches in the Department of History at the United States Military Academy and resides at West Point with his family.

The Naval Institute Press is the book-publishing arm of the U.S. Naval Institute, a private, nonprofit, membership society for sea service professionals and others who share an interest in naval and maritime affairs. Established in 1873 at the U.S. Naval Academy in Annapolis, Maryland, where its offices remain today, the Naval Institute has members worldwide.

Members of the Naval Institute support the education programs of the society and receive the influential monthly magazine *Proceedings* or the colorful bimonthly magazine *Naval History* and discounts on fine nautical prints and on ship and aircraft photos. They also have access to the transcripts of the Institute's Oral History Program and get discounted admission to any of the Institute-sponsored seminars offered around the country.

The Naval Institute's book-publishing program, begun in 1898 with basic guides to naval practices, has broadened its scope to include books of more general interest. Now the Naval Institute Press publishes about seventy titles each year, ranging from how-to books on boating and navigation to battle histories, biographies, ship and aircraft guides, and novels. Institute members receive significant discounts on the Press' more than eight hundred books in print.

Full-time students are eligible for special half-price membership rates. Life memberships are also available.

For more information about Naval Institute Press books that are currently available, visit www.usni.org/press/books. To learn about joining the U.S. Naval Institute, please write to:

Member Services
U.S. Naval Institute
291 Wood Road
Annapolis, MD 21402-5034
Telephone: (800) 233-8764
Fax: (410) 571-1703
Web address: www.usni.org